The Making of Felony Procedure in Middle English Literature

LAW AND LITERATURE

The Law and Literature series publishes work that connects legal ideas to literary and cultural history, texts, and artefacts. The series encompasses a wide range of historical periods, literary genres, legal fields and theories, and transnational subjects, focusing on interdisciplinary books that engage with legal and literary forms, methods, concepts, dispositions, and media. It seeks innovative studies of every kind, including but not limited to work that examines race, ethnicity, gender, national identity, criminal and civil law, legal institutions and actors, digital media, intellectual property, economic markets, and corporate power, while also foregrounding current interpretive methods in the humanities, using these methods as dynamic tools that are themselves subject to scrutiny.

Series Editors
Robert Spoo, University of Tulsa
Simon Stern, University of Toronto

The Making of Felony Procedure in Middle English Literature

ELISE WANG

OXFORD
UNIVERSITY PRESS

Great Clarendon Street, Oxford, OX2 6DP,
United Kingdom

Oxford University Press is a department of the University of Oxford.
It furthers the University's objective of excellence in research, scholarship,
and education by publishing worldwide. Oxford is a registered trade mark of
Oxford University Press in the UK and in certain other countries

© Elise Wang 2024

The moral rights of the author have been asserted

All rights reserved. No part of this publication may be reproduced, stored in
a retrieval system, or transmitted, in any form or by any means, without the
prior permission in writing of Oxford University Press, or as expressly permitted
by law, by licence or under terms agreed with the appropriate reprographics
rights organization. Enquiries concerning reproduction outside the scope of the
above should be sent to the Rights Department, Oxford University Press, at the
address above

You must not circulate this work in any other form
and you must impose this same condition on any acquirer

Published in the United States of America by Oxford University Press
198 Madison Avenue, New York, NY 10016, United States of America

British Library Cataloguing in Publication Data
Data available

Library of Congress Control Number: 2023947795

ISBN 9780192870728

DOI: 10.1093/9780191967023.001.0001

Printed and bound in the UK by
Clays Ltd, Elcograf S.p.A.

Links to third party websites are provided by Oxford in good faith and
for information only. Oxford disclaims any responsibility for the materials
contained in any third party website referenced in this work.

Contents

Acknowledgments   vi

   Introduction   1
1. Death Investigation: *St. Erkenwald's* Bright Body   23
2. The Plea: *Placita Corone* and Narrative Satisfaction   50
3. Testimony: *The Pistil of Swete Susan* and the Oathworthy Witness   75
4. The Records: Roberd the Robbere and Documentary Technology   96
5. Standing Mute: Silence and Consent in Law and Literature   119
   Epilogue   140

Works Cited   148
Index   163

Acknowledgments

I am fortunate to have had so many people show me kindnesses during the conception and writing of this book, and it is a pleasure to be able to thank them here. My thinking about crime, punishment, and literature developed in my dissertation work, with the guidance of Peter Brooks, Andrew Cole, Bill Jordan, and Vance Smith. I am especially grateful to Vance for his brilliant guidance and enduring friendship; his works and his presence continue to be an inspiration. I have Peter to thank for the law and literature framing of this work, because he helped me conceptualize the stakes of the project and generously set me on my disciplinary feet. Just as importantly, his work with graduate students provided a model of compassionate and substantive mentorship. The guidance and encouragement of Andrew and Bill were invaluable at different stages of the project. In addition to being gracious mentors, all four are also beautiful writers. I have read and reread their work so often that I hope their voices sound through this book.

Special thanks go to Simon Stern, who encouraged this manuscript from the beginning and gave feedback throughout; he has truly been the ideal editor and shepherd for this project. I am grateful to both him and Bob Spoo for their faith in the book. Many thanks to my editor at OUP, Jo Spillane, for her generosity and patience. I would also like to thank my anonymous reviewer for their exceptionally detailed, incisive, and kind feedback, without which this would be a very different book. Jen Jahner and Karl Shoemaker provided detailed and incredibly generous feedback on my first chapter, and it is through discussions with them that my methodology took shape. I want especially to thank Sara Butler for her critique of the fourth chapter, which is a completely changed (and much better) object for her intervention. Elizabeth Fowler asked just the right question about the law's agency to inform the epilogue, and I am grateful to John Parker for sharing his thoughts on Christ's madness and silence in the mystery plays. Seth Strickland has been my first stop for all things *Piers Plowman*, and for discussions with that magical combination of big ideas and precision. I am especially grateful to Lukas Norling, who patiently offered feedback on every chapter and helped me get the manuscript into shape for submission. S. C. Kaplan provided exceptionally astute copyedits in the final stages. Last and most, I want to thank Maria Bo for her expert and thoughtful feedback on every page of this manuscript, and for her invaluable companionship in the writing process.

Few words from the dissertation appear here; it served primarily to introduce me to the archives, sources, and frames that I needed to approach the problems I cared about. But writing it taught me to think and to do the work, and I am indebted to everyone who made that learning possible—intellectually, materially, and emotionally. Thanks to Rita Copeland and Jeff Dolven, who often intervened at just the right moment with just the right reference or reframing. Time is funny in graduate school; you never feel you have enough, but in fact you have more than anyone around you. I am grateful to those who were always generous with theirs: Wendy Belcher, Sandy Bermann, Erin Huang, Lital Levy, and Eileen Reeves. I am thankful also to the graduate school colleagues who carried me through: Katlyn Carter, Clifton Granby, Anjuli Gunaratne, Nikhil Menon, Friederike Funk, and Ron Wilson.

I am more grateful every day to have found a collegial department that supports me and my work. Lana Dalley, Stephen Mexal, Marty Blaine, Irena Praitis, and Chris Westgate have been especially kind with their guidance and encouragement in these early, settling-in years. I owe a great debt to my students, whose thoughtfulness and enthusiasm have buoyed me through this project. I bring them all the texts I don't understand, in hopes they will explain them to me. And they do; my reading of Geoffrey Chaucer's *Man of Law's Tale* took shape in the discussion of my ENGL 315 Chaucer course in Spring 2022. Constantly on my mind are my students from my six years teaching at Garden State Youth Correctional Facility. I taught medieval literature for the first time in those classrooms; it is where I learned to be a teacher. It is with them in mind that I strive in this book to speak clearly about things that matter. The Epilogue is for them.

I have been lucky throughout my career to have found so many friendly spaces to discuss my work, and so many institutions to support it. I have presented versions of this work at various stages at the International Congress of Medieval Studies, the New Chaucer Society, the Piers Plowman Society, and the Works in Progress Series for Law and Literature out of University of Toronto, and the generous feedback I received at each has brought this book into shape. A version of the first chapter appeared in New Medieval Literatures, and I am grateful to Phil Knox for his help in the process. I am thankful for grants and support from the Rhodes Scholarship, Princeton University, the Charlotte Newcombe Fellowship, the Graduate Prize Fellowship at the University Center for Human Values, and the Princeton Department of Religion.

I am especially grateful to the UCHV for their support and for the community they provided as I finished my dissertation.

Behind every set of acknowledgments are the largest debts. Mine are to Beth Coughlin, David Wang, Aaron Wang, Hannah Wang, Liesl Yamaguchi, and my husband and two daughters. If only I had the words to say.

Introduction

Felony is the offense for which one forfeits a good life. This has been true from the category's beginnings in medieval English common law to the present day. While in the medieval context a felony conviction could mean the literal loss of life, its primary consequence was the loss of goods and property—those things that anchored one to the world.[1] As Jeremy Bentham quipped of the medieval felon allowed to live: "He lost his fief, the only source of his importance, and with it all that was worth living for."[2] Likewise, a modern felony conviction often entails not just imprisonment, but also the permanent loss of all those things "worth living for" that prison did not extinguish: a meaningful profession, democratic participation in society, social support, and dignified old age.[3] Criminality is usually punished with some exclusion from the goods of society, but the extremity and finality of these consequences frame felony as the essence of crime. It is the crime of which all other crimes are lesser versions.

One might think that the term that represents crime itself to the law would need an especially firm footing. But instead, the concept of felony rests on an absence and a shared fiction: the law has never defined the act of felony, and its prosecution proceeds as though it has. As Frederic Maitland observed, medieval felony can only be known "by its legal effects; any definition that would turn on the quality of the crime is unattainable."[4] The modern category

---

[1] As William Blackstone observed, one must look to property, not life, in trying to determine if a historical crime was considered a felony: "the true criterion of felony is forfeiture" (*Commentaries on the Laws of England in Four Volumes*, vol. 4 [Philadelphia, PA: Lippincott Company, 1893], p. 97). Note that, as Alice Ristroph points out about this definition, this is a historical criterion, not a description of felony's character ("Farewell to the Felonry," *Harvard Civil Rights-Civil Liberties Law Review* 53 [2018]: p. 567).

[2] Jeremy Bentham, *The Rationale of Punishment* (London: Robert Heward, 1830), p. 369.

[3] The "collateral consequences" of felony conviction include (most famously) disenfranchisement, but they can also include the denial of social services such as housing, food, and health care assistance. They can bar one from licensing in a variety of professions and preclude hiring in many professions that serve the public. A felony conviction can even be grounds for divorce and the termination of parental rights. I address these (their number and their variety) at more length in my Epilogue, but for good introductions to the concept see: Sarah Berson, "Beyond the Sentence—Understanding Collateral Consequences," *National Institute of Justice Journal* 25 (2013): pp. 25, and Christopher Uggen and Robert Stewart, "Piling on: Collateral Consequences and Community Supervision," *Minnesota Law Review* 99 (2014): pp. 1871–1910.

[4] Frederick Pollack and Frederic Maitland, *The History of English Law Before the Time of Edward I*, vol. 1 (Cambridge University Press, 1895), p. 467.

of felony in Anglo-American law retains this consequentialist definition; felony in the United States is "any crime punishable by more than a year in prison."[5] In other words, the quality of felony lies not in the act, but in how the law responds to that act. The act of felony cannot be known before the law has treated it as a felony, but in order to treat it as a felony, the law must pretend that it recognizes its object.

We can perceive both this lack and its compensating fiction where Geoffrey Chaucer added the character Felonye to his Italian source material for The Knight's Tale. As the walls of the temple of Mars are revealed, Felonye himself never comes into focus; he can only be known by the company he keeps, his "derke ymaginyng":

> Ther saugh I first the derke ymaginyng
> Of Felonye, and al the compassying;
> The crueel Ire, reed as any gleede;
> The pykepurs, and eek the pale Drede;
> The smylere with the knyf under the cloke;
> The shepne brennynge with the blake smoke;
> The tresoun of the mordrynge in the bedde;
> The open werre, with woundes al bibledde.

> There saw I first the dark imagining
> Of Felony, and all the company;
> The cruel Ire, red as any coal;
> The pick-pocket, and also the pale Dread;
> The smiler with the knife under the cloak;
> The sheepbarn burning with the black smoke;
> The treason of the murdering in the bed;
> The open war, with wounds all bled.[6]

The scene's images veer around the act itself: the smiler with the (yet unused) knife, the barn already burning, the war's wounds made to bleed with blows struck offstage. Chaucer's literary swerve traces the legal one, which perpetually avoids describing the act itself in favor of describing its own reaction to the act. But Chaucer's "dark imagining" also presents the shared fiction that

---

[5] The UK abolished the category in the Criminal Law Act of 1967, but the US retains it from the Anglo-American tradition.

[6] Geoffrey Chaucer, "The Knight's Tale," I ll. 1995–2002, in *The Riverside Chaucer*, ed. Larry Dean Benson, and F.N Robinson (Boston: Houghton Mifflin, 1987).

compensates for this tautology; these scenes help the reader to fantasize that we would know Felonye if we saw him. The litany of colors, emotions, and images pass so quickly in these lines that we might be forgiven for imagining that this scene *does* describe felony. The specificity of these images masks the fact that felony itself never materializes.

These peculiarities and their origins are the subject of this book. In it, I explore felony's beginnings in thirteenth- to fifteenth-century English common law, and I argue that both felony's lack of definition and our unspoken but certain sense that it must have one derive from the fact that felony—unlike most legal categories—was left to laymen to define. In medieval common law, felonies constituted the most serious class of crimes, but professional lawmen generally found the matter "boring and distasteful."[7] "Crime has never been the business of lawyers," as S.F.C. Milsom reminds us, so although felony fell under royal purview, crown justices were happy to let its procedure—from collecting evidence to determining guilt—fall to the local community.[8] This meant that people who were almost always untrained in the law were tasked with pursuing the case from act until the last moment of the trial.

Left with difficult questions but few legal concepts, they turned to cultural ones, archived in sermons they heard, plays they had seen, poetry they knew. A juror investigating a neighbor for a robbery might want to know: what makes an act felonious, as opposed to just wrong? Does this quality lie in the act itself, or in the manner or spirit in which it was committed? How does one choose which witnesses to trust and which to exclude? What amount or quality of proof would be sufficient, for both the law and one's own conscience, to put this neighbor to death? Unhelpfully, the entire chapter on felony robbery in the medieval judicial treatise *Glanvill* reads: "The crime of robbery need not be discussed, for it poses no special problems."[9] And so he might supply his own answers: it is not the murdering, it is the treason of slaying someone to whose bed you have access; it is not the burning of the barn, it is the malevolence of setting a fire among wooden dwellings; it is not what you might do with the knife, it is that you smiled as you concealed it.

This intellectual work created felony, a category made real by the force of law but whose boundaries were drawn by narrative, penitential, and poetic

---

[7] John G. Bellamy, *The Criminal Trial in Later Medieval England: Felony Before the Courts from Edward I to the Sixteenth Century* (Toronto: University of Toronto Press, 1998), p. 13.

[8] S.F.C. Milsom, *Historical Foundations of the Common Law* (London: Butterworths, 1969), p. 374.

[9] "Crimen quoque Roberiae sine specialibus intercurrentibus praeteritur," G.D.G. Hall, ed. and trans., *The Treatise on the Laws and Customs of the Realm of England Commonly Called Glanvill* (Oxford: Clarendon Press, 1994), pp. 174–175.

understandings of guilt, proof, and punishment. In each chapter of this book, I consider as one body of work the texts that made felony procedure: the literary treatments of its major concepts (like evidence, witnessing, and culpability) alongside the documents of its practice, from coroners' rolls to records of the eyre. I argue that felony was created by the procedure that prosecuted it, and that its capacious stock of sources informed a concept that, to this day, remains suspended between crime and imaginary construct. This suspension has ensured the category's longevity over more than seven centuries; the legal category of felony has been sustained by the fact that its conceptualization has always lain outside of the law, out of reach of any shift or reform.

As a result, this book's argument lies primarily in its sources and methodology. Most scholarship in medieval law and literature from the discipline of literature has focused on statute and theory, drawing from the instantiating texts of English law: acts of Parliament, judicial treatises, the Magna Carta.[10] There are good reasons for this. For one thing, as members of an educated elite, poets were generally closer in station to judges and members of Parliament than they were to the usual cast that filled a criminal courtroom. The two groups were more likely to share both material concerns and cultural perspectives. For another, these texts are far more promising to a literary eye. They are longer, full of references and reasoning, and the lineage of their ideas is often discoverable. In addition, they were made (in a literal sense) for this reading; both their authors and their contemporary audiences understood them to be creating the law, which means that scholars can read them as they were intended to be read.

But felony was its procedure, and it requires different sources. For the most part, the records I examine—of coroners' inquests, indictments, and trials—were created for administrative and fiscal purposes, and are accordingly abundant but formulaic, terse, and partial. The specifics they give are of all the wrong sort for an inquiry into state of mind; they record fines and sureties in great detail, but do not seek to demystify how a jury chose witnesses, for example, nor discuss what coroners thought of evidentiary standards. This colorlessness is likely why few studies of law and literature focus on procedure.

---

[10] This has been by far the norm, so there are too many to list here, but some excellent recent examples of this kind of work upon which I have drawn include Candace Barrington and Emily Steiner, eds., *Cambridge Companion to Medieval English Law and Literature* (Cambridge: Cambridge University Press, 2019), Jennifer Jahner's *Literature and Law in the Era of Magna Carta* (Oxford: Oxford University Press, 2019), and Emily Steiner, *Documentary Culture and the Making of English Literature* (Cambridge University Press, 2003). Andrew Rabin and Anya Adair, eds., *Law, Literature, and Social Regulation in Early Medieval England*, (Woodbridge: Boydell Press, 2023) is an example of this method applied to the early medieval period; even though it reaches back before most judicial treatises, most of its essays focus on law codes and legal writings by kings and bishops.

But I argue that in the case of felony, they provide an unusually direct site of interaction between literary and legal ideas, a conversation that can be brought out when set beside literary counterparts.

Similarly, the literary texts I have chosen are obviously legally minded but are not the most obvious sources for a work of law and literature because they rarely feature scenes of trials. Instead, I chose them because they engage with the concepts necessary to designing criminal procedure, issues like what constitutes evidence, whose testimony can be trusted, what written records can and cannot achieve. I suggest that like most medieval people, poets were more familiar with the rituals of the law's everyday practice than they were with its theory. When they wanted to work out their ideas about social harm and its repair, they turned to the forms they knew. In turn, the moral discourse they produced on felony generated its own vernacular theorization of guilt, proof, and verification that then guided legal practice.

Chaucer's smiler provides a good example of the story I seek to tell here, of how this intellectual production—between law, literature, and religious writing—took place. Duplicity—smiling while concealing a knife—was the first definition of felony, but it does not seem to have originated in a single tradition. Rather, felony/*felonia* as a crime of duplicity entered literature, penitential writing, and secular law simultaneously around the turn of the fourteenth century. The manuscripts of the Middle English romance *Beves of Hamtoun* (c. 1300) describe Beves interchangeably as "that wike lad, that fule treitour" and "that wekyd lad, that ffelown," and the penitential manual *Handlyng Synne* (1303) calls Judas, the arch-betrayer, "foul felun," who "weytede Ihu wyth tresun."[11] Beves and Judas committed different acts; their shared status as felons derived from having betrayed someone they had seemed to love. That is, their felony derived from their stories, a feature that would not seem to translate well to a legal category.

And yet around the same moment in 1300, *Britton* (the first judicial treatise to use the category as a crime) describes felony as "any mischief, which a man knowingly does, or procures to be done, to one to whom he pretends to be a friend," mirroring the literary definition almost exactly.[12] This definition is

---

[11] E. Kölbing, ed., *The Romance of Sir Beues of Hamtoun* (London: N. Trübner, 1885), ll. 479–480, and Robert of Brunne, *Robert of Brunne's* Handlyng Synne, *A.D. 1303: With those Parts of the Anglo-French Treatise on which It Was Founded, William of Wadington's* Manuel des pechiez, ed. Frederick Furnivall (London: EETS, 1901), p. 142.

[12] The dating of *Britton* is not known, but it refers to several statutes passed in the 1290s—including the important land statute "Quia Emptores"—which suggests a date between 1295 and 1300. Jean le Breton, *Summa de legibus Angliae que vocatur Bretone*, ed. Francis Nichols, vol. 1 (Oxford: Clarendon Press, 1865), p. 40.

far more polemical than technical; the records clearly show that not just "any mischief" could be considered a felony, and how exactly would the law propose to identify a pretense of friendship? The eventual prosecution of felony provided specifics (murder, robbery, rape, and arson were the mischiefs in question) but the original, cross-disciplinary sense of felony as betrayal—of crown, of friend, of community—lingered perceptibly in the background of coroners' inquests, indictments, and judicial comment, and returned vividly in Chaucer's smiler almost a hundred years later. Even as enforcement provided some practical parameters, felony's essential quality remained narrative.

Calling the creation of felony procedure a "dark imagining" gets closest to the way I understand it in this book: as a diffuse intellectual project built by day-to-day practice, mired in and elevated by ideals of justice drawn from every corner of life. This perception has guided my method. Each chapter pairs one or two case records (in one instance, a procedural manual) with a literary text that I believe helps us perceive a movement of thought or an activity that had been obscured, either in the legal texts themselves or in the procedure more generally. In one case, I suggest a close reading of a literary text can reveal details of the practice of law that did not make it into the law's own records. In another, I argue that a poet observed an instability in the pursuit of the law and tried to work it out in their own lines, and that perceiving this critique helps us see that the same analysis was playing out in the law as well. In other cases, there is no clear trail, and rather than attempting to trace a lineage of thought, I have sought to surface a conversation I believe was taking place in both literature and the law. In each chapter, I begin with a legal text, move to a literary one, and then return to the legal, applying the perceptual lessons we can draw from traversing the texts as a single discourse. Throughout, I have focused repeating a methodological gesture to discover the variety of conclusions it can offer.

In framing felony procedure as an intellectual project, I am also wading into a conversation about the motivations and interests of the local jury to suggest that they brought to their work more integrity and rigor than has been assumed. Most scholars have agreed that the medieval jury was largely left to its own devices when it came to investigating the crime, gathering evidence, interviewing witnesses, and coming to a conclusion. The ideal of a modern juror is someone who is representatively "average" and uninformed about the case. The medieval juror, by contrast, was high status, and prized for his (or in some rare cases, her) information about both the issue and the parties. This dynamic has led many to assume that juries simply decided cases on the basis of reputation and what was the best outcome for them personally. As Richard Firth

Green memorably put it, the local jury judged "the *trouthe* of the man not the truth of the accusations made against him."[13] The dynamic of the jury clearly opened the door to self-dealing and mixed motives, issues I discuss at length in Chapter 3. But throughout this study, I have found a great deal of good faith engagement—among thinkers both legal and literary—with felony procedure's urgent conceptual questions: what evidence should be valued most highly for proof (Chapter 1), whether guilt is binary or lies on a spectrum (Chapter 4), and what danger our love of a good story poses to justice (Chapter 2).

In doing so, I also intervene in a related conversation on the struggle between local and royal power, both over jurisdiction for crime and over larger political issues.[14] The standard story goes that local communities resisted and resented royal courts as crown overreach, butting into community matters in which they had no business. Evidence for this tension is everywhere: in literature like "The Song on the Venality of Judges" and "The Outlaw of Trailbaston" that lambasted the corruption and overzealousness of the judiciary, or in the numerous cases (as in Chapter 3) where local power brokers successfully derailed court proceedings.[15] In the Peasant Rebellion of 1381, one of the central aims of the rebels had been to kill as many lawmen as they could find, based on the general understanding that the increasing specialization of the profession and the bureaucratic complications of legal procedures were barring them from what they understood to be their own law: the ancient, natural law of England.[16] And so this story of tension has been strongly enforced by associating these positions with "the peasantry." Modern scholars have read this evidence as reflective of a united local resistance to crown intrusion, calling coroners mere "tax gatherers," arguing that "the judicial authority of the

---

[13] Richard Firth Green, *A Crisis of Truth: Literature and Law in Ricardian England* (Philadelphia: University of Pennsylvania Press, 1999), p. 131.
[14] For a recent example, see Luke Sunderland, *Rebel Barons: Resisting Royal power in Medieval Culture* (Oxford: Oxford University Press, 2017). This assumption is also the basis for Green's argument in *A Crisis of Truth* that the documentation the courts required was resented for having assumed the authority of truth.
[15] Although as Wendy Scase has pointed out, both of these poems are written in Anglo-Norman and clearly represent the perspective of a local lord who considered himself ousted from his rightful position, and hardly an underdog story: *Literature and Complaint in England, 1272–1553* (Oxford: Oxford University Press, 2007), pp. 85–100.
[16] As Green has pointed out, this intention is attested in *Anonimalle Chronicle*, Walsingham's *Historia*, and *Knighton's Chronicle* (*A Crisis of Truth*, p. 198). For these works, see in order: Wendy Childs and John Taylor, eds., *The Anonimalle Chronicle, 1307 to 1334: From Brotherton Collection MS 29* (Cambridge: Cambridge University Press, 2013); Thomas de Walsingham, *Historia Anglicana*, ed. Henry Thomas Riley, 2 vols. (London: Longman et al., 1862–1864); and Henry Knighton, *Knighton's Chronicle, 1337–1396*, ed. and trans. G.H. Martin (Oxford: Oxford University Press, 1996). Steven Justice has argued that they showed a sophisticated understanding of the principles and practice of English law, and considered professional lawmen an assault on the "true" law of England, to which they had a natural right (*Writing and Rebellion: England in 1381* [Berkeley: University of California Press, 1994], pp. 44–48).

crown was a public nuisance," and positioning even the documentation these courts required as a resented intrusion into local ways of creating truth.[17]

But a thread that runs throughout the examples of this book is that this binary encounter had a third party: the local victims. In fact, the book's subject is the participation of those same local communities in the prosecution of offenses *for* the crown, participation that seems often active, even eager. Of course, local authorities are not always universally loved by their own communities. The abuses perpetrated by local power-holders could be the most destructive to their own communities, and royal jurisdiction offered victims an opportunity to seek—if not true accountability—then at least a record of their grievances and perhaps some reputational damage for the perpetrators. While the Anglo-Norman "Outlaw of Trailbaston" bemoaned the overzealousness of the courts, commons complaints most often deplored the laxity of those same courts and begged for more, not fewer, indictments and convictions. Partly because felony was a way to leverage the struggle between local and royal power, and partly because its offenses were of the grave, violent sort, a good number of felony cases I discuss here target offenders who had previously escaped punishment by way of their power (whether social, political, economic, or relational; see Chapters 3 and 4). While local authorities might have resented sharing power with crown justices, these cases caution us that we should not assume that their attitudes were representative of every member of their communities.[18]

As the field of law and literature has settled from its spotlight in the early 2000s, I believe its unique methodologies have come into sharper focus. This book is inspired by recent works from the disciplines of literature, history, and law that have taken expansive approaches to sources and methodology. In literary studies, Jamie Taylor and Emma Lipton's work on witnessing both literary and legal has demonstrated that the two are, in Lipton's words, "mutually constitutive perceptual habits."[19] Both books harness theoretical concepts to make startlingly concrete claims about what it meant to perceive in community,

---

[17] Paul Matthews, "Involuntary Manslaughter: A View from the Coroner's Court," *Journal of Criminal Law* 60, no. 2 (1996): pp. 189–200; Michael Clanchy, "Law, Government, and Society in Medieval England: Review of *Crime and Public Order in England* in the Later Middle Ages by John Bellamy," *History* 59, no. 195 (1974): p. 78; Green, *A Crisis of Truth*, especially pp. 166–201.

[18] Ian Forrest's work on "trustworthy men" does an excellent job of complicating the local/royal divide by delving into what exactly made a person "trustworthy" and how the confluence of power conferred by that title created space for local abuses and the complications of local politics: *Trustworthy Men: How Inequality and Faith Made the Medieval Church* (Princeton, NJ: Princeton University Press, 2020).

[19] Emma Lipton, *Cultures of Witnessing: Law and the York Plays* (Philadelphia: University of Pennsylvania Press, 2022), p. 24; Jamie Taylor, *Fictions of Witnessing: Witnessing, Literature, and Community in the Late Middle Ages* (Columbus, OH: Ohio State University Press, 2019).

claims that reach beyond the texts to the society around them, as this book seeks to. Legal historian Sara Butler's books define fields, and her most recent book on *peine forte et dure* (the torture that would coerce a defiant defendant into entering a plea) is a work of law and literature as well as legal history. She uses literary sources to cast a wide-angle lens on the issue of torture and protest in the period, using literary depictions of torture to help us understand its valences in this context.[20] Elizabeth Kamali, writing for both a legal and legal-historical audience, demonstrated with both legal and penitential sources that medieval jurors had a robust concept of *mens rea*, a conclusion difficult to discern from case records alone.[21]

In my mind, this book could not have existed before now, because it draws so gratefully on very recent scholarship in both medieval literary studies (like the investigations into medieval narrative theory that inform Chapter 2) and legal history (like Ian Forrest's work on trustworthy men that enabled Chapter 3). As a result, the book, like the procedure it identifies, participates in conversations in both disciplines. The creators of felony procedure drew freely from both arenas in order to build a practice of law that accorded with their values. Therefore, rather than tracing a familiar path of influence from theory to practice or from law to literature, this book tells the story of ideas born in the inquest and the courtroom: the notions about justice the participants brought with them, the literary representations of wrongdoing that informed these notions, the procedures and documentary systems that brought them to life, and their influence on writers who created poetry in order to imagine a more just disposition for their world.

The remainder of this Introduction follows a format more familiar to historians than to literary scholars, one meant to lay the groundwork of the material rather than the groundwork of the ideas. This is partly because some of the legal material might be less familiar to readers from literature, and partly because the heart of my argument lies in the practice of my methodology, in the efficacy (or failure) of the chapters themselves. Thus, I will begin with an outline of the steps of felony procedure, which might be of use for readers to reference because it is a roadmap that I struggled to locate when I began this project. I will then provide some context for my legal and literary sources, and discuss the obvious issue of language in the project (my literary sources are all in English, while most legal records are in Latin and Anglo-Norman). I end the

---

[20] Sara Butler, *Pain, Penanace, and Protest:* Peine Forte et Dure *in Medieval England* (Cambridge: Cambridge University Press, 2022).
[21] Elizabeth Papp Kamali, *Felony and the Guilty Mind in Medieval England* (Cambridge: Cambridge University Press, 2019).

introduction with a summary of the chapters and a reflection on the project's self-imposed limitations.

Felony and its Procedure

Felony was a common law category of crime punishable by the loss of life and property. By the thirteenth century, its list of offenses was short (murder, rape, robbery, arson, treason), and they overlapped neatly with the early medieval "bōtlēas" crimes, offenses too serious to be resolved by remuneration (bōte) because they betrayed the very notion of community.[22] As a result, unlike most crimes, felony fell under the purview of the crown; it was investigated by the crown's coroners and tried by the crown's justices. Its prosecution became a primary subject of the eyres, assizes, and special commissions the king sent in circuits around the country. And yet, as John Bellamy puts it, "there has survived no great wealth of material which describes the actual process of the criminal trial—rather the reverse ... there is little that can be called direct and informed contemporary content."[23]

This makes its details difficult to reconstruct, but also demonstrates a primary contention of this book: felony procedure was a matter of the public, not the lawyers. Not only did most of it take place in public, barely any part of medieval society was exempt from participation in it, and this participation started from the moment a crime was discovered. Townspeople performed law enforcement duties as well as responsibilities like pledging, witnessing, serving on juries, providing expert opinions, and paying fines when the vill had failed in any one of these duties. Anyone who came across a body or witnessed a crime was considered a "first-finder," and was bound to raise the hue and cry, which anyone within earshot was required to respond to.[24] The first finder would also be required to give testimony to the coroner when he arrived, and perhaps the indicting and trial juries as well.[25] As I show in Chapter 1, those who arrived after the hue and cry were responsible for

---

[22] Felix Liebermann, ed. and trans., *Die Gesetze der Angelsachsen*, vol. 1 (Halle: Niemeyer, 1903–1916), pp. 88–89.

[23] Bellamy, *The Criminal Trial in Later Medieval England*, p. 8.

[24] Samantha Sagui, "The Hue and Cry in Medieval English Towns," *Historical Research* 87, no. 236 (2014): pp. 179–193.

[25] R.F. Hunnisett details these amerceable duties of the first finder in *The Medieval Coroner* (Cambridge: Cambridge University Press, 1961), pp. 10–11, 24. These are only the duties for which the first finder could be fined if they did not complete them; their presence throughout the procedure indicates a high level of participation for the first finder, suggesting that there might have also been more informal duties or voluntary participation.

investigating the crime, examining the body, seizing suspects, and protecting the scene.

When the coroner arrived (sometimes days later) he would hold an inquest, to which all men over the age of 14 from the four neighboring vills had to come, and his enrollment would rely largely on the fruits of the crowd's investigation, as communicated to him by a jury.[26] This jury, like all others in the procedure, would be drawn from local "oathworthy" men. While virtually everyone was required to participate at some point in the criminal prosecution, not everyone's word was weighted equally. Those who were called upon to serve on juries, provide sureties, and give witness testimony were men who already held local power and significance, an overlap in social and legal power that is the subject of Chapter 3. If the suspect had not already fled or claimed sanctuary in a church, he would be attached to stand trial, either through imprisonment or release on sureties, again provided by oathworthy men.

Indictment could come in several ways, all of which involved the support of the public. To bring indictments indirectly, a indicting jury could propose cases to the judge, or somebody (or a number of somebodies) might bring a bill to a judge who would then pass it to the jury to verify.[27] The aggrieved or a family member could also bring a direct appeal, but even this involved the many; any accusation would need to be announced at several consecutive sheriff's tourns (which many prominent townspeople were obligated to attend) and county court sessions. The publicity of the sheriff's tourn was invoked in a variety of situations where the public could be of service, like when the accused had fled and needed to be captured, or to enforce abjuration (when a suspect vowed to abjure the realm and make directly for the nearest port rather than standing trial).[28] As it was the period when both the charge and the defense came into focus, the indictment stage was where most of witness-interrogating, document-sifting, and evidence-weighing took place.

---

[26] While Hunnisett doubts this requirement, there are many instances of neighboring vills being amerced for their failure to appear. See for example the eyre of Kent in 1313–1314, when the justice admonished that because Overland, Weddington, Rolwing, and Dene (the four neighboring vills) had not attended the coroner's inquest for the death of John Bunter, they were all in mercy. Frederic W. Maitland, Leveson W. Vernon Harcourt, and William C. Boland, eds. *The Eyre of Kent of 6 and 7 Edward II (1313–1314)* (London: Selden Society, 1909), p. 139. See also Charles Gross, *Select Cases from the Coroners' Rolls, A.D. 1265–1413, with a Brief Account of the History of the Office of Coroner* (London: Bernard Quaritch, 1896), pp. 42–45.

[27] Bellamy provides a thorough discussion of indicting juries and their overlap (or nonoverlap) with trial juries, and the attempts to keep these functions separate (*The Criminal Trial*, pp. 26–27).

[28] For a summary of the ways the public was involved (both formally and informally) in law enforcement in towns, see: H.R.T. Summerson, "The Structure of Law Enforcement in Thirteenth Century England," *American Journal of Legal History* 23, no. 4 (1979): pp. 313–327.

By the time the accused stood at the bar to plead his case, possibly with help of a professional pleader (the subject of Chapter 2), it is hard to imagine any in the audience were new to the story. The involvement of the crowd at every stage of the procedure also meant that they probably felt more than a passive investment in the case. This meant that when the justice read the charge and asked the accused, "How do you wish to acquit yourself?," the audience was filled with people who considered this their business. If the accused dutifully pled "guilty" or "not guilty," the trial commenced. If the accused refused to plead and instead "stood mute," he could be put to *peine forte et dure*, a form of torture designed to coerce his compliance. In Chapter 5, I consider this example and how an invested and literarily informed audience might have shaped what such a refusal signified for the accused and the power of the court.

The trial itself proceeded at a breakneck pace. Witnesses were rarely called, and most scholars have agreed with Ralph Pugh's estimate that, on average, criminal trials took less than fifteen minutes.[29] Within this quarter of an hour, charges and pleas would be spoken, any necessary negotiation or clarification would be hastily resolved, and a verdict would be reached. The accused would be remanded to prison for hanging, remanded with a recommendation of pardon, or released, and the next defendant called. One reason that criminal procedure has seemed an unpromising interlocutor for literature is a predictable result of this brevity: as Robert Davis observed, "courtroom trial scenes are rare in medieval English literature, and, when they do appear, few are detailed."[30] But in the context of the entire procedure, this is hardly surprising. By the time the case had made it to a courtroom, most matters of interest and any drama had already taken place. For the purposes of exploring meaning-making in criminal procedure, the trial might be the least significant component, and as a result I do not dedicate a chapter to it in this book.

The Records of Felony Procedure

The records this process produced are the main legal sources of this book. Vast and carefully preserved, their documentary technology oriented them toward an interconnected archive. This orientation made for a repetitive record, but one that was designed to take part in a single conversation. As a result, they

---

[29] R.B. Pugh, "The Duration of Criminal Trials in Medieval England," in *Law, Litigants and the Legal Profession*, eds. E.W. Ives and A.H. Manchester (London: Royal Historical Society, 1983), pp. 104–115, p. 108.

[30] Robert Evan Davis, "Medieval Law in The Tale of Beryn," *Classica and Mediaevalia* 36 (1985): p. 261.

were zealously organized and protected. In the opening proceedings of the Northamptonshire Eyre of 1339–40, Chief Justice Scrope called (as was customary) for "all coroners who had held office since the last eyre, that is since 1285" to produce their records, and that they be delivered "in white bags marked with the name of the coroner and the name of the one who delivered them up and the period when the coroner held office."[31] A fantasy of perfect preservation (over more than fifty years) layers upon itself the fantasies of perfect organization and recollection, white bags and all. And this was no empty formula; the records of the next several days are filled with questioning, threatening, and arresting errant coroners and their heirs. In one case the chief justice arrested and fined a coroner because, although he presented himself, remembered the incident, and claims to have recorded it in his rolls, "they were searched and nothing was found."[32] It was not enough that the man was present and had the information they needed; the document itself was essential.

Criminal jurisdiction in medieval England was overlapping and complex, and it created a wide range of source materials, so I will briefly describe here the case records I use and where they can be found. Coroners' rolls contain a record of the inquest held by the coroner with the aid of a local jury. Some of the enrollments have been published; most can be found in the JUST 2 series of the National Archives.[33] Gaol delivery records, some published and most found in the JUST 3 series and the KB (King's Bench) series of the National Archives, were produced when the prisoners from a jail were delivered to stand trial.[34] Gaol delivery became a more routine practice toward the end of the fourteenth century, so more of the records are from this period up to the latter half of the fifteenth century.

---

[31] "Touz les coroners (...) qi vnt este coroners pus le drein eir, ceo est assauer pus lan .xiij"/"en blanches bagges titlez du noun le coroner et du noun celi qi les liure et du tens qil fut en le office." Oxford, Bodleian Library, Tanner MS. 13, fol. 162r. This note, absent from other records of the eyre, is also attested in the other manuscript produced at Lincoln, Lincoln Cathedral Library MS 169. These notes only appear in two rolls copied at Lincoln that, as Donald Sutherland points out in his edition, are identical in arrangement but have not been copied from one another, suggesting that the notes were added programmatically with a knowledgeable sense of what would enhance the documents' usefulness (Donald Sutherland, eds. and trans., *The Eyre of Northhamptonshire: 3-4 Edward III, A.D. 1329–1330*, vol. 1 [London: Selden Society, 1983], pp. lxix–lxxi). Although I take Sutherland's translations as a guide, I have used my own here because the manuscripts I was working from vary from his edition.

[32] "les quex furent quis et rien troue" (Bod. Lib., Tanner MS. 13, f. 162r).

[33] In addition to the collections I use in Chapter 1, another example is: R.F. Hunnisett, ed. and trans., *Bedfordshire Coroners' Rolls* (Streatley: Bedfordshire Historical Record Society, 1961).

[34] Published examples include: Elisabeth G. Kimball, ed. and trans., *A Cambridgeshire Gaol Delivery Roll, 1332–1334* (Cambridge: Cambridge Antiquarian Records Society, 1978); Barbara A. Hanawalt, ed. and trans., *Crime in East Anglia in the Fourteenth Century: Norfolk Gaol Delivery Rolls, 1307–1316* (Norwich: Norfolk Record Society, 1976); Ralph B. Pugh, ed. and trans., *Wiltshire Gaol Delivery and Trailbaston Trials* (Devizes: Wiltshire Archaeological and Natural History Society, 1978).

I also discuss plea rolls of the eyre, assize, and *oyer and terminer* tribunals, all of which were itinerant courts sent by the crown to try cases across the counties. The eyre was a visitation by an itinerant justice to try criminal and civil pleas, and its jurisdiction overlapped with that of the assizes, which originally tried property issues but began to try gaol deliveries in the late thirteenth century. *Oyer and terminer* commissions, which included the notorious Trailbaston proceedings, tried certain categories of crimes, including felonies, that seemed necessary to keeping the king's peace. Some of these records (particularly those of the eyre) have been published, in the form in which they were disseminated in the aftermath of the circuit.[35] The unpublished material is mostly available in the JUST 1 series of the National Archives.

Finally, I draw from the Year Books, which were compilations of unofficial records of important or peculiar cases that might be useful to lawyers in the course of their duties. They directly quote the arguments of justices and counsel much more often than case records do, and therefore offer more direct information on issues of reasoning and argumentation. Because they were designed to build the common law, they were circulated in a great number of manuscripts during the medieval period and printed in the sixteenth century. The so-called "Vulgate" edition that I often cite was printed at the end of the seventeenth century.[36] These texts are not representative; like most texts produced by professional lawmen, they are far more interested in civil matters than criminal, and they often selected criminal cases that were unusual or unique.

English in the Courtroom

All of the above records are composed in either Anglo-Norman or Latin. But it is obviously essential to my argument that all parties shared a language, if not in writing then at least in speaking and reading. At the initial stages of criminal procedure, I believe we may assume that those who investigated

---

[35] In addition to *The Eyre of Northhamptonshire* collection that I cite above, see for example: Herbert G. Fowler, *Calendar of the Roll of the Justices on Eyre, 1247* (Aspley Guise: Bedfordshire Historical Record Society, 1939); C.A.F. Meekings, ed. and trans., *Crown Pleas of the Wiltshire Eyre, 1249* (Devizes: Wiltshire Archaeological and Natural History Society, 1961); R. Stewart-Brown, ed. and trans., *Calendar of County Court, City Court and Eyre Rolls of Chester, 1259–1297* (Manchester: Chetham Society, 1925).

[36] For each citation of the Year Books, I include the standard citation (term, regnal year, case number, and folio) and the published reference, but also the Seipp number, to make it easier to locate. See David Seipp and Carol Lee, eds., *Medieval English Legal History: An Index and Paraphrase of Printed Year Book Reports, 1268–1535* (Boston: Boston University School of Law, 2003).

the crime, consulted one another on what happened, and protected the scene would have used their mother tongue to communicate with one another. There is good evidence that coroners' inquests were conducted in English, even if they were recorded in Latin, and as Sara Butler notes, the oaths required for those giving evidence and performing law enforcement duties both existed in the vernacular.[37] But as the procedure moved toward its more formal steps, the linguistic landscape became more mixed. The courtroom—with all its bureaucracies and documentary demands—would naturally be the most hostile space to English within the procedure, with all other spaces less so. If we assume this, we can examine the state of English in the courtroom and extrapolate linguistic tolerance outwards from there.

The much-discussed Statute of Pleading of 1362 proclaimed that English should be used in all courts pertaining to royal matters for accessibility and fairness reasons; "since (cases) are pleaded, counted, and judged in the French language, which is very much unknown in the said realm, so that people who plead or are impleaded in the king's courts and the courts of others have no understanding or knowledge of what is said for them or against them," all cases before any court henceforth "shall be pleaded and counted in the English language."[38] Modern scholars have alternately taken this Statute as a definitive turning point toward the vernacular or assumed that the legal profession ignored it and carried on in French.[39] But as W.M. Ormrod has painstakingly shown, it was attended by so many similar policies and by other supportive political changes that it seems more likely to have been just one move in a larger trend toward viva voce proceedings in English that began long before and were already the strong norm.[40]

---

[37] See Sara Butler, *Forensic Medicine and Death Investigation in Medieval England* (Milton Park: Taylor & Francis, 2014), pp. 40, 80–81.

[38] C. Given-Wilson et al., eds., *The Parliament Rolls of Medieval England*, vol. 2 (Leicester: Scholarly Editions, 2005), 273, http://sd-editions.com; translation by W.M. Ormrod,"The Use of English: Language, Law, and Political Culture in Fourteenth-Century England," *Speculum* 78, no. 3 (2003): pp. 756–757.

[39] For the former, see for example Janet Coleman, *English Literature in History, 1350–1400: Medieval Readers and Writers* (London: Hutchinson, 1981), Ethan Knapp, *The Bureaucratic Muse: Thomas Hoccleve and the Literature of Late Medieval England* (University Park, PA: Pennsylvania State University Press, 2001); and Emily Steiner and Candace Barrington, "Introduction," in *The Letter of the Law: Legal Practice and Literary Production in Medieval England*, ed. Emily Steiner and Candace Barrington (Ithaca, NY: Cornell University Press, 2002), pp. 1–11. For the latter, see Jean Devaux, "From the Court of Hainault to the Court of England: The Example of Jean Froissart," in *War, Government, and Power in Late Medieval France*, ed. Christopher Allmand (Liverpool: Liverpool University Press, 2000), pp. 1–20.

[40] Ormrod, "The Use of English," see especially pp. 752–753.

Interestingly, the exception the Statute provides is for the "terms and processes" of the law, which can continue in Anglo-Norman.[41] As John Baker argues, "terms and processes" refer to the highly technical count, or plea, an argument corroborated by Sir John Fortescue's observation that "the English ... were used to pleading in French, until the custom was much restricted by force of a certain statute; even so, it has been impossible hitherto to abolish the custom in its entirety, partly because of certain terms which pleaders express more accurately in French than in English."[42] As Ormrod points out, the claim that lawmen blithely ignored this Statute and carried on in French seems to rest on a misunderstanding of this clause; because "pleading" can refer to both the formal "plea" or "count" and all the discussion and negotiation that takes place in court, scholars have mistaken this reference to the formal mechanics of the plea to mean the entire trial procedure. This linguistic division between the language of the plea and other aspects of the trial is reflected in the fact that the manual on pleading I discuss in Chapter 2 is my only longer text in French.

Relevant to this study, the Statute's only regulatory precedent seems to have been in the criminal and petty sphere of the sheriff's tourn; in 1356, the mayor and aldermen of London ordered that the proceedings in the sheriff's court of the city should be held in English.[43] This meant that all felony accusations pronounced at successive sheriffs' tourns would be given in English, as would all requests for people to corroborate or deny these accusations. Likewise, any requests to find felons who had fled or to enforce abjuration would also be disseminated in the local vernacular. This setting would make good sense as the first location of mandated English if the picture upon which this study rests is true: that criminal procedure was largely an affair of local labor (and local language), even when it fell under royal jurisdiction. If there was any place in the crown jurisdiction where the demands of Anglo-Norman and Latin eroded quickest, it would be in the legal system manned by laymen.

English was increasingly becoming the language of testimony in religious spheres as well. Throughout the book, I use penitential and sermon examples because they provided these laymen an organized and familiar system

---

[41] David Mellinkoff, *The Language of the Law* (Boston, MA: Resource Publications, 1963), pp. 111–112.

[42] John Baker, *The Common Law Tradition* (London: Hambledon Press, 2000), pp. 225–246; Sir John Fortescue, *De laudibus legum Angliae*, ed. and trans. S.B. Chrimes (Cambridge: Cambridge University Press, 1949), p. 115.

[43] R.R. Sharpe, ed., *Calendar of the Letter Books of the City of London*, 11 vols (London: John Edward Francis, 1899–1907), p. 73. See also Anthony Musson, *Medieval Law in Context: The Growth of Legal Consciousness from Magna Carta to the Peasant's Revolt* (Manchester: Manchester University Press, 2001), pp. 208–209.

for deciding questions of guilt and its severity. Lateran IV—the landmark church reform that addressed issues from the sacraments to criminal justice—mandated annual confession in 1215, and over the next 200 years this requirement sparked the creation of a genre of literature aimed at guiding priests and penitents through this new procedure, the majority of which was written in English in order to tend to the lay. In addition, townspeople in many places would have an annual example of trials held entirely in the local language in the Mystery Plays, annual pageants depicting the stories of the Bible, put on by the town. The trials of Christ were spread across two days of the celebration, and in them the proceedings from arrest to execution would be conducted in the vernacular.

Thus, the discourse in which I am interested—and the spaces in which it took place—was primarily English, even though its records were made in Latin and Anglo-Norman. This suggests that—even if there had been an abundance of professional legal treatises on felony law—it might still make sense to turn to vernacular and public sources in a book such as this one. The accessibility of the medium and the language would make their understandings of guilt, evidence, and proof closer to hand to the layman than the Latin judicial treatise or the Anglo-Norman procedural manual. The fact that those sources for criminal procedure do not exist as they do for other forms of the law, in other words, is not the only reason they would not be the best ones for this study.

Literature and the Law in the Making of Felony Procedure

I have intentionally confined my method to making small demonstrative gestures drawn from a few texts, rather than larger claims drawn from an accumulation of evidence. My argument in each chapter has deferred to what seem to me to be each text's primary concerns, while also seeking to open a wider angle for future discussion. As a result, although each chapter focuses on a different moment in felony procedure, roughly pacing through a case from beginning to end, it cannot aim to sketch the full field of interactions between literary texts and the documents of felony procedure. Rather, the chapters together seek to demonstrate a variety of possible angles on the issue and suggest new ways of conceiving it. In some, I speak more directly to conversations in legal history; in others, more directly to concerns of medieval literary studies, and the direction of each intervention has been dictated by what I believe the texts in question can and cannot tell us.

In Chapter 1, I argue that *St. Erkenwald*, a *miraculum* in which a bishop of London reanimates the long-forgotten corpse of a pagan judge, offers a rare portrait of medieval death investigation. Because the bishop uses the judge's reanimation and subsequent baptism to knit together pagan and Christian England into a single national history, most scholarship on the poem has focused on its historiographical work. But of course, the poem is also an investigation of a dead body, and the body is a judge of the eyre, whose just and blameless life in the law is what made him worthy of belated salvation. Once we perceive its legal valences, we can see that the poem meticulously recreates a death inquest by bringing to life the form of a coroner's enrollment, acting out what was meant to be only a textual form. It offers us a vivid glimpse of investigative procedure, particularly of aspects that are absent or only vaguely outlined in legal records, like the investigation of a community after a body is found but before the coroner arrives. I consider the poem next to two coroners' enrollments in order to see what this new perspective reveals about previously hidden aspects of the procedure.

I also suggest that, in this portrait of that liminal moment, we can detect a deep ethical interest in evidence and proof procedures that emanated from the crowd's investigative practice itself. The fact that evidentiary standards were not recorded until much later has been taken to mean that physical evidence was not much valued in earlier moments, much less in unguided and informal investigations such as these. But I argue that the behavior of the crowd in the poem suggests an active investigative ideal, one in which physical evidence could be of the highest value, provided it could be made to speak. I also argue that the poem expresses a logical anxiety about the crowd's activities that must have been concerning from the crown's perspective; once communities were in the business of collecting the evidence, determining the culprit, and arresting him, why not go further? Why not simply continue to judgment and punishment, all without help of the coroner? The poem imposes a linguistic limit on this possibility; the zealous amateurs are stymied by words on the tomb that they cannot bring "to mouthe."[44] Thus, the poem hazards a kind of miraculous investigative procedure, in which the evidence is simply reanimated and made to speak for itself, and the helpful but unruly crowd knows when to fall silent.

In Chapter 2, I consider the curious text commonly called the *Placita Corone*, the only extant manual designed to guide criminal pleading. The text survives in more than twenty manuscripts; from the perspective of legal

---

[44] Clifford Peterson, ed., *Saint Erkenwald* (Philadelphia: University of Pennsylvania Press, 1977), l. 54.

treatises—particularly criminal ones—it was exceptionally popular. And yet the text is filled with so many procedural inconsistencies, uneven legal advice, and obvious procedural mistakes that its "very unreliability as a guide to the practice of the courts" has caused scholars to wonder what possible purpose it could have served.[45] In this chapter I suggest that its business was not to teach the rules of a plea but the narrative expectations of the courtroom and how to satisfy them. The plea, bringing as it does the story of the case to the courtroom, is a logical place to consider narrative in medieval criminal procedure. But while modern law and literature studies have long applied narrative theory to legal texts and contexts, such a study is more difficult to undertake on texts created long before the novels from which that theory was drawn.

I argue that we can harness a medieval theory of narrative if we approach from the perspective of audience expectations, which have especially high stakes when that audience will be deciding your (or your client's) fate. What that audience expected to hear—a story? an argument?—necessarily dictated the shape of the plea, and so it makes sense that anticipating that expectation would be as urgent a business of pleaders as would the up-to-date procedural rules. I put the treatise beside literary pleaders, including the sages in the *Seven Sages of Rome*, Chaucer's Man of Law, and John Gower's ideal pleader, to delineate a shared conversation about the construction and dangers of narrative satisfaction to the law. I argue that this conversation was made for a medieval reader—trained by the most popular literary genres to relish repetition and stitch up connections between discontinuous episodes—and that for such a reader, the eccentricities of the treatise slipped into place.

In Chapter 3, I turn to the power of the "oathworthy" witness, a man of standing in the community who could participate in juries, be called to testify in legal matters, and whose word was considered trustworthy enough to provide oaths for a variety of legal purposes. Though there are no descriptions of what made a man "oathworthy," we know that they generally overlapped with other forms of social power, such as local office-holding, wealth, and proximity to other powerful people. The fact that no critique of this system's obvious vulnerability to corruption exists in judicial treatises, combined with the fact that hearsay and reputation were routinely admitted as evidence for centuries after, has seemed to suggest that medieval legal thinkers themselves saw little danger in this system. I argue that we can locate such a critique in legal-minded literature, where false talk and its dangers are central problems, and

---

[45] J.B. Post, "Placita Corone," in *Legal Record and Historical Reality*, ed. Thomas G. Watkin (London: Hambledon Press, 1989), p. 5.

that recognizing its shape in literature can help us perceive a similar critique in the legal record.

I focus on the anonymous poem *The Pistil of Swete Susan*, a Middle English adaptation of the story of Susannah and the Elders from Daniel, in which the virtuous Susannah is falsely accused of adultery after spurning the advances of the lecherous Elders. Taken in both legal and penitential literature as the essential example of false witnessing, I argue that while in most contexts it was understood to be a procedural triumph (Daniel saves the day by separating the Elders and interviewing them separately), *The Pistil* treats it as a failure. The poem, I argue, is less interested in Daniel's *deus ex machina* and more in the system whose structural vulnerability to corruption trapped the innocent woman in the first place. I pair this with a case in which a justice baldly attempts to cajole, threaten, and beg a group of oathworthy men into accepting some token accountability for their criminal actions to demonstrate that the case and the justice's forthrightness partake in the same understanding of the testimonial system's inherent instabilities.

Chapter 4 turns to the vast records that these previous processes have occasioned and considers the documentary system as a whole. I focus on the crime of robbery, an offense roundly and hotly condemned in both judicial and social comment, but hazily defined and rarely punished. With this example, I consider the strangeness (and literariness) of a documentary procedure that routinely records so much failure, indeed, conviction rates (usually less than 20% by most estimates) ensured that the failure was the archive's primary subject.[46] I turn to the Good Thief in William Langland's *Piers Plowman*, a character reduced from a role model to a robber, and who plagues Will, the main character, with his unearned salvation. The poem returns again and again to the Thief, but never resolves its basic problem. Like the robbers that were hauled up repeatedly before the court only to slip the noose, however you tell the story, the Thief is always saved.

I argue that the poem's repetitions offer the reader cumulative opportunities to think through the problem of guilt and offer us an opportunity to consider what the self-consciously interconnected archive of felony might have been

---

[46] For example, in Essex sessions of the peace between 1377–1379, only 18.7 percent of those accused of robbery were convicted, and Kathleen Garay estimates the felony conviction rate in English counties as a whole between 1388 and 1399 to have been about 14 percent. Data drawn from Elizabeth Chapin Furber, ed., *Essex Sessions of the Peace, 1377–1379* (Colchester: Wiles & Sons Ltd for the Essex Archaeological Society, 1953), pp. 59–60, and K.E. Garay, "'No Peace nor Love in England': An Examination of Crime and Punishment in the English Counties, 1388–1409" (PhD dissertation, University of Toronto, 1977), pp. 338–339. Bellamy offers a thorough summary of the statistical studies of conviction rates in *The Criminal Trial*, pp. 96–98.

able to accomplish besides conviction. I turn to two cases of robbery—in which the jury attempts to record something beyond strict guilt or innocence—to consider what they might tell us about the archive's communicative function. Judicial comment and acts of parliament paint a dark picture of robbery's definition—as the natural and vicious end of beggars and wasters—but literary depictions (and the records themselves) often document robbery as an abuse of the powerful. I argue that in these cases we can see juries building their own definition, one that attempted to reconcile robbery's contradictory social valences and create a record that not only did the right thing, but said the right thing.

In each of the first four chapters, I focus on a different stage of the felony trial: the investigation, pleading, witness testimony, and judgment. In Chapter 5, I consider a practice unique to felony procedure that could end the trial before it even began. As I mentioned above, when the accused came to the bar, the judge asked, "How do you wish to acquit yourself?" This was originally meant to be a question of manner, but as the ordeal and trial by battle (which was never available to some defendants) fell out of use, the only true answer was jury trial, and the accused's answer of "guilty" or "not guilty" was really an indication of consent to be tried by jury. But if she said nothing, if she did not consent, the trial could not go on. The court had its own answer to this—*peine forte et dure*, a torture designed to coerce compliance—but I am interested in the silence itself. What kind of "saying nothing" was this? What did it signify to the audience, and what did it accomplish for the accused?

I consider several cases of "standing mute," as it was called, alongside some possible frameworks for understanding this silence. I examine the case of the silent Christ in the trials of the Mystery Plays (particularly the York example, but also others) to discuss the possibility of seeing the silence as a statement of protest against an unjust regime, and the consolidation of an identity as a Christian, English martyr. I note that the dramatization of the scene argues powerfully for that interpretation, but Christ's words themselves caution against interpreting messages in silence. Of course, there was another strong (political) tradition that considered silence to be anti-social recalcitrance, akin to the wasters who refuse to give their labor to their own community. I turn to the personification of silence in the poem *Mum and the Sothsegger*, a political poem from the *Piers Plowman* tradition, to seek a physical instantiation of "standing mute." I argue that—although Mum is clearly the villain—the poem helps us reflect on the disruptive power of silence, why it makes us uncomfortable, and what it reveals about the contradictory demands of the law.

I finish the body of the book with this chapter on silence because its conclusion forms a method that became important to me in its writing. As a necessary part of the work, I have tried to make these records speak, even when they were not designed to say what I sought. This has yielded big hypotheses from small practices. The neighbors who happened to hear the hue and cry and came running established standards of evidence and verification in their investigation. The terse, colorless gaol delivery rolls sought to theorize the definition of a crime. And the women who—out of terror or defiance or something else—refused to plead and stood silent before the court could destabilize the authority of the procedure itself. These habits of law and literature are exciting; they open more interpretive possibilities than they shut down, and allow us to find, in the contours of a few people's words, a clear shape of the world. But for me, the best lesson of combining the efforts of literary and legal historical approaches has been to be careful with that deep attention. Even as we turn a text over again and again in our hands, we must know that there is a limit to what it can offer up, and that that limit should be respected. I hope that I have done that here.

Chapter 1
Death Investigation

St. Erkenwald's Bright Body

Like all good detective stories, *St. Erkenwald* begins with a dead body. The townspeople of seventh-century London stumble on a tomb no one has seen before. They call for their bishop, Erkenwald, but before he arrives they open the lid, revealing a perfectly preserved, royally arrayed, and entirely unknown man. They comb their records and their memories for any sign of him, but are stumped until Erkenwald arrives and miraculously returns the body to a "goste lyfe" (l. 192).[1] The corpse itself testifies that he was a pagan judge who lived a blameless life before Christ, but that after burial, he lay unbaptized without decay under the church for centuries, suspended between death and judgment. Upon hearing this sad story, Erkenwald asks him to wait "as longe as I mygt lacche water / And cast vpon thi faire cors and carpe thes wordes" ("until I might find water / And cast it upon your fair corpse and say these words [of baptism]," ll. 316–17). But as the bishop speaks his plan, his tears fall upon the body. The judge reveals that the baptism is accomplished and has already restored him to his proper place; in an instant, his body has decayed as it ought to have, and his soul is in heaven as it ought to be. By Erkenwald's miracle, the good of pagan England is reclaimed.

St. Erkenwald practically demands a historicist reading. Its explicit project is to rehabilitate England's non-Christian past by unearthing the good in it and sublimating it into the Christian world. Facing the inconvenient fact that England had not always been Christian, the poem opens with the demolition, refounding, and renaming of the churches of London to represent the conquest of English history in the name of the newly Christian English identity.

---

[1] "Þurghe sum lant goste lyfe" (Peterson, *St. Erkenwald*, l. 192) All citations of *St. Erkenwald* are taken from Clifford Peterson, ed., *Saint Erkenwald* (Philadelphia: University of Pennsylvania Press, 1977), hereafter cited parenthetically in the text; all modern English translations are mine. To my knowledge, two modern English translations of the poem exist: Clifford Peterson, ed., *The Complete Works of the Pearl Poet*, trans. Casey Finch (Berkeley: University of California Press, 1993) and Christopher Cameron, "A Translation of the Middle English *St. Erkenwald*" (MA thesis, Emporia University, 1993). While my translations are indebted to both, neither work well as a citation text for this chapter: Finch's because of the liberties it takes to capture the poetry, and Cameron's because it renders the text in prose without line breaks.

Written during a politically unstable moment of Richard II's rocky reign, the poem makes a forceful argument for the longevity, durability, and essential Christianity of Englishness. As a result, studies have dissected at length what Ruth Nissé calls its "strikingly anxious" attitude toward historical discontinuities, examining its perspective on the strengths and failures of the historical archive, detailing the theory of history it proposes, and illuminating its nationalistic attempt to wrench England's many political and religious discontinuities into harmony with one another.[2] But perhaps the clarity with which the poem announces its historicist agenda has distracted us from its form, which is in fact a death investigation.

The townspeople and Erkenwald follow standard procedure for a medieval coroner's inquest: the people of London raise the hue and cry and investigate the matter by searching their records, questioning neighbors, and—of course—gossiping. When Erkenwald takes on the role of coroner, he hears from witnesses, examines the body, and he skillfully elicits from the evidence the truth of the matter from the evidence. This is no ordinary death investigation—after all, the dead body itself testifies. But the supernatural elements do not override the mundane procedure; on the contrary, they perfect it. A coroner's enrollment usually took the form of an imagined dialogue between the coroner and his jury, who spoke for the evidence. But in this case, the evidence can talk, so the poem is able to stage this dialogue directly between coroner and evidence, bringing what was a fictionalized recordkeeping format to life. The result is not just a death investigation, but a perfect one. After all, what could be tidier than simply animating the evidence and demanding that it speak for itself?

In this chapter, I suggest that as an idealized death investigation, *St. Erkenwald* offers both literary and legal scholars something unique. For literary scholars, it reveals that its more obvious historicist project is grounded in the practice of English law, and that its formal eccentricities are the result of

---

[2] Ruth Nissé, "'A Coroun Ful Riche': The Rule of History in *St. Erkenwald*," *English Literary History* 65, no. 2 (1998): p. 277. Following Nissé's work, Stefan Schustereder ("Coming to Terms with a Pagan Past: The Story of *St. Erkenwald*," *Studia Anglica Posnaniensia* 48, no. 2 [2013]: pp. 71–92), Cynthia Turner Camp ("Spatial Memory, Historiographic Fantasy, and the Touch of the Past in *St. Erkenwald*," *New Literary History* 44, no. 3 [2013]: pp. 471–491), and John Scattergood ("*St. Erkenwald* and the Custody of the Past," in *The Lost Tradition: Essays in Middle English Alliterative Poetry* [Dublin: Four Courts Press, 2000], pp. 184–195) have all delved into the poem's explicit project to reimagine English history not as it was, but as it should have been for the purposes of late fourteenth-century English society. On the same subject but with a different focus, D. Vance Smith reveals the theory of history it proposes by anchoring its imagined past in it the cityscape of its present ("Crypt and Decryption: *Erkenwald* Terminable and Interminable," *New Medieval Literatures* 5 [2002]: pp. 59–85), and Phillip Schwyzer delves into the explicit nationalism of its historical project ("Exhumation and Ethnic Conflict: From *St. Erkenwald* to Spenser in Ireland," *Representations* 95 [2006]: pp.26).

reconciling the demands of narrative with the demands of procedural justice. After all, the thread with which the poem stitches together England's history is the body of a justice of the eyre, and the historical St. Eorcenwald is credited with helping to draft the groundbreaking *Leges Inae*. *St. Erkenwald* and the law are thus deeply entwined.[3] Perceiving its indebtedness to legal forms like the coroner's enrollment also allows us to disentangle its dialogic shape, and its interest in the temporal demands of justice can help us understand the poem's bizarre temporality. This engagement does not negate its incarnations as a *miraculum* or as historical theory, but rather reveals how pervasive these mundane legal forms were, and that the poet understood their rhythms to be an essential part of Englishness.

For scholars of law and literature as well as legal history, the poem offers a rare portrait of medieval investigation, one that illuminates the role that evidence and proof procedures played in the process, correcting the impression that they were not a part of criminal procedure. The fact that standards for oral testimony and evidence were not written down until much later has been taken to mean that the medieval criminal process did not need them; the jury served as witnesses, and they required no evidence.[4] Most have agreed (following Daniel Klerman's article) that "self-informing" is a more or less accurate term for medieval trial juries, and "self-informing" has sometimes come to mean valuing reputation over evidence.[5] Green has influentially argued that,

---

[3] When the poem's canvas of history reaches its subject, it introduces him as the bishop of London who "teaches the law" ("Now of þis Augustynes art is Erkenwolde bischop / At loue London toun and the laghe teches," ll. 33–34). Ine grandly referred to Eorcenwald as "my bishop," though Ine probably only controlled the Surrey portion of Eorcenwald's bishopric (see Barbara Yorke, *Kings and Kingdoms of Early Anglo-Saxon England* [Oxford: Taylor & Francis, 2002], p. 187). Trajan, the closest analogue for the judge and certainly the tradition upon which the author drew, is actually saved for a juridical act, according to the Whitby account (An Anonymous Monk of Whitby, *The Earliest Life of Gregory the Great*, ed. and trans. Bertram Colgrave [Lawrence: University of Kansas Press, 1968], p. 29).

[4] See for example James B. Thayer, *A Preliminary Treatise on Evidence at the Common Law* (Boston: Little, Brown, and Co., 1898), pp. 85–136; John H. Wigmore, *A Treatise on the Anglo-American System of Evidence*, vol. 1 (Boston: Little, Brown, and Co., 1940), p. 235, and vol. 5, pp. 10–12.

[5] Our understanding of the jury's "self-informing" nature has evolved to recognize that juries could not have operated purely on previous knowledge, especially as we have realized that by the fourteenth century few juries for any stage of criminal procedure were drawn from the vill where a crime occurred, or even the same hundred. On this topic, see Daniel Klerman, "Was the Jury Ever Self-Informing?" *Southern California Law Review* 77 (2003): pp. 123–149. For jury composition, see Edward Powell, "Jury Trial at Gaol Delivery in the Late Middle Ages: The Midland Circuit, 1400–1429," in J.S. Cockburn and Thomas A. Green (eds.), *Twelve Good Men* (Princeton, NJ: Princeton University Press, 1988), p. 78; Thomas A. Green, "The Jury and the English Law of Homicide, 1200–1600," *Michigan Law Review* 74 (1976): pp. 423–499. See also, in *Twelve Good Men*, J.B. Post, "Jury Lists and Juries in the Late Fourteenth Century," pp. 73–75; and Bernard W. McLane, "Juror Attitudes toward Local Disorders: The Evidence of the 1328 Trailbaston Proceedings," pp. 56–67. Nevertheless, the idea of the medieval jury as witnesses, either to character or even to the event itself, has persisted, especially when contrasted to the formal introduction of witnesses and evidence to trial. However, Sara Butler is a notable counterexample to this scholarship, and I have relied on her groundbreaking and capacious work on the medieval coroner, which demonstrates that we can find signs of standards for evidence and

"for all their esoteric procedures, the king's courts do not seem to have brought superior forensic techniques to bear on the cases they removed from local jurisdiction," and James Whitman has argued that if medieval juries often acquitted, it was because they feared for their souls, not because they sought a factually correct verdict.[6] Both characterize medieval law as a kind of holding pattern before the progress of later centuries.[7] Scholars such as Barbara Shapiro and Sara Butler have methodically chipped away at aspects of this impression, but it remains prominent, especially in transhistorical studies that seek to place medieval criminal procedure in the context of later reforms and works of law and literature.[8]

But *St. Erkenwald's* idealized inquest actively seeks to set standards for the use of witnesses and evidence in the pursuit of justice. These standards, it shows us, pertained long before the trial and perhaps even before the coroner arrived. The poem's inquest gives us a glimpse of how these investigations might have worked in practice, and also reveals the areas in which these procedures were subject to doubt and debate, a process that indicates ongoing interest in refining and perfecting these practices. It bolsters historical work that indicates that witnesses and evidence were essential to medieval criminal procedure, even though they may not have been recorded. The poem's formal engagement with the rhythms and moral questions of investigation suggests that these practices were deeply embedded in daily life and thus made their way into the literature that came out of that culture.

---

witness reliability in coroners' enrollments, even when the enrollments were not designed to document such standards: Butler, *Forensic Medicine*.

[6] Green, *A Crisis of Truth*, p. 131. James Whitman, *The Origins of Reasonable Doubt: Theological Roots of the Criminal Trial* (New Haven, CT: Yale University Press, 2008). Both of these studies rely on Thomas A. Green, *Verdict According to Conscience: Perspectives on the English Criminal Trial Jury, 1200–1800* (Chicago: University of Chicago Press, 1985), which argues that medieval trial juries might modify the facts of the case to conform better to the (very narrow) statutory definitions of crimes (such that, for example, an unusual number of accused murderers the juries believed had been acting in self-defense just happened to have found a weapon of convenience in a fight and had no choice but to defend themselves). However, this does not necessarily mean they judged however they liked; it could be that they found the definitions too restrictive to accommodate what they believed to be factually true (that the accused acted in self-defense, for example). Whitman has argued that jurors sought "moral comfort" rather than "factual proof," and that if juries often acquitted it was because they thought it was the "safer way" for their souls, rather than the factually correct conclusion. (*Origins of Reasonable Doubt*, pp. 125–128).

[7] As Green puts it, in the fourteenth century, "though the administration of law was becoming more complex, the principles of evidence and the concept of proof underwent no dramatic transformation" (*A Crisis of Truth*, p. 132).

[8] Shapiro's work focuses primarily on later periods, but convincingly argues that the standards of proof whose origins lay in the medieval legal system (like "satisfied understanding" and "moral certainty") implied a "high standard of belief based on evidence." For her overview of the field and rebuttal to Whitman's history of "reasonable doubt," see Barbara Shapiro, "Beyond Reasonable Doubt Doctrine: 'Moral Comfort' or Standard of Proof?" *Law and Humanities* 2, no. 2 (2008): pp. 149–173. See also Butler, *Forensic Medicine*.

I will begin by examining two coroners' enrollments to map the form I see reproduced in *St. Erkenwald* and to discover what details of investigative procedure remain hidden from us. This systematization will help me to animate *St. Erkenwald*'s contribution, which fills in a few gaps but more crucially brings to life the rationalizing effort behind death investigation procedure, even at a local level. The first of these gaps is the community's investigation that took place before the arrival of the coroner, a routine part of the process that almost never left traces in legal records. Then I examine Erkenwald's performance of inquest procedure, which reveals a hierarchy of evidence in death investigations in which material evidence actually held the highest place—provided it was certain. Finally, I turn to the issue of delay, which plagues the poem from its very first lines. In attempting to both harness and conquer delay in its idealized investigation, the poem expresses this negotiation in its form, forcing the reader to experience delay. I argue that the poem's delays willingly risk jeopardizing the reader's enjoyment in order to caution against confusing the temporal demands of narrative for satisfaction in justice. Throughout, my method is not to propose that the legal sources offer context to the literary, or that the literary outpaces the legal, but that, read in concert, they offer a new picture of medieval investigation's principles and priorities.

Coroners' Enrollments: Two Examples

A coroner would generally be called when there was a sudden or unnatural death, but he could also be summoned when unexplained objects or treasure were found.[9] The judge is a unique case but nevertheless combines several of these functions; his body is buried but not properly, and there is no explanation for his death. His tomb is also obviously expensive (which is why it attracts such notice), so it could fall under the category of treasure as well. A coroner served a whole county, so the delay we see with St. Erkenwald—he takes nearly a week to arrive at the body—was common and much lamented, because the body could not be moved until he did. When he arrived, he would summon a jury to give information about the death and together they would go through all available evidence: the scene, the body, any weapons, witness testimony, and rumor. As Butler puts it, this was a process of "assigning meaning to death," with all the legal, reputational, and personal consequences that might

---

[9] For the coroner's responsibility to examine, value, and protect treasure and wrecks that are discovered see Hunnisett, *The Medieval Coroner*, p. 6.

entail.[10] With the help of a clerk who travelled with him, the coroner would then create an enrollment that communicated this meaning and advocated for its adoption at any subsequent trial or exaction of fees.

A coroner's enrollment was above all a functional document, one generically constrained by its purposes.[11] As I will discuss in Chapter 4, the documents of criminal procedure were designed with an eye to their future use—an indictment, for example, might note events like flight or notoriety that would be relevant to a trial jury. Coroners' records fulfilled several different purposes. First, enrollments helped everyone avoid amercement and legal jeopardy by recording that all legal obligations were fulfilled: the enrollment confirmed that the first finder, jurors, coroners, and pledges all did their jobs. Second, they kept books for the king: each enrollment listed the money owed to the king through forfeiture of chattel and deodand (any object implicated in the death, the value of which was forfeit).[12] Third, they could summarily close a case by ruling the death accidental or natural. Finally, if the case was not closed, the inquest contained a story to instruct an indicting or trial jury on what to do by tailoring the narrative to point clearly toward acquittal, conviction, or pardon. This last purpose conceals many matters of interest. Who created this story, and how? Where did they get their information, and how did they know it was credible? Did they examine evidence, like the scene, body, or weapon?

In the first record, Robert Curteys was found dead in the street on a Tuesday in May, 1322:

> [The] Coroner ... diligently enquired how it happened. The jurors say that when on the preceding Monday about the time of sun-set the said Robert made an assault on Amicia, wife of John Pope as she stood at the door of the shop ... by reason of an old quarrel between them, and had badly beaten her with a staff ... there came up the said John Pope holding in his hand a drawn knife which he used in service of William Prodhomme, fishmonger, and approached the said Robert Curteys to pacify his anger by fair means, if possible; and that when the said Robert saw him coming, he assaulted and beat him pursuing him as far as the wall ... that, at length, the said John Pope struck the said Robert with the knife under the left breast, inflicting a mortal

---

[10] Butler, *Forensic Medicine*, p. 176.

[11] In her essay on the form, Carrie Smith discusses how much historians can reliably draw from coroners' rolls ("Medieval Coroners' Rolls: Legal Fiction or Historical Fact," in *Courts, Counties, and the Capital in the Later Middle Ages*, ed. Diana E.S. Dunn [London: St. Martin's Press, 1996], pp. 93–116). My question is slightly different: what were the legal functions of coroners' rolls that shaped what information was included and what form it would take?

[12] Hunnisett details this function at length, characterizing coroners as revenue-generators for the crown in *The Medieval Coroner*, see in particular pp. 2, 32, 113–114, and 148.

wound an inch long and two inches deep; that the said Robert, so wounded, followed the said John in order to kill him, as far as the place where he lay dead, and there he fell and forthwith died of the wound aforesaid. Thereupon the said John took refuge in the church of St. Margaret in the said Ward. Being asked who was present when this happened, the jurors say the said Robert, John, Amicia his wife, and a certain Isabella de Bristoll who was the first to find the corpse of Robert and to raise the cry so that the country came. Being asked if the said Amicia or Isabella abetted the felony, they say No, nor do they suspect any man or woman of the felony save the said John Pope ... The corpse viewed whereon the said wound appeared and no other hurt.[13]

Like most enrollments, this one takes the form of a dialogue ("The coroner diligently enquired / the jurors say, being asked / the jurors say"). Butler argues that this format did not reflect the process of the inquest itself, but merely served as "a useful framework to arrange the record," though it seems likely that it also represented the nature of the inquiry in a general sense (that is, the coroner asked questions which the jury answered).[14] The first benefit of this arrangement is that it allows the enrollment to interject details discovered at any stage of the investigation into any point in the narrative they might be useful, without regard to chronology. For example, it is unlikely that the coroner inquired about who was present at the scene last, but it makes more logical sense at the end of the enrollment because it helps tie up loose ends, namely the question of whether anyone else is suspected. Likewise, even John probably did not note the wound location and size at the moment of the stabbing, yet its dimensions are noted *in medias res*. The wound was measured during the examination of the body (which is not mentioned until the last line), and the information inserted into the story at the right moment.

The second benefit of this dialogic arrangement is that it allows the record to frame a narrative argument for the trial jury. The argument here is that John Pope killed Robert Curteys in self-defense and in defense of his wife, without premeditation, and should therefore be pardoned. Besides the fact that John arrives when his wife has already been attacked, the record also specifies that his knife was a tool of his trade (and therefore not carried for violence) and that Robert attacked first, pursued him, and perpetrated significant violence "at length" before John struck back.[15] Just as the form accommodates details

---

[13] Reginald Sharpe, ed., *Calendar of Coroners Rolls of the City of London, 1300–1378* (Suffolk: Richard Clay and Sons, Ltd, 1913), p. 54.
[14] Butler, *Forensic Medicine*, p. 145.
[15] As Green notes, in order to qualify a pardon for self-defense, it was necessary to show that one had retreated as far as was possible, so juries often used the phrase "to the wall" in order to signal that

gleaned from the investigation in any order, it allows the argument to deal with counterarguments within the story itself. How do we know Robert was not acting out of self-defense, having been approached with a knife? The record answers: because John hoped to resolve the matter fairly, but Robert intended to kill John. Was anyone else suspected? The record answers: no, witnesses say not. Mixed in with the precision of the wound measurement and other verifiable details, these speculations seem out of place, and it is this muddling of traditional evidence with unevidenced speculation that has led many scholars to assume that standards in investigation as a whole (including evidence, proof, and witness testimony) were not crucial to medieval criminal procedure, and that perhaps reputation and the jurors' own interests were more important to the process.

But in the context of the constrained form of the enrollments and the limited uses to which they might be put, this type of information might take more effort to unearth. As J.B. Post noted, one of the limitations of these enrollments is that they do not often offer information that seemed extraneous to their purposes, and therefore give little direct information about the process of investigation.[16] In a system in which a trial jury had to come to their decision with only the judge and the coroner's roll as guidance, extraneous information would be a hindrance, not a help.

Can we find any signs that coroners or their juries were invested in investigative standards? There are some clear signs in this enrollment and the next that witness credibility mattered. For example, it could be significant that Isabella was attached as a witness. The question, "who was present?" might have been a way to solicit a witness other than Amicia, who was not credible by virtue of being involved and married to the accused. This indicates a commonsense standard, even though the enrollment does not specify the reasoning.

If we turn to the second enrollment, we can see a more protracted attempt to corroborate testimony, which suggests that not only was there a credibility standard, but that coroners sought additional verification when it was not met:

the accused had been justified in self-defense (Verdict According to Conscience, p. 41). In one case from 1455, judicial comment detailed the necessary elements of a "self-defense" argument: "quar si un home vous assaute de vou batre n'e loial pour vous a dire que vous voiles luy tuer, et de luy menasser de vie et de membre: mes si l'cas soit tiel, q'il ad vous a tiel advantage que par entendment il voilloit vous tuer come si voiles fuir, et il est plus courrant que vous estes, et alia apres vous, issint que ne vous poies luy escaper; ou autrement que vous estes desouh luy al' terre; ou s'il ad enchace vous a un mure ou un hedge ou dike, issint que vous ne poies luy escape, donq' est loial pour vous adire que s'il ne veut departir de vous, q'vous en salvatio de vostre vie luy voiles tuer, et issint vous poies luy menasser pour tiel special cause." YB Pasch. 33 Hen. 6.10, 18b (Seipp 1455.037), published in C.H. Williams, ed., *Year Books of the Reign of Henry VI, 1422–1461* (London: Selden Society, 1895), p. 10.

[16] J.B. Post, "Crime in Later Medieval England: Some Historiographical Limitations," *Continuity and Change* 2, no. 2 (1987): p. 215.

Robert struck his wife with a staff called a "wombedstaf"[17] on the neck as she stood by the stair in said solar, so that with the blow she fell down the stair and broke her neck ... Because information was given to the Coroner, that Robert son of the aforesaid Robert of Portesmouthe had been arrested on suspicion of causing the death of the said Alice his step-mother and had been taken to Neugate, precept was issued to the Sherriffs to summon other jurors of the Ward of Queenhithe for the following Tuesday in order that further enquiry might be made. Accordingly on that day there came [the second group of jurors, listed by name], who said on oath that on the aforesaid day the said Robert, the son, struck the said Alice with his hand, whilst the father struck her with a "wombedstaff" on the neck from which blow the said Alice died, and that the death of said Alice was not hastened by the blow from the hand of the said son. The corpse viewed, the neck of which was seen to be broken by the blow of the staff.[18]

The first record offered a single story of what took place; this one offers three, each produced by a different source. The first jury says that Robert (the elder) worked alone, killing his wife Alice with a blow that sent her down the stairs, which broke her neck. But the second jury adds the son, whom they say also struck Alice but was not responsible for his death. The final source is the corpse itself, which testifies that her neck was broken by the blow of the staff, not from falling down the stairs or by the strike of a hand.

All ultimately more or less corroborate one another, but the subtle differences trace a practice of verification. The first jury's credibility is put into doubt when the coroner discovers the arrest of the son, so a second jury is called to offer further information. They give their opinion, but even though they mostly agree with the first, this is not enough to settle the matter. The coroner turns to the body for final testimony, and while it confirms the distribution of guilt, it disagrees with the method (the staff broke her neck, not the fall). It is difficult to tell, but it seems possible that because the first jury offered an incomplete account, the credibility of both juries was put into doubt, and the body's information was needed to settle the matter.

Clearly, credibility mattered, verification and corroboration were active practices, and material evidence held at least some sway. But the second question, where these standards pertained in the process, and how an investigation

---

[17] Reginald Sharpe defines this unusual weapon as "a variety of the bedstaff commonly used to keep bed clothes in their proper place," and thus a weapon that might have been found in the bedroom (*Calendar of Coroners Rolls*, p. xxiii).

[18] Sharpe, *Calendar of Coroners Rolls*, p. 245.

actually took place, is a more difficult one to answer. Like many wrongful deaths, these are private incidents; no one of the jury was present, much less the coroner. And the stories are not straightforward; the detail about the old quarrel between Amicia and Robert Curteys would take some questioning to reveal, and it would have been necessary to unravel the history of the two Roberts and Alice to guess what happened behind closed doors. Discovery of these stories would have required an active investigation, including questioning a variety of witnesses and perhaps even searching records for previous altercations. Who investigated these matters, and how? Evidence clearly held some sway, but how much? And how do we straighten out the chronological mess of both the enrollments and the process they represented, which (like the modern justice system) was plagued by delay? In the rest of the chapter, I will take each of these questions in turn (crowd investigation, evidence, delay), considering what *St. Erkenwald* can reveal about the rationalizing effort that went into the investigative process.

The Crowd Investigates

St. Erkenwald is a clamorous poem. The mystery of it begins and ends with noise, and in between the people of the town repeatedly swell with cries and then quieten, marking the emotional trajectory of the plot with their sounds. A "cry" brings Erkenwald to London, a "crakit" ("clamour," l. 110) informs him of the mystery, and the judge's testimony is marked by "a gronynge ful grete" (l. 283). When "all the belles in the burgh beryd at ones," ("all the bells in the city sounded at once," l. 352) the poem is over. But of course, a medieval death investigation was a noisy affair. Residents themselves were responsible for most of medieval law enforcement, and the noise of the poem reminds us that much of this was accomplished not by individuals, but by crowds. When a body was found, every adult resident of the vill was obligated respond to the hue and cry, and when the coroner did arrive, all men over the age of twelve from the four neighboring vills were required to attend the inquest, just as the coroner for Robert Curteys "summoned good men of that Ward and of the three nearest wards." The crowd must indeed have been full "wyt ryngande noyce" (l. 61).[19]

---

[19] Carol Loar discusses the problem of keeping crowds at bay in a coroner's inquest in the seventeenth century, but given the requirement for such large numbers crowd control must have also been a serious problem at medieval inquests. Carol Loar, "Medical Knowledge and the Early Modern English Coroner's Inquest," *Social History of Medicine* 23, no. 3 (2010): pp. 475–491. We can also see enforcement of this requirement in the eyre of Kent in 1313–1314, when the justice admonished that because Overland, Weddington, Rolwing, and Dene (the four neighboring vills) had not attended the coroner's inquest for the death of John Bunter, they were all in mercy (Maitland, Vernon Harcourt, Boland, eds. *The Eyre of Kent of 6 and 7 Edward II (1313–1314)*, p. 139).

The time in between the discovery of a body and the arrival of the coroner is hard to parse in the legal records. The information we do have tends to reveal instances where something went wrong, such as moments where the community failed to protect the body or moved it. Very occasionally, we get a sense that that the failure was a lack of investigative activity on the part of the community. In Sussex, for example, a jury twice asked for (and were granted) an adjournment because "they were still not well informed" on the matter, and the inquest could not move forward until they completed their own investigation. This hints that it was their investigation, and not that of the coroner, that was responsible for uncovering the facts of the case.[20] But such examples in legal records are unusual and always suggestive rather than illustrative.

However, in *St. Erkenwald*, we are able to follow along in this liminal time, because nearly a third of the poem passes before the bishop arrives. The poem illustrates that the crowd that rushed to a dead body was also there to perform an investigative role, offering a rare glimpse into this process, and tracking a detection method that we might now call "crowdsourced." It also offers the poet's critique of this process; the crowd's excellent work coupled with its failure to solve the mystery suggests that the poet advocated an inquiry that was thorough but (implausibly) knew its own limits. It would be easy to characterize this scene and these investigations as extra-legal, since only hints of this work can be found in coroners' enrollments. But I posit that the poet's efforts to idealize this labor helps us see that a strongly felt responsibility toward the criminal process pushed communities to create a rational procedure.

The crowd pursues their investigation scrupulously. They fulfill their legal obligations: they raise the hue and cry ("suche a cry aboute a cors, crakit euer-more," l. 110) and everyone comes running ("mony hundrid hende men highide thider sone" | "many hundred worthy men hurried to the tomb," l. 58), they do not move the body, they protect the scene (the mayor's "meynye ... the sayntuaré thai kepten" | the mayor's "retainers ... guarded the sanctuary," ll. 65–6), and the first finder, the mayor, reports the facts to Erkenwald when he finally arrives.[21] They also proceed rationally, seeking out clues like a practiced investigative body. The people who arrive at the scene of the tomb begin by examining the scene, which they approach with a practiced eye to what each object might mean. The mayor arrives and requests that the tomb be opened.

---

[20] This record is from approximately 50 years after the assumed date of *St. Erkenwald*, but I argue that the fact that the coroner seems to have accepted this excuse as a matter of course (not once, but twice) suggests that it might have been an established understanding. R.F. Hunnisett, ed., *Sussex Coroners' Inquests* (Lewes: Sussex Record Society, 1985), p. 18.

[21] See Hunnisett, *The Medieval Coroner*, chapter 8 for details on the first finder and their responsibilities.

Many men are at hand to open the tomb, and the next passage allows us to view the body for the first time together with the crowd, as though we are peering over their shoulders:

> Al wyt glisnande golde his gowne wos hemmyd,
> Wyt mony a precious perle picchit ther-on,
> And a gurdille of golde bigripide his mydelle,
> A meche mantel on-lofte wyt menyuer furrit
> The clothe of camelyn ful clene wyt cumly bordures (ll. 78–82)

> All with glistening gold his gown was trimmed,
> With many precious pearls set there,
> A girdle of gold encircled his waist
> A large gown was trimmed on top with miniver fur
> The cloth of a flawless wool and silk with handsome borders

The details treat us to a vivid first impression, and as in any detective story, we become willing co-investigators. And as in a detective story, the narrative draws our eyes specifically to the interpretable evidence—that is, clues. The fur is miniver, the wool is well-made, and the silk has a handsome border, all of which translate to wealth and importance, an impression amplified by "a coron ful riche / And a semely septure" ("a very ornate crown / And a dignified scepter," ll. 83–4), which lead the crowd to believe that the body was royal.

Having thus more or less answered *what* lies before them (a king), they turn to the question of which one, or *who*. This proves trickier, and their next observations lead us through their logical inquiry.

> Als wemles were his wedes wyt-outen any tecche
> …
> And als freshe hym the face and the fleshe nakyde
> Bi his eres and bi his hondes and that openly shewid
> Wyt ronke rode. (ll. 85–91)

> Spotless were his clothes, without any blemish
> …
> And he was fresh in the face, and on his bare skin
> By his ears and by his hands that showed
> A rosy red.

This, they observe, makes it seem "As thai hade yepely in that yorde bene yisturday shapen ... As he in sounde sodanly were slippide opon slepe" ("As though they had been skillfully shaped yesterday ... As if he were in sound health and had suddenly slipped into sleep," ll. 88–92) Given his clearly recent death, they interview witnesses ("spyr vch on othir" | "inquire to each other," l. 93) and search their records, but discover that he is not remembered "ne by tale nothir / That euer wos bruyt in burghe ne in boke notyde" ("not in any tale / That was brought into that city or noted in a book," ll. 102–3). This suggests that a community investigation depended on not just gossip, but also institutional sources like written records and lore. The body's absence from their records leads them to reconsider their first conclusion, which was that he had recently died. They circle back to the question they got wrong the first time, which "ylke weghe askyd" ("every man asked," l. 96): "How longe had he ther layne"? (l. 95). This is only one of many questions that might spring to mind upon finding a dead body; their focus on it is the fruit of a progressive inquiry that has identified the question that will unravel the rest.

Returning to the matter of Robert Curteys, we can now imagine better what might have taken place. Most likely, Isabella heard the fight because she was a neighbor to the shop. Perhaps she ran out into the street. When she saw Robert die, she raised the hue, which brought the neighbors running. Isabella immediately relayed what she had seen to the crowd, perhaps even a look on Robert's face or words he spoke to indicate an intent to kill. Isabella or someone else would have provided other crucial evidence, like Amicia and Robert's longstanding quarrel, John's profession, and where he got that knife. In Alice's death, we can imagine that (while the enrollment does not list a first finder) her neighbors arrived on the scene first, perhaps having heard screams. During the inquest, Robert the younger is already in Newgate gaol, which suggests that these same neighbors suspected and arrested him on the spot. Surely, gossip told them there was reason to suspect the son. However, the story they deliver first to the coroner is that the father was responsible, which suggests that after arresting the son they examined the body, questioned the father, and revised their understanding.

In both example enrollments, we can see that the primary investigators who provided the evidence were the people who arrived at the hue and cry, not the coroner and not even the jury. While jurors were responsible for delivering the information to the coroner, they could not know they would be called before he arrived. And the timeline in this case is very short. The first set of jurors are called on Monday and testify the same day, and the second set of jurors are called on Tuesday and testify the same day. It seems implausible that each set could launch its own investigation and develop its own explanation in so short a time. And yet investigations clearly took place, ones that arrested suspects, located fugitives, and even revisited their own understandings of the matter, before the coroner arrived and the jury was convened. Given this timing and *St. Erkenwald's* demonstration of the crowd's responsibility toward its own discoveries, the only possible answer is that the crowd gathered by the hue investigated the matter itself.

But the community's investigation in *St. Erkenwald*, of course, is a failure. Not for a lack of effort, or for corruption; the crowd fails because it is naturally inadequate to the task. This inadequacy is expressed as a linguistic failure, in which they identify letters but cannot interpret them, like evidence that is clearly significant but cannot be brought to a coherent narrative. When "mony clerkes in that clos wyt crownes ful brode" ("many clerks with broad tonsures," l. 55) apply their own expertise to interpret the tomb's markings, they are unable to "brynge hom in words" (l. 56), neither "to mouthe" (l. 54) nor to meaning. This metaphor suggests a crowd capable of collecting raw evidence but not of interpreting it. But the poet goes a step further to emphasize the crowd's inadequacy; these letters are so foreign, the poet writes, that "roynyshe were the resones that ther on row stoden" ("obscure were the reasons that they stood in a row," l. 52). This ignorance describes a state below illiteracy, in which one is unfamiliar with even the concept of writing. Yet letters are letters because they form words, just like evidence is only evidence when it can be interpreted and fit into a narrative. That is, the clerks' interpretive powers are inconsistent; they can recognize the building blocks of writing, but upon doing so they become completely ignorant of the practice itself. Likewise, it is implausible that one might be able to collect all the relevant pieces of the story but refrain from assembling them.

In the artificiality of this limit, we encounter the anxiety the poet is attempting to address. After all, once communities are in the business of collecting the evidence, piecing together the events, determining the motive, and arresting the culprit, what would stop them from going further? Why not decide guilt, choose a punishment, and execute it, all without the interference of outside parties and rule of law? Looking back, we can see that the town began its work before the men of the law arrived. But where did that work end? The firm line the poem attempts to draw between evidence and interpretation shows how difficult it was to negotiate the limits of the community's role in an increasingly professionalized legal system. The question of jurisdiction between local and crown authorities was a notorious flashpoint, so the poem wisely uses an argument about capacity to delimit community involvement instead. It is simply that they are naturally insufficient to the task, and that the procedures the coroner provides are necessary to complete it.

The Evidence Speaks

In his foundational book on "truth" in medieval English literature and law, Green reads an example from a book of pleas that seems to mimic a modern evidence-based case but "in reality is nothing of the sort ... . The justice is not seeking to establish a factual case against the accused, merely to maneuver him into an untenable position."[22] The medieval accused, he concludes, was judged on the basis of his reputation, not the facts of the crime or the evidence available. Milsom puts it another way; the evidence was available, it was just undesirable. He argues that English juries felt that their task was to judge the criminal, and not the crime, and that therefore evidence was counterproductive. "Jurors," if faced with evidence that contradicted their allegiances to their neighbors, "made unacceptable rules produce acceptable results by adjusting the facts."[23]

This picture does not accord with the careful attention the jurors in the two coroner's reports give evidence, nor with the picture *St. Erkenwald* offers. But it is true that would-be lawmen saw strict proceduralism as an aid to turn rumor into good evidence. In fact, procedure is the remedy Bracton recommends for rumor gone awry. *De legibus et consuetudinibus Angliae* (commonly called Bracton) allows for indictment by way of rumor, so long as it arises among "good and responsible men," but in a section immediately following and of equal length, Bracton emphasizes that in such cases the judge must first inquire diligently into the jurors' sources and their sources' sources, conducting a whole chain of witness interviews.[24] The text speculates that the jurors when asked might all admit they learned the matter "from one of their fellow jurors, and he under interrogation will perhaps say he learned it from such a one, and so by question and answer (*interrogatio et responsio*) the judge may descend from person to person ... . For by such inquiries ... many scandalous things may be discovered."[25] In other words, rumor could offer a starting point, but methodical interrogations as required by coroner procedure provided the

---

[22] Green, *A Crisis of Truth*, p. 131.
[23] Milsom, *Historical Foundations*, p. 422.
[24] "bonos et graves." George Woodbine, ed., *Bracton on the Laws and Customs of England*, trans. Samuel Thorne, vol. 2 (Cambridge: Belknap Press, 1968), p. 403.
[25] Woodbine, *Bracton*, vol. 2, p. 404.

discovery of facts, at which point the matter ceased to be rumor and became witness accounts.

In fact, the body in *St. Erkenwald* (before he is awoken) offers a uniquely reputation-less mystery. Reputation requires a social context, and as the crowd observes, "Ther is no lede opon lyfe of so longe age / That may mene ... his nome ne his note" ("there is no man alive from so long ago / who can ... speak of either his name nor his reputation," ll. 150–1). Scholars have argued that the almost pedantic emphasis on procedure in the poem reminded readers of the importance of the sacraments to salvation, even for those who led the most blameless of lives.[26] But in the context of a death investigation it also provides an alternative to rumor; a recourse when reputation has failed. Erkenwald's interrogation of the body yields results where the crowd's does not, but that is not because he holds the answer or even the interpretation of the answer. Rather, his proper execution of procedure unlocks the ability of the evidence not only to present but also interpret itself, providing both fact and narrative.

Erkenwald's part in the investigation performs a strikingly modern fantasy, one in which material evidence is both certain and auto-exemplifying, only awaiting the right procedure to awaken it. This fantasy suggests that the body and material evidence were far more important than previously thought, given certainty and the right procedure to bring it to life. Erkenwald finds the same evidence the crowd does; it just speaks to him in a way it does not to them. The crowd's investigation has followed its own leads, first asking "what" and "who," and turning quickly when stymied to "how long?" and "how is this possible?" But Erkenwald maps out the entire investigation as soon as he addresses the body. He asks the same questions as the crowd, but in a set interrogatory format borrowed from penitential manuals designed to help a confessor investigate the full truth of a sin.

Boethius advises pursuing a series of specific "causes," distinct from general "propositions" or theses, that form the seven circumstances fundamental to the arts of prosecution and defense.[27] The Fourth Lateran Council later adapted this series to guide a confessor in his investigation of sin, and Aquinas standardized them into the formulation that, by the fourteenth century, most confessors' manuals followed: *quis, quid, cur, ubi, quando, quomodo, quibus*

---

[26] See especially Anne Schuurman, "Materials of Wonder: Miraculous Objects and Poetic Form in *Saint Erkenwald*," *Studies in the Age of Chaucer* 39 (2017): pp. 275–296 and Jennifer L. Sisk, "The Uneasy Orthodoxy of *St. Erkenwald*," *English Literary History* 74 (2007): pp. 89–115.

[27] Boethius, "De topicis differentiis libri quatuor," in *Patrilogia Latina*, vol. 64, ed. Jacques Paul Migne (Paris: Garnier, 1860), p. 1212.

auxiliis.[28] When Erkenwald returns the body to a "ghost-life" he fastidiously follows this form:

> Sithen we wot not qwo thou art witere vs thiselwen
> In world quat weghe thou was and quy thou thus ligges,
> How longe thou hast layne here and quat laghe thou vsyt
> Quether art thou ioyned to ioy othir iuggid to pyne. (ll. 185–8)

> Since we know not who you are, tell us yourself,
> In the world what you were and why you thus lie,
> How long have you lain there and what law you used
> Whether you are joined to joy or judged to pain.

Since we know not who (*quis*) you are, Erkenwald explains, we will ask what (*quid*) you were, why (*cur*) you lie here (*ubi*), how long (*quando*) you have thus lain, and in what manner (*quomodo*), joined to joy or judged to pain. Erkenwald plays both confessor and coroner here. Naomi Hurnard has pointed out that jury testimony from this period was frequently "reminiscent of the passages from penitentials and the works of canonists."[29] Such borrowing was common, especially since penitential manuals were far more common than manuals of legal procedure and dealt with many of the same issues of discovering, categorizing, and punishing wrong deeds.

The question of *ubi* here also contributes to the slippage between Erkenwald's functions as ecclesiastical officer and county coroner, because in a penitential context it came to represent a jurisdictional question. As John Mirk puts it in his *Instructions for Parish Priests*, "Were hyt was, wyte thou also / In holy place or no" ("Where it was, know thou also, in [a] holy place or not," ll. 1451–2).[30] St. Paul's in this moment is confusingly a bit of both; it is in the process of being built, preconsecration, and therefore its role as a church technically still lies in its future. And yet, the significance of the judge lies in tying his nonreligious beginning to his Christian end, in parallel with the reconsecration of the church, so the fact that he is found in the foundation of the central cathedral of the English faith is sort of the whole story. The fantasy Erkenwald represents is that all of these differences are so insignificant that

---

[28] Thomas Aquinas, *Summa Theologica*, trans. The Fathers of the Dominican Province (Cincinnati, OH: Benziger Bros., 1947), I–II, Q. VII, Art. III; For an example, see John of Salisbury, *Metalogicon*, ed. C.C.J. Webb (Oxford: Clarendon Press, 1929), pp. 83–84.

[29] Naomi Hurnard, *The King's Pardon for Homicide before 1307* (Oxford: Clarendon Press, 1969), p. 77.

[30] John Mirk, *Instructions for Parish Priests*, ed. E. Peacock (London: Bernard Quaritch for the Selden Society, 1898), p. 45.

they can be united in a single person, a single office efficacious enough to unite secular and ecclesiastical jurisdictions such that the church was never not a church and England was never not Christian.[31]

Although Erkenwald asks the same questions the crowd does, his systematization of them unlocks the answers. He arranges their organic inquiry into the proper interrogatory format, and his transformation bestows new efficacy on the same questions that previously yielded nothing. That is, it is his proper execution of procedure that unlocks the ability of the evidence to present and interpret itself, providing both fact and narrative. This fantasy suggests that the body and material evidence were more important than previously thought, given certainty and the right procedure to bring it to life. These were high standards that were almost never satisfied, so these priorities do not necessarily represent practice so much as what people thought they desired from evidence. But desires are not nothing; they indicate a nascent direction that would guide future evolution of the practice.

While Erkenwald has prayed for God to "fulsen me to kenne / The mysterie of this meruaile" ("help [him] explain / the mystery of this marvel," ll. 124–5) he does not interpret the evidence; it is the body that explains. The body answers each of Erkenwald's questions in turn, neatly mapping his life and death onto Erkenwald's format. Erkenwald interrupts only twice to ask questions. The first asks the judge to provide an interpretation—to "reveal [his] reason" and explain why he is dressed as a king if he was not one—which he readily does: "I was ryȝtwise and reken and redy of the lawe ... thus to bounty my body thai buriet in golde" ("I was righteous, upright, and quick of the law ... thus to my honor they buried my body in gold," ll. 245–8). The second asks him for an explanation, more scientific in nature:

> Thi body may be enbawmyd, hit bashis me noght
> That hit thar ryue ne rote ne no ronke wormes,
> But thi coloure ne thi clothe—I know in no wise
> How hit myȝt lye, by monnes lore, and last so longe (ll. 261–4)

> Your body may be embalmed; it does not disconcert me
> That no rot touched it, nor any loathsome worms,
> But the color of your cloth—I know no manner
> In which it might remain, by man's science, and last so long

---

[31] Kathryn Kerby-Fulton's recent excavation of the poem's likely authorship heightens these issues of jurisdiction; she argues that—given the loving specificity with which the cathedral itself is described—the author may have worked at St. Paul's: *The Clerical Proletariat and the Resurgence of Medieval English Poetry* (Philadelphia: University of Pennsylvania Press, 2021), pp. 275–276.

Erkenwald's question reveals up-to-date scientific knowledge. Recent work has shown that embalming developed rapidly in sophistication over the fourteenth century because of the popularity of relics and the association of foul smells with sin.[32] Romedio Schmitz-Esser's encyclopedic work on dead bodies in the medieval period shows that embalmed bodies on the continent sometimes played a role in political legitimation (wherein "having the body" meant "having the authority") and in high profile murder trials, where the body stood in for a kind of quasi-accuser.[33] This question and his physical examination of the body supports a growing sense that even medieval coroners had some access to medical knowledge, and in this context shows how scientific knowledge was already coming to underpin the procedures that revealed the truth of evidence.

I read the judge here not as a witness under investigation (although his testimony could be read in that light) but as material evidence. In his speech, he refers to himself as two people ("myselfe and my soule," l. 300), and discusses his soul as a third party not present "my soule may sitte ther in sorow and sike ful colde" ("my soul may sit there in sorrow and also great cold" l. 305), which means that it is only his body, only the material, that speaks. It both makes good sense and accords with medieval practice to turn to the body for final say. Both the legal treatise *Summa de legibus Anglie que vocatur Bretone* (commonly called Britton) and the Anglo-Norman *Mirror of Justices* prescribe punishments for people who fail to preserve the body so that "one cannot tell how death happened."[34]

This division of responsibility matches the example enrollments, which gather all evidence and all witness testimony into the single voice of the jury, and in which the examination of the body almost always comes last, often having the last word. In the case of Robert Curteys, the examination of the corpse ends the enrollment and confirms the story Isabella told ("The corpse viewed whereon the said wound appeared and no other hurt"). This form handily relieves the coroner of revisiting what must have been the investigation's most tricky tasks; weighing multiple narratives and the knowledge of the community, determining the reliability of witnesses, and all the other messy details and doubts of inquiry. But as convenient as this form is, *St. Erkenwald*

---

[32] See Paul Brazinski and Allegra Fryxell, "The Smell of Relics: Authenticating Saintly Bones and the Role of Scent in the Sensory Experience of Medieval Christian Veneration," *Papers from the Institute of Archaeology* 23, no. 1 (2013): p. 15.

[33] Romedio Schmitz-Esser, *Der Leichnam im Mittelalter: Einbalsamierung, Verbrennung und die kulturelle Konstruktion des toten Körpers* (Berlin: Jan Thorbecke Verlag Gmbh & Co., 2014).

[34] Le Breton, *Summa de legibus angliae que vocatur Bretone*, vol. 1, p. 9; Andrew Horne, *Mirror of Justices*, ed. William Joseph Whittaker (London: Selden Society, 1895), p. 30.

perfects it still further, excising the middleman of the jury and having the evidence literally speak for itself. Where the circumstances and material of the body created the mystery for the townspeople, it now resolves it, thanks to Erkenwald's essential but essentially content-less procedural intervention. In all of this, particularly the fantasy of simply animating the corpse and having it speak for itself, there is a hierarchy of proof in which the body, the material evidence, is at the top. If reputation were paramount, for example, the testimony of others would carry the narrative, perhaps from the grave, perhaps through written or oral accounts. Instead, this demonstrates an investigative ideal in which material evidence was central to the investigation, whether or not that ideal always played out in practice. Returning to Alice's enrollment, we can see this in action; the examination of the corpse ends the enrollment and supersedes the jury's authority by offering its own story (that Alice died from the blow, and not from the fall). It does not contradict Robert the elder's guilt, but it does contradict the jury's version of events. It even reveals him to be *more* at fault than the first jury's story, in which the fall was what killed her. In fact, *St. Erkenwald's* fantasy of self-interpreting evidence suggests frustration with the equivocations and silences of material evidence; that it gives so little when it means so much. This does not mean that reputation did not count as evidence, but *St. Erkenwald* reveals that material evidence, both in practice in the enrollments I give as examples and as an ideal, was a more desirable source of information than reputation, so long as it spoke clearly and univocally, as the judge does.

The final caveat is a major one, and medieval law's high standards for material evidence are probably a major reason it is difficult to find cases that hinge entirely on such details.[35] Sara Butler points out that "the medieval rules of evidence generally were more stringent than modern expectations."[36] As Barbara Shapiro elegantly puts it, the standard of proof is a reflection of "the culture's general understanding of how we 'know' things to be true," and the "sense of certainty" that would now allow a jury to convict someone on a preponderance of circumstantial evidence would have intervened here to prevent the same outcome.[37] Perhaps a better way to articulate what *St. Erkenwald* demonstrates about the balance between reputation and material evidence is this. Reputation gave confident information but could contribute only a small

---

[35] The list of types of evidence that could substantially sway an indicting jury was very narrow. Bracton recommends searching the scene, but notes that while having stolen goods ("the hand-having thief") or the still-bloody murder weapon on your person could be persuasive, circumstantial evidence would not be (Woodbine, *Bracton*, vol. 2, pp. 343, 429).

[36] Butler, *Forensic Medicine*, p. 131.

[37] Barbara Shapiro, *Beyond Reasonable Doubt and Probable Cause: Historical Perspectives on the Anglo-American Law of Evidence* (Berkeley, CA: University of California Press, 1991), p. 2.

quantity toward proof. Material evidence was hardly ever certain but could contribute a very large quantity when it was. Thus the fantasy that *St. Erkenwald* presents is that reputation, with its lesser proof value, fails, so no one is put in the uneasy position of having to rely on hearsay. Instead, proper investigative procedure reveals material evidence that is not only absolutely certain but auto-exemplifying, and its higher proof value makes reputation unnecessary. In fact, the fantasy of this poem's propaganda for the value of procedures and evidence is that reputation as a source of truth could become obsolete, if only material evidence could become more certain.

The Poem Delays

When the moment of judgment finally arrives, Erkenwald holds back. He instead a subjunctive hope for baptism:

> Oure lord lene, quoth that lede, that thou lyfe hades,
> By Goddes leue, as longe as I myght lacche water
> ... and carpe thes wordes,
> "I folwe the in the Fader nome." (ll. 315–18)

> Our lord allow, said that man, that you might have life
> By God's leave, until I might find water
> ... and say these words,
> "I baptise you in your Father's name."

In this hypothetical, he pronounces the words of the sacrament as reported speech, not as the speech act itself, and we only realize that these words and the bishop's tears have accidentally achieved baptism when the body speaks again. In a line, the poem jolts from the subjunctive—the possible—to the preterite— the achieved: "The fyrst slent that on me slode slekkyd al my tene. / Ryght now to sper my soule is sette at the table" ("The first drop that touched me had relieved all my suffering. / Right now to supper my soul is set at the table," ll. 331–2).

In revealing his salvation, he also reveals his baptism, which a recursive narrative has hidden from view; the "now" of the supper table brings a second temporality to life, one that adds to the first without negating it, instead doubling the experience. Erkenwald is hoping for a future baptism (now), but the judge is also "sette at the table" (now), and both coincide with a baptism (also now). It is a strange choice to conceal the triumph of procedure and history from the reader, but from its opening lines, the poem has struggled to establish progressive narrative momentum. "At London in Englonde noght fulle longe sythen" ("In London in England not very long since," l. 1) inspires conventional assumptions that the story will begin "not long since" the reader's present and proceed forward through time in an orderly manner. But the second line immediately supersedes this with a clarification: "Sythen Crist" (l. 2) shuffles the referent of since from the poem's present to Christ, and reverses its direction from backward to forward in time. This process only expands in the following thirty lines, giving a sense of many layers of the present but very little narrative sequence. *St. Erkenwald* is a poem preoccupied with an orderly, sequential, and contiguous representation of history. Why then does it refuse to do the same for its form?

I argue that the poem's form is a result of grappling with two competing temporal imperatives for justice—to foster delay and to conquer it. The dangers of delay to justice are obvious; its benefits are more difficult to locate, in both criminal procedure and narrative. And yet this is where the poem makes its most important intervention; evidence takes time, time to discover, interpret, deliberate, and revise. The coroner often took days to arrive, and his inquest took a few more. In *St. Erkenwald*, this time is dilated to a full week, and we linger with the bishop as he delays the body's final judgment, time passed only partly in active inquiry. The poem does not just praise procedure, it performs it in its form, even at the risk of wasting the reader's attention, the greatest sin of narrative time. But of course, a just investigation almost never makes a satisfying narrative. By forcing the reader to experience delay, even at the risk of thwarting their enjoyment, the poem warns against letting narrative enjoyment drive our expectations for criminal procedure.

Medieval legal thought had long understood that deferral of justice is akin to denial, and *servientes ad legem* (like Chaucer's "serjeant of the lawe, war and wys") regularly took oaths to serve the King's people and to never "defer or delay their causes willingly."[38] And yet, as in modern criminal justice, delay was an endemic feature of the medieval trial. A juror might fail to appear, the defendant might flee or be difficult to locate, or a writ might simply be late in reaching the sheriff, as one pled, all resulting in harm both to the victims and to the accused.[39] As a result, commons petitions to Parliament are filled with

---

[38] Geoffrey Chaucer, "General Prologue," l. 311 in *The Riverside Chaucer*; Edward H. Warren, "Serjeants-at-Law: The Order of the Coif," *Virginia Law Review* 28, no. 7 (1942): p. 925. Britton, the book of authority, cautioned against any delay, even *propter difficultatem*: "Difficulty of judgment is a shameful reason for delay: because the king, who ought to govern the people by law, ought not to be ignorant of it" (Francis Morgan Nichols, ed. and trans., *Britton*, vol. 1 [Washington: John Byrne & Co, 1901], p. 313).

[39] "quod iste breve tarde michi deliberatum fuit quod propter brevitatem temporis nullam inde facere potui executionem." Cited in James F. Willard and William Alfred Morris, *The English Government at Work: 1327–1336* (Cambridge: Medieval Academy of America, 1940), p. 266.

complaints of delay, especially regarding felony cases. In one case, the commons complained of local delay, when men of the county took commissions to determine felonies but "then delayed and did nothing, whereby those who were thus indicted caused great evil, that is to say they assaulted and threatened the good people by whom they were indicted." In another, they complained that the justices themselves caused delays, because they were supposed to hold gaol delivery at every session but failed to, "on account of which executions to be made on felons and the deliveries of others indicted falsely and by procurement are greatly delayed, to the damage of our lord the king."[40] Satisfaction in justice imagines perfect sequence, a world without delay in which act, investigation, judgment, and punishment all follow upon one another like beads on a string. Both of these petitions recognized that, in addition to the practical problems delay created, it irrevocably taints the quality of justice in a way that quantity cannot mend.

Delay in narrative is similarly disruptive, and for this reason medieval narratives tend to avoid causing the reader delay, even when the story told is one of deferral, frustration, or prolonged suffering for the character. As Thomas Wilson cautions in his 1553 *Arte of Rhetorique*, "Consideryng the dulnesse of mannes nature, that neither it can be attentiue to heare, nor yet stirred to like or allowe, any tale long tolde, except it be refreshed, or finde some swete delite."[41] When Gawain is forced to wait a year to meet the Green Knight in combat, the poem turns its attention away from his stasis and delay to the constant movement and change of the natural world. The poem describes in gorgeous detail the colors and movements of the grass, seeds, sun, dust, wind, and light, and Gawain only returns to its lines when he is ready to set off.[42] While we journey through years of events with Sir Orfeo in the eponymous romance, Heurodis languishes in suspension; she sleeps, she rides, and sleeps again, but the reader only experiences her time when she is before Sir Orfeo's eyes.[43]

A moral reason to avoid such a description was that time spent in waiting was freighted with implications of idleness and waste. Idleness as a spiritual

---

[40] "Edward III: February 1334," in Given-Wilson, et al. Internet Version, http://sd-editions.com (Leicester: Scholarly Editions, 2005).

[41] Thomas Wilson, *Arte of Rhetorique*, ed. G.H. Mair (Oxford: Clarendon Press, 1909), p. 74.

[42] "Til Meʒelmas mone / Watz cumen wyth wynter wage. / Then thenkkez Gawan ful sone / Of his anious uyage" ("Until Michaelmas moon / Was coming with waging winter. / Then Gawain thought how soon / Was his anxious voyage"). Malcolm Andrew and Ronald Waldron, eds. *The Poems of the Pearl Manuscript* (Liverpool: Liverpool University Press, 2008), ll. 531–535, translation mine. If we had dwelt with Gawain himself in wearisome anticipation of his "anious uyage" for those passing seasons, we might weigh the timeline of the adventure differently. I am grateful to Vance Smith for bringing my attention to this reference to Gawain's delay.

[43] She disappears from line 60 to line 362: "Sir Orfeo" in Anne Laskaya and Eve Salisbury, eds., *The Middle English Breton Lays* (Kalamazoo, MI: Medieval Institute Publications, 1995).

offense was linked in medieval penitential texts with a variety of other wasteful excesses: "Thus wasteth the wrecche," charges the *Ayenbite of Inwyt*, "his time and his wyttes and his guodes and wretheth God and harmeth his bodi and more his zaule." ("Thus the wretch wastes his time and his wits and his goods and provokes God and harms his body and more his soul").[44] Waste was a useful way to recast the cardinal sins to highlight their effects; gluttony wasted food, lust wasted the body, and sloth wasted both resources and time. The spiritual waste of time was, like other forms of waste, deeply linked with the material. After Chaucer's Host carefully calculates the passage of the day before inviting the Man of Law to speak, he cautions his companions: "los of tyme shendeth us," quod he ... / Lat us nat mowlen thus in ydelness" ("the loss of time shames us, he said ... / Let us not mold thus in idleness").[45] Idleness strips away precious things that cannot be recovered, and the time itself "molds" those who are idle.[46]

And yet, *St. Erkenwald* repeatedly risks wasting the reader's time. Even after he belatedly arrives, Erkenwald's first act is not to hurry to the body but to avoid it: "He passyd in-to his palais and pes he comaundit, / And deuoydit fro the dede and ditte the durre after" ("He passed into his palace and commanded silence / He avoided the dead and bolted the door after himself," ll. 115–16). The reader experiences the frustration of this delay with the crowd, passing idle time in descriptions of his night of prayer and the mass he holds, and in stopping to hear the mayor's summation of what we already know. By the time he lifts the judge's eyelids seven days have already passed, an unusual delay in a death investigation.

Even when urging God's haste to return the judge to history, Erkenwald "tok hym a tome" ("took himself some time," l. 316) to compose himself. By the time Erkenwald prays that the baptism of the body be delayed "not one grue lenger" ("not one bit longer," line 319) the reader might be forgiven for feeling skeptical of his belated haste. And disoriented, for the poem has replaced the familiar sequencers ("first," "and then," and "after") with a single marker: "now." Its

---

[44] Richard Morris and Pamela Gradon, eds., *Dan Michel's Ayenbite of Inwyt: Or, Remorse of Conscience; Richard Morris's Transcription* (Oxford: Early English Text Society, 1965), p. 52.

[45] Chaucer, "Introduction to the Man of Law's Tale," in *The Riverside Chaucer*, ll. 31–32.

[46] As Eleanor Johnson has shown, this kind of waste can bedevil anyone, even good workers. In the debate poem *Wynnere and Wastoure*, Wastoure is repeatedly accused of profligacy with his labor and his goods, but Wastoure also accuses Wynnere of choosing to wait to repair his storehouses when he should have acted immediately: "With wronge thou wastes thi tyme." Thus, as Johnson argues, the true transgression of the poem is that Wynnere has in fact wasted Wastoure's time. Eleanor Johnson, "The Poetics of Waste," *PMLA* 127, no. 3 (2012): pp. 460–476. For the text, see Warren Ginsberg, ed., *Wynnere and Wastour and The Parlement of Thre Ages* (Kalamazoo, MI: Medieval Institute Publications, 1992).

repetitions of "now" do not anchor the narrative; they dislocate it. In the opening section, where the poem quickly traverses the highlights of English history (out of order), "now" is the time of the reader ("Now that London is neuenyd—hatte the New Troie," l. 25), but it is also the time of Erkenwald ("Now of this Augustynes art is Erkewolde bischop," l. 33), as well as the ambiguous time of the judge's soul ("Ryght now to sper my soule is sette at the table," l. 332).

Suzanne Fleishmann has observed that while in nonnarrative language the present tense is unmarked, in medieval literature the past is the unmarked one, and that "the present tense ... is marked with respect to one or more of a set of properties that together define the unmarked tense of narration, the past."[47] The present tense's markedness, when it occurs, disrupts the unremarkable progression of the narrative. In *St. Erkenwald*, "now" signals a change, initiating a new temporal orientation but allowing multiples "nows" to exist at once. The motivation of the poem is to repair the judge's unearned delay, but the solution, the way to return the judge to timeliness, is to take more time. This tension, this attempt to repair the judge's disrupted timeline, perturbs the poem's own, and results in the disrupted form that conceals the most important moment of the poem from Erkenwald and its readers. In this way, it cautions the reader against enjoying this detective story too much. By thwarting the reader's experience, it demonstrates the danger of mapping narrative expectations onto investigative process, even when they borrow from one another and come together so satisfyingly.

*

The judgment that ends the poem is hidden, but its consequences are not.

> Bot sodenly his swete chere swyndid and faylide
> And alle the blee of his body wos blakke as the moldes,
> As roten as the rottok that rises in powdere ...
> Meche mournynge and myrthe was mellyd to-geder;
> Thai passyd forthe in processioun and alle the pepulle folowid
> And alle the belles in the burghe beryd at ones. (ll. 324–52)

> Suddenly, his sweet cheer dwindled and faded,
> And all the blood of his body was black as mold
> As rotten as the dust that rises in powder ...
> Much mourning and mirth were mixed together

---

[47] Suzanne Fleischman, *Tense and Narrativity: From Medieval Performance to Modern Fiction* (Austin, TX: University of Texas Press, 2010), p. 5.

They passed forth in procession and all the people followed
And all the bells in that city rang out at once.

The celebration in which "mourning and mirth were mixed together" demonstrates how mixed satisfaction in both narrative and justice can be. The body is returned to the dust it ought to have been all along, but just as his death was delayed, so too was his mourning. When time starts again, we have to pick up where we left off, with losing him. Ending the poem means losing the judge, and even though the judgment is perfectly certain it carries with it a tinge of regret.

Certainly, a community that self-investigated and found violence or hatred within itself would be torn between justice and mourning. For instance, Alice's inquest has some suspicious holes in it. If there was an altercation involving Alice and the two Roberts, and the neighbors arrived in time to arrest the son, would they not have also caught the father? Yet if there were a conspiracy in favor of the father, then why did the juries name him guilty rather than the son, who was already in jail and made a far more convenient target? We have no way of knowing. Perhaps the father had higher standing in the community than did his son, but also a history of violence toward his wife that was well known. Surely it would have been apparent to all that he had finally killed her. So to charge the son with her murder when everyone knew otherwise would have undermined trust in both the law and those who represented the community to it. Torn between the obvious facts and desire to protect the abuser, they might have found that proclaiming the father guilty but letting him live in exile was the least bad option.

St. Erkenwald—with its fantasy of an ideal investigation in which everyone plays their role, evidence reveals and explains itself, and doubt is completely allayed—hopes for a different version of medieval investigation than we have thought medieval people desired. It imagines an investigation where the uncorruptible community gathers before the coroner, collects all the right information, but knows when to stop. The coroner's procedure picks up the investigation seamlessly, unlocking the meaning of the evidence with absolute certainty. And in this ideal, no one mistakes the desire for speed or satisfaction with justice, and it all proceeds with whatever delays the investigation demands. I do not imagine this ideal existed, or that anyone pursued the truth with the steadfastness of *St. Erkenwald's* Londoners. But that is not what ideals show us; they reveal how we hope one day to be able to act.

Perhaps one reason these standards have been difficult to locate is the way in which the modern trial incorporates these elements. Many aspects of the investigation and nearly all of the judgment take place within the confines of the modern trial itself. Evidence is presented, witnesses testify and are cross-examined, experts give their interpretation of the facts, and the jury takes in all of this information and deliberates. A modern felony case can last months or years. As I discussed in the Introduction, a typical felony trial in the fourteenth century took between fifteen and thirty minutes.[48] Evidence was generally not part of the proceedings; witnesses who did appear usually spoke to reputation. As Nicola Lacey has pointed out, it is hard to imagine that much deliberation took place in so short a time.[49]

Yet there is proof even in statistics that evidence mattered; Anthony Musson's count puts a 98 percent exoneration rate for those appealed by approver—that is, those whose reputations had been impeached by those who would know—in the first half of the fourteenth century in Norfolk, compared to a 63 percent acquittal rate on cases brought through coroners' inquests.[50] Some of the low rate for approvers is surely a result of finding admitted criminals untrustworthy in general, but not all; cases brought by a procedure that produced evidence succeeded at eighteen times the rate of those brought purely by reputation. So it seems to me that while a bad reputation eased the way to the gallows and a good one was strong protection, reputation's power did not mean that medieval investigative procedure did not value evidence or the "factual case."

St. Erkenwald is a poem about Englishness: its history, its politics, its law. Its nationalism pushes it to untenable fantasies of auto-exemplifying mysteries and perfectly contiguous histories, both of which in the end seem more anxious than confident, more self-justifying than justified. But its sincerest engagement with the culture it hopes to represent lies in its portrait of a worried community horrified by finding a dead body in their midst for which they cannot account, their sense of responsibility toward its fate, and their earnest attempts to set it right. Its melding of religious and historical registers allows it to create a sophisticated and sensitive commentary on proof. That is, the story of the judge helps elucidate a legal standard we might not otherwise glimpse.

---

[48] R.B. Pugh, "The Duration of Criminal Trials in Medieval England," in *Law, Litigants and the Legal Profession*, eds. E.W. Ives and A.H. Manchester (London: Royal Historical Society, 1983), pp. 104–115, p. 108.

[49] Nicola Lacey, *In Search of Criminal Responsibility: Ideas, Interests, and Institutions* (Oxford: Oxford University Press, 2016), pp. 93–99.

[50] Approvers were felons who turned "king's evidence" in order for delays in their sentencing and other unspecified benefits. Anthony Musson, *Medieval Law in Context: The Growth of Legal Consciousness from Magna Carta to The Peasants' Revolt* (Manchester: Manchester University Press, 2001), p. 115.

Chapter 2
The Plea

Placita Corone and Narrative Satisfaction

There is a longstanding and lively conversation in law and literature about the utility of using narrative theories developed for literature to understand modern law's oral arguments and judicial decisions.[1] But there is less work in this vein in the medieval context; while scholars often use the term "stories" or "storytelling" to describe medieval legal case records, it is usually not in a technical or argumentative sense.[2] For one thing, applying narrative theory developed for the nineteenth-century novel to the medieval context has seemed fraught and unhelpful, to both narrative theorists and medievalists alike. For another, much of the data useful to the conversation on the modern context (what judges themselves say about narrative in their decisions, for example) are not available in the medieval one.

But one way we might approach the relationship between narrative theory and legal writing in the medieval period is through the plea. The plea brought the case to the courtroom; it formed an argument about the act (what happened) and the issue (how that matters to the law). Because it interfaced with statutes and customary procedure, any story it told was highly crafted and technical. And yet, the language of narrative suffused the medieval plea. Pleas and tales share the same terminology; "to count," the word for "to plead" from the

---

[1] For a good summary of the field, see Greta Olson, "Narration and Narrative in Legal Discourse," in Peter Hühn et al. (eds.), *Handbook of Narratology*, vol. 1, ed. Peter Hühn et al., 2nd ed. (Berlin: De Gruyter, 2014), pp. 371–383. See also the excellent collection by Peter Brooks and Paul Gewirtz, eds., *Law's Stories: Narrative and Rhetoric in the Law* (New Haven, CT: Yale University Press, 1996), pp. 61–83. Simon Stern's more recent essay on the limitations of seeing narrative in all legal texts has been especially helpful in identifying the contours of this chapter: "Narrative in the Legal Text: Judicial Opinions and Their Narratives," in *Narrative and Metaphor in the Law*, ed. Michael Hanne and Robert Weisberg (Cambridge: Cambridge University Press, 2018), pp. 121–139.

[2] See, for instance, Trevor Dean's treatment of criminal pleas in *Crime in Medieval Europe, 1200–1500* (London: Routledge, 2014), and Teresa Phipps's study of women's pleas in her chapter "Violence, Property and 'Bad Speech': Women and Trespass Litigation," in her *Medieval Women and Urban Justice: Commerce, Crime and Community in England, 1300–1500* (Manchester: Manchester University Press, 2020), pp. 111–152. In a fantastic older but still relevant state-of-the-field reflection, Barbara Hanawalt discusses the modern interest in hearing stories in medieval legal records, though not in pleas specifically: "The Voices and Audiences of Social History Records," *Social Science History* 15, no. 2 (1991): pp. 159–175.

The Making of Felony Procedure in Middle English Literature. Elise Wang, Oxford University Press.
© Elise Wang (2024). DOI: 10.1093/9780191967023.003.0003

Anglo-Norman verb *conter*, could apply in both literary and legal arenas, as could the Latin term for professional pleader, *narrator*, from which English later derived its terms "narrator" and "narrative."[3] In criminal cases, the act was generally an event, a catastrophe best related chronologically, with context and character descriptions. And like any good story not yet worked into shape, the plea could even be revised; Frederic Maitland notes that if a justice indicated a plea was not likely to succeed, the party could often disavow his hired *narrator*'s words (not having spoken them himself) and try again.[4]

In this chapter, I argue that the overlap in terminology and methodology is not merely incidental, but that pleaders themselves were explicitly interested in narrative satisfaction. I focus on the only extant manual of criminal pleading, commonly called the *Placita Corone*, to suggest that its primary lesson is not about legal procedure but narrative construction: how a compelling narrative is created, what effect it can have in the courtroom, and what shape works best for the audience of a plea. The slim tome's procedural inaccuracy, uneven narration, and "unreliability as a guide to the practice of the courts" has caused scholars to wonder what possible purpose it could have served its many readers.[5] But I argue that if we recognize narrative as the book's central concern, we can see that the legal manual considers learning to satisfy narrative expectations as an area of study in itself, and that it draws deftly upon the literary training of the medieval reader to further this education. In other words, I believe this instructional text demonstrates that not only did pleaders recognize that they were telling stories, they were also invested in honing that craft.

Narrative satisfaction is not the only way to approach this question, but I center it here for two reasons. The first is practical: recent scholarship on medieval narrative theory has focused on the reader's experience, offering my investigation coordinates from which to begin.[6] While modern narrative

---

[3] A typical legal use of *conter*: "yl n'y ad serjant en terre qe savereit counter le counte en ceo cas" ("there is not a serjeant on earth who would know how to count the count in this case," S.J. Stoljar et al., *Year Books of Edward II*, vol. 27 [London: Selden Society, 1988], p. 12, my translation), and a typical literary one: "Jo ai oi sovent cunter K'en bois soloient converser" (Gaston Paris and Alphonse Bos, *La Vie de saint Gilles, poème du XIIe siècle par Guillaume de Berneville* [Paris: SATF, 1881], p. 1809). For a discussion of the use of *narrator* in the legal context, see: Paul Brand, "The Language of the English Legal Profession: The Emergence of a Distinctive Legal Lexicon in Insular French," in *The Anglo-Norman Language and Its Contexts*, ed. Richard Ingham (York: York Medieval Press, 2010), p. 97. A.C. Spearing discusses the use of *narrator* in its literary context, informed by narrative theory, in "What is a Narrator? Narrator Theory and Medieval Narratives," *Digital Philology* 4 (2015): pp. 59–105.

[4] Pollack and Maitland, *The History of English Law*, p. 191.

[5] Post, "Placita Corone," p. 5.

[6] See "Stories and the Medieval Reader" below for a more detailed discussion, but here are some primary examples: Julie Orlemanski, "Who Has Fiction? Modernity, Fictionality, and the Middle Ages,"

theory addresses audience expectations as one part of the larger work, much of what scholars have observed in the medieval context pertains to what the audience expected, and how that foreknowledge allowed a medieval reader to handle narratives that seem difficult to the modern one. Episodic, discontinuous, and repetitive narratives are common in medieval literature, and the literary theory that scholars have begun to excavate from the period helps us better understand the reader for whom these tricky narratives were made.

The second reason is that in a legal context, audience reception of a text has especially high stakes. How the courtroom audience—the judge and jury, but also the gathered crowd—received the text had immediate ramifications for the pleader, his client, and future cases. What this audience expected to hear, and their standards for satisfaction—for both its technical or narrative components—dictated the shape of a successful plea. Centering audience satisfaction frames some primary questions for this chapter: did the audience come to a plea about horse-thieving or homicide expecting "a story," and if so, what was necessary to satisfy that expectation? What role did the story's truth value play in this expectation, and how did the story signal it? Did narrative—and in particular, its relationship to fiction—seem to the compositors or audience to pose any challenges to justice?

I begin with the premise of the chapter: that the *Placita Corone* is explicitly invested in narrative. Turning to a (helpfully direct) scene in which a judge dismisses a procedurally accurate response and demands a story instead, I suggest that its puzzling failure as a guide to procedure is a symptom of prioritizing good stories over procedural accuracy. Then I turn to medieval theories of narrative to understand how the medieval reader navigated the relationship between story and truth. I consider how three examples of pleading in literary texts deal with this question: the tale-telling competition of *The Seven Sages of Rome*, John Gower's trial of Cataline in his *Confessio Amantis*, and the accusations of Custance in Geoffrey Chaucer's "Man of Law's Tale." These examples offer a literary perspective on the possible pitfalls of prioritizing good stories in a court of law. Finally, I return to a scene of three trials in the *Placita Corone* that has always seemed a damning portrait of the abuses of criminal procedure when taken as a faithful reflection of courtroom conduct. But I suggest that if we bring a medieval reader's active evaluation to the scene, we can not

---

New Literary History 50, no. 2 (2019): pp. 145–170; Steven Justice, "Did the Middle Ages Believe in Their Miracles?" *Representations* 103, no. 1 (2008): pp. 1–29; Elizabeth Allen, "Episodes," in Paul Strohm (ed.), *Middle English (Oxford Twenty-First Century Approaches)* (Oxford: Oxford University Press, 2007), pp. 191–206; Gabrielle M. Spiegel, "Forging the Past: The Language of Historical Truth in the Middle Ages," *The History Teacher* 17, no. 2 (1984): pp. 267–288.

only discern a different answer to the problem of stories in the law than the one literature provided, but we might also find startling narrative satisfaction ourselves.

The Pleas of the Crown

Pleading was a precise business; the opening of the *Placita Corone* cautions the would-be pleader to carefully review his count, "that he may not fail in any one particular or detail."[7] Generally, professional pleaders—standing beside their clients—would deliver a version of the issue, to which the defendant would respond, and because the parties themselves had not spoken the plea they could disavow what their *narrators* had said if the justice indicated it was prudent.[8] Thus, the professional pleader existed both for his expertise in the form and to distance the parties from their pleas for the sake of later revision. But in criminal pleas, which often involved parties not wealthy or informed enough to hire professionals, many were left to do this work themselves. Therefore, this scene usually involved two, not four, and considerably less polish, which might have led the justice to lend his expertise and take a more active role in the plea stage.

The *Placita Corone*, as criminal pleading's only extant treatise, reflects these rough edges. Its blow-by-blow account of accusations, questions, and defenses is unusually lively; its speech sounds like speech. Because it is the only one of its kind, this color has been taken as verisimilitude, as a robust portrait of the felony courtroom, something the rolls offer only in partial, accidental glimpses. But its use as a historical source is mitigated by a second peculiarity; it is a procedural mess. There is no discernible structure or order to it, and it leaps from case to case without so much as a connecting thought. It haphazardly mixes old-fashioned proof procedures with later prosecution methods, often misrepresenting both.[9] It mistakes basic procedural rules and confuses the names of parties midstream. Its modern editor, Joel Kaye, lamented that for the scholar

---

[7] "ke il ne faille de nul article ne de nul point," Joel Kaye, ed. and trans., *Placita Corone or La Corone Pledee devant Justices* (London: Selden Society, 1966), p. 1. While I have referred to Kaye's translations, all modern English translations from all texts in this chapter are mine.

[8] As Baker notes, this is the source of "advocatus," or forespeaker, who "stood beside the litigant and spoke for him" (John Baker, *Introduction to English Legal History*, 5th ed. [Oxford: Oxford University Press, 2019], p. 156).

[9] It was actively copied and amended from the late 1200s to the early 1500s, a period of significant procedural change. Though Kaye in his introduction marks the earliest date of composition as 1278, Donald Sutherland points out that this rests on a mistranslation of "vintime" as "fifth" instead of "twentieth;" the twentieth year of Edward I's reign being 1291–1292. Therefore, the manuscripts of this treatise probably date from the 1290s to the early fifteenth century, with some of the latest hands

or practitioner of procedure, it contains "little in it above the level of routine," and shows "no evidence of profound legal knowledge or love of technicality for its own sake," as most manuals of pleading do.[10] J.B. Post calls its attitude toward details "reckless," noting that it contains quite a few basic inaccuracies that no trained lawman would make.[11] And yet, at least 22 manuscripts (many different enough to suggest intermediary copies) survive; for a medieval legal text, this was a bestseller.

Who could possibly have use for a text whose carelessness renders it useless for pedagogy, and whose cases jumble together more than a century's worth of procedural changes? Kaye posits that it had once been more like the Year Books, but that "as time went on the treatise gradually contracted in size, the number of precedents becoming smaller, each individual precedent losing much of its original detail, and the explanatory matter being steadily cut away."[12] And yet, he also notes that "there is (still) far too much material in it which has no relevance to pleading or indeed to the professional lawyer's normal sphere of activities."[13] Its only reliable value has seemed to lie in its insights into the conduct of the parties in court, and for that it is fairly bleak evidence.[14] Based on these scenes, J.G. Bellamy calls the plea stage a "confrontational free-for-all," and Green observes that success in the plea stage was "primarily a matter of punctilious observance of procedural rules ... in which the accused opened his mouth at his peril."[15]

This portrait offers us a sadly diminished—yet somehow also damning—view of the text, but it still does not answer the question of how it commanded interest for so long. But I suggest that if we leave aside the question of what might have been lost or mangled, we can perceive what it has retained over its many copies. The prologue and explanatory matter differ from manuscript to manuscript, but all copies retain several of the same lively, memorable scenes. The explanatory matter on these scenes expands and contracts depending on the overall length of the manuscript, and sometimes the names of the parties

---

appearing to copy some of the earliest versions. Donald Sutherland, "Review: *Placita Corone, or La Corone Pledee devant Justices* by J.M. Kaye," *Speculum* 43, no.1 (1968): pp. 167–170.

[10] Kaye, *Placita Corone*, p. xx.

[11] Post, "Placita Corone," p. 4.

[12] Sutherland, "Review," p. 167; Kaye, *Placita Corone*, p. x. Kaye does note that this would be very unusual, since most legal treatises in use for as long as the *Placita Corone* were intended to be added to, not degraded.

[13] Kaye, *Placita Corone*, p. xxiii.

[14] Besides those I list, see also Kamali, *Felony and the Guilty Mind*, pp. 327–328. Sutherland challenges some aspects of this impression, arguing that the various aggressive judicial moves amount to "a judge who was determined to go beyond the hallowed formalities in order to get at the truth" ("Review," p. 169). Few scholars have commented on the nature of the text as a whole (I address most here).

[15] Bellamy, *The Criminal Trial in Later Medieval England*, p. 110; Richard Firth Green, *A Crisis of Truth*, pp. 131–132.

change, but the essential shape of these scenes remain. It is true that the manual does not evince a "love of technicality," but in all its copies, it does seem to have an ear for a good story.

In one scene that occurs in all manuscripts, Alice de C delivers a brutally specific plea; she alleges that Adam "called her vile names" and carried her under an oak tree, tying her hands with the cord of his yew bow. She pleads that he exclaimed, "I have wanted you for a long time—and here you are," after which, "with his right hand he forced open her legs and thighs, and, by violence and against her free will, (he) raped her in such a way that she was forced completely."[16] Her plea is both vivid and procedurally well-crafted. It gives the time, place, and circumstances, stipulates premeditation ("I have wanted you a long time"), violence, and abduction, checking all the boxes for a successful plea of rape.[17] Asked to respond, Adam says that he "never assailed her with vile words, in premeditated attack, feloniously as a felon; nor laid her down beneath an oak tree or any other tree," he claims, reflecting her plea point by point.[18] His answer is procedurally orthodox; in a criminal case, "the formal defense consisted ... of a technical exception to the appeal followed by the ancient *thwertutnay*, a flat denial of the whole charge."[19]

But the justice, with palpable impatience, breaks in: "Tell us the truth, for we shall find it out from the country if you do not recount (*recomtet*) it."[20] The threat of a jury trial seems to do the trick, because Adam suddenly takes

---

[16] "le assailli de mauvese parole et vileines ... 'longtens vous ay desire: et ore estes vos venue tot a point' ... de sa meyn deytre overyt ses gambes et ses quices et a force, encontre son gre et sa bone volunte, la ravy son pucelage et en tele manire ly focyt totoure" (*Placita Corone*, p. 8).

[17] Both Glanvill and Bracton define the charge of rape identically as "a woman (who) charges a man with violating her by force in the peace of the lord king" ("Placitum de crimine raptus," in G.D.G. Hall, ed. and trans., *The Treatise on the Laws and Customs of the Realm of England Commonly Called Glanvill* [Oxford: Clarendon Press, 1994], XIV, vi, p. 175; "De placitis corone," in Woodbine, *Bracton*, pp. 414–415). The Statute of Westminster declares, "It is provided henceforth that if a man ravishes a married woman, a maiden, or other woman, without her consent before or afterwards, he shall have judgement of life and limb." (This is taken from Post's version of the statute in "Ravishment of Women" because, as he notes, there is no satisfactory text for it; his is based on Corporation of London Records Office, CS/01/002 [*Liber Horn*], and the translation from Henry Rothwell, ed., *English Historical Documents*, vol. 3: 1189–1327 [London: Eyre and Spottiswoode, 1975], p. 400, C34, 164). Post, like Hanawalt, also notes that abduction and rape were often prosecuted and discussed together, a rape being a "carrying off" of a woman's value (Barbara Hanawalt, *Crime and Conflict in English Communities, 1300–1348* [Cambridge, MA: Harvard University Press, 1979], p. 106). In her article tracing the status of rape law from pre-conquest England to the thirteenth century, Corinne Saunders shows that pleas regarding rape had to note both lack of consent and violence, and that the most successful pleas usually claimed previous virginity, as this one does ("Medieval Law of Rape," *Kings College Law Journal* 11 [2000]: pp. 19–48). Caroline Dunn's work, *Stolen Women in Medieval England: Rape, Abduction, and Adultery, 1100–1500* (Cambridge: Cambridge University Press, 2013), p. 85, demonstrates that jurors placed high importance on premeditation and (lack of) consent in deciding ravishment cases.

[18] "ne lassaillit de mauveise paroles en assaut purpense felonessement com felon; ne desuz cheigne, ne desuz nul autre arbre" (*Placita Corone*, p. 8).

[19] Sutherland, "Review," p. 169.

[20] "Dites nous la verite kar par pays le attendruns bin si vous ne la recomtet" (*Placita Corone*, p. 8).

a different tone—fluid, informal, and narrative: "Sir, she has been a loose woman in body and mind for years. There once came a time that I made her acquaintance in such a town—we met at a market—and for the money I gave her, specifically a penny, she gave me her services at that time, and after." He continues to say that she offers her services to many others, and that they have maintained their professional relationship ever since.[21] In this improved response, he introduces a character (a "loose woman") and opens conventionally ("There once came a time"), which begins a brief narrative. They meet, and we hear about her character and the money before we hear about her services, which allows us time to anticipate what he will say and then experience having our expectations met. His account also sounds like speech, with vocatives ("Sir") and digressions ("we met at a market," "specifically a penny"). In other words, the justice demands "the truth," and Adam tells a story.

By staging an unsatisfying but accurate performance of procedure and interrupting it to bring us a narrative, this scene elevates the lay impression that the plea is where one tells one's story over the understanding that it is a technical construction of act and issue. The justice's demand for the truth assumes that the *thwertutnay* did not provide it. At this point in the text, the frame narrative also launches into the hypothetical. After the justice demands that Adam "recount" the truth, the treatise exchanges its more standard indicative mood ("fet la Justice") for the subjunctive ("deit dire la Justice"), and it stays in this hypothetical space to the end.[22] The case ends abruptly with yet another subjunctive note that—should this case proceed—it could only be decided by jury trial, not by battle.[23] It does not note an outcome, but in this subjunctive space we do not expect one.

Leaving the case in the hypothetical pointedly hands the reader the task of judgment. We might find we have invested ourselves in Alice, Adam, and their conflict. When we find Adam's story more satisfying than his procedurally correct response (as I believe we are meant to), we are left to consider the differences between the two accounts and—if we are pleaders learning our craft—how we might create the latter. We also probably find one story more compelling than the other, which leads us to examine why we feel that way,

---

[21] "Sire, ele ad este fole femme de cors et de corage, jourx et aunz: si ke avint une foyz ke je my aquenitay de li a tele vile, a un marche ou nous encontrames, et pur de men donant, nomeement un denier, ke ele servyt de teu mestir a tel hure, et apres" (*Placita Corone*, pp. 8–9).
[22] Kaye, *Placita Corone*, p. 9.
[23] This was because a man could not meet a woman in battle, though it does not acknowledge the well-established possibility that she could have a champion fight on her behalf. Perhaps we are meant to understand that she really was a prostitute, and therefore not of the standing to hire or call upon a champion, though the vast majority of women could not do so either.

given that we have no outcome to confirm our feeling. Perhaps details like the yew bow or oak tree or penny "feel true" to us, in the sense that they give us what Roland Barthes calls the "reality effect."[24] Or perhaps we find Alice's inclusion of Adam's speech ("I have wanted you a long time, and here you are") compelling in its recreation of the scene. Both the pleas individually and together call upon expectations of narrative satisfaction, and the case's refusal to conclude with an authoritative answer leaves us with only those expectations to reflect upon.

Our evaluation of the stories of Alice and Adam and the literary sensibility we bring to bear in doing so uncovers the treatise's pedagogy. It offers examples like all procedural manuals, but these examples are not meant to guide proper procedure or even instruct pleaders step by step on the construction of pleas. Indeed, they contain little explanation and lurch abruptly from one to the next in no particular order. Instead, the examples help readers reflect on narrative satisfaction and its relationship to truth by inviting them to explore these mechanisms within their own reactions.

In our own responses to this short scene, we might find some important points of reflection. If we agree with Adam and the justice that the "truth" (at least what will be taken for it in court) is a story, can falsehood also be a story? Can we trust ourselves and what we like in stories to know the difference? That is, given that stories in their native territory of literature happily accommodate fiction, does this frame for the truth work against—or at least orthogonally to—justice? These are not questions that the slim pleading manual takes up directly. But the *Placita Corone* depends on habits readers cultivated on literary ground, so we might turn to this field next to understand how the medieval reader approached the relationship between story and truth.

Stories and the Medieval Reader

What does medieval literary theory teach us about how readers approached texts that accommodated fiction but also claimed some truth? Such genres were common; romances and histories were self-consciously creative while also claiming some basis in historical fact. But as scholars of medieval literature have pointed out, a nuanced discussion of these genres has been flattened

---

[24] While I use the famous term here, it is worth noting that Barthes himself did not think this applied to medieval literature. He felt that medieval readers were not equipped to experience a reality effect and therefore medieval authors did not attempt to create one. Roland Barthes, *The Rustle of Language*, trans. Richard Howard (Berkeley, CA: University of California Press, 1986), pp. 143–144.

by a general assumption that medieval readers could not have approached this issue with sophistication. Especially in earlier scholarship on the medieval period, the medieval reader often fell prey to the modern one's desire to distance himself from all childish things, gullibility and credulousness in particular. The matter of fiction—or as Catherine Gallagher puts it, "believable stories that (do) not solicit belief"—has been a site for this exercise.[25] Gallagher, for example, excludes medieval literature from fiction on the grounds that its readers responded to believable stories by believing them.[26]

Part of this impression surely derives from what Monica Fludernik and A.C. Spearing note about the foundational texts of narrative theory; that they generally take texts from the eighteenth to early twentieth century as their subject, referring to medieval narrative only as a foil for the modern incarnation.[27] Julie Orlemanski convincingly associates these stark claims with the secularization thesis: that the linear progression of Western society can be tracked by the rise of skepticism and decline in unexamined belief.[28] Such logic necessitates that those at the start of the progression be narratively naive, responding to imaginative literatures as though they were truth claims.[29]

In fact, medieval literary theory's "oldest and most constant generic taxonomy" classified texts according to their relationship to truth.[30] Drawing from Ciceronian rhetorical texts, most theories lay the three primary literary genres on a spectrum: *fabula* was not true and did not mimic the style of truth, *argumentum* used realistic conventions for invented subjects, and *historia*

---

[25] Catherine Gallagher, "The Rise of Fictionality," in Franco Moretti (ed.), *The Novel* (Princeton, NJ: Princeton University Press, 2006), p. 340.

[26] Gallagher, "The Rise of Fictionality."

[27] A.C. Spearing, "What is a Narrator?: Narrator Theory and Medieval Narratives," *Digital Philology* 4 (2015): p. 65. See Monika Fludernik's engagement with the medievalist responses to Gallagher in "Medieval Fictionality from a Narratological Perspective," *New Literary History* 51 no. 1 (2020): pp. 259–263.

[28] Orlemanski, "Who Has Fiction?," pp. 145–170. Her definition for fiction that accounts for the medieval context is "the interface between language's fundamental capacity to portray the nonactual and the various regularizations of that capacity" (p. 146), to which Fludernik has offered some useful critiques ("Medieval Fictionality").

[29] On this subject, there has been a great deal of reflection. See, among others, Jeffrey Jerome Cohen, ed., *The Postcolonial Middle Ages* (New York, NY: St. Martin's Press, 2000); John Dagenais and Margaret Greer, eds., "Decolonizing the Middle Ages," *Journal of Medieval and Early Modern Studies* 30, no. 3 (2000): pp. 431–448; Patricia Clare Ingham and Michelle R. Warren, eds., *Postcolonial Moves: Medieval through Modern* (New York, NY: Palgrave Macmillan, 2003); Kathleen Davis, *Periodization and Sovereignty: How Ideas of Feudalism and Secularization Govern the Politics of Time* (Philadelphia, PA: University of Pennsylvania Press, 2008); Davis and Nadia Altschul, eds., *Medievalisms in the Postcolonial World: The Idea of "the Middle Ages" Outside Europe* (Baltimore, MD: Johns Hopkins University Press, 2009); and Carol Symes, "When We Talk about Modernity," *American Historical Review* 116, no. 3 (2011): pp. 715–726.

[30] Rita Copeland and Ineke Sluiter, "General Introduction," in *Medieval Grammar and Rhetoric: Language Arts and Literary Theory, AD 300–1475*, ed. Rita Copeland and Ineke Sluiter (Oxford: Oxford University Press, 2009), p. 42.

contained actual events presented in a compellingly imaginative way.[31] Even when not using this schema, medieval authors found a text's relationship to truth a useful way to classify narratives. As Paul Strohm outlines, Chaucer used generic terms to denote a narrative's level of truthfulness rather than its form; *storie* or *tretys* lie close to the truth, while *tale* or *fable* lie further away.[32] The popular medieval grammarian Servius demonstrated how this work might be done: the medieval Christian reader of the *Aeneid* must recognize that it "contains true things alongside fictions (*fictis*), for it is obvious that Aeneas did come to Italy, but it is understood that Venus speaking with Jove or Mercury being sent as messenger is made-up (*conpositum*)."[33] Thus, as Orlemanski argues, medieval readers "took certain claims—about the existence and nature of the pagan gods especially—to be literally false but worth entertaining as true in limited ways."[34]

The *historia* or *storie* end of the spectrum—the genres that contain actual events but maintain a relationship to fiction—have caused the most confusion for modern readers because there are no clear modern analogues.[35] *Historia* was not an opportunity for a spectacle of imagination; medieval authors self-consciously framed it as a factual genre. And yet, as Christopher Cannon puts it, "the Middle Ages prized *historia* for its invention, classing it with poetry."[36] While Aristotle excludes *historia* from mythos, Ralph Hanna has shown that the medieval definition of history-writing was "capacious enough to contain 'the romantic'", and that (as he puts it) the separation between medieval law, romance, and history was a "doubly osmotic membrane."[37]

Recent work on medieval readers has productively undermined the modern fixation on credulousness (as though the most interesting thing about a

---

[31] Spiegel, "Forging the Past," pp. 267–283.

[32] Paul Strohm, "Some Generic Distinctions in the Canterbury Tales," *Modern Philology* 68 (1971): pp. 321–328. See also the classic engagement with chronicles as stories in chapter 4 of Evelyn Birge Vitz's *Medieval Narrative and Modern Narratology: Subjects and Objects of Desire* (New York: New York University Press, 1989), pp. 126–165.

[33] Servius, *Servii grammatici qui feruntur in Vergilii carmina commentarii*, ed. Georgius Thilo and Hermannus Hagen, vol. 1 (Hildesheim: Georg Olms, 1961), p. 4, quoted in Orlemanski, "Who Has Fiction," p. 161.

[34] Orlemanski, "Who Has Fiction," p. 161.

[35] Historical fiction has been suggested, but modern readers of historical fiction generally expect a "true" and perhaps familiar frame in which an "invented" story has been placed, while medieval readers of *historia* expected both the frame and story to be more or less "true" and probably familiar. Thus, the modern reader of historical fiction will agreeably go along with much of the invention, while previous versions of the tale will persistently haunt the medieval reader, offering an active conversation between the versions.

[36] Christopher Cannon, *The Grounds of English Literature* (Oxford: Oxford University Press, 2004), p. 29.

[37] Ralph Hanna, *London Literature, 1300–1380* (Cambridge: Cambridge University Press, 2005), p. 83.

reader's response to a work of literature is whether or not she believes it to be true) and returned to the question of belief as an experience rather than a permanent state.[38] This active discernment demanded an especially engaged reader, one who was then primed not just for discerning believability, but experiencing belief. Michelle Karnes uses the example of marvels to argue that medieval literature intentionally played with the line between real and imaginary by telling two stories about marvels simultaneously: "one about their believability and one about their impossibility."[39] That is, the medieval reader approached this project without skepticism not because he was gullible, but because the point was to enjoy believing in marvelous things.

These practices also meant that the medieval reader was more accustomed to disjunction, revision, and repetition than the modern one is. Scholars have long noted that the contingencies of manuscripts contributed to an episodic and fragmented reading practice.[40] Tale anthologies like the *Canterbury Tales* and John Gower's *Confessio Amantis*, and compendia of sermons, penitential advice, and saints' lives like the *Legenda aurea* were not only episodic and compiled the same tales again and again, they were also designed to be collected miscellaneously themselves in vast collections, like the Auchinleck, Vernon, and Simeon manuscripts.[41] Even single narratives, like dream narratives and romances like *Beves of Hamtoun*, took on the episodic disjunction familiar to these collections. This textual material trained a reader to handle many versions of the same material, presented with the assumption that the basic counters, causal links, and characterizations were already known. Thus, the narratives themselves could "avoid clear causation and even subordination," Elizabeth Allen notes, "relying on readers to connect one scene to another." Fragmentation can disorient, but "such ruptures also encourage symbolic or associative connection," teaching readers to stitch together discontinuous episodes themselves.[42]

---

[38] Laura Ashe takes the approach of placing the invention of fiction in the twelfth century instead ("1155 and the Beginnings of Fiction," *History Today* 65, no. 1 [2015]: p. 41), and Steven Justice ("Did the Middle Ages Believe in Their Miracles?" *Representations* 103, no. 1 [2008]: pp. 1–29) confronts the misconception that belief came easily to medieval people.

[39] Michelle Karnes, "The Possibilities of Medieval Fiction," *New Literary History* 51, no. 1 (2020): pp. 209–228, p. 211.

[40] For example, Paul Zumthor, *Toward a Medieval Poetic*, trans. Philip Bennett (Minneapolis: University of Minnesota Press, 1992), Ralph Hanna, *Pursuing History: Middle English Manuscripts and their Texts* (Stanford, CA: Stanford University Press, 1996), Morton W. Bloomfield, "Episodic Motivation and Marvels in Epic and Romance," in *Essays and Explorations: Studies in Ideas, Language, and Literature* (Cambridge, MA: Harvard University Press, 1970), and Douglas Kelly, "Fortune and Narrative Proliferation," *Speculum* 51, no. 1 (1976): pp. 6–22.

[41] Edinburgh, National Library of Scotland, Adv. MS 19.2.1; Oxford, Bodleian Library, MS English Poet, a. 1; and London, British Library, MS Add. 22283, respectively.

[42] Allen, "Episodes," p. 191.

The medieval reader was deeply familiar with the complex relationship between narrative and truth, accustomed to navigating it but also accustomed to reflecting on that navigation with self-awareness. With this perspective, we can see even more clearly that the scene of Alice and Adam is an invitation for the reader to judge the credibility of the two stories, like a repetition of the same tale. The reader cannot make a determination on evidence she does not have, so if she finds one story closer to the truth than the other, she must make that decision based on the story's form. Then she is left to reflect on what brought her to that choice (was it Adam's easy and casual digressions? Alice's graphic description of his hands on her legs?), and the ethics of judging truth based on form and style. In the next section, I will consider the obvious and perilous question—what are the dangers of a good story to the truth?—from the perspective of literary texts.

Finding Truth in Medieval Literary Pleas

As Peter Brooks notes, in the modern context "story is not generally a category that the law wishes to recognize," and when it does acknowledge it, "it is most often to treat it with suspicion."[43] But in the medieval context, it is literature that is consistently suspicious of stories in the law, and in this section I will discuss three treatments of this issue. In *The Seven Sages of Rome*, the truth and the reader's love of a good story are at war with one another; the Empress almost condemns the innocent prince because her narratives are too neat, too satisfying. John Gower, both professional pleader and poet, proposes a solution to this conflict: constructing a plea with "plain" style will prevent the allures of narrative from occluding the truth. But this solution assumes that the audience has been misled. Geoffrey Chaucer's Man of Law, another pleader and poet, demonstrates that this is not always the case; sometimes it is not that the truth becomes hard to discern, but that it becomes undesirable.

In *The Seven Sages of Rome*, the poem frames the desire for narrative satisfaction as antipathetic to justice. Originally from Persian, Sanskrit, or Hebrew, the *Seven Sages* made its way to Middle English through Arabic. Its frame narrative is a trial before Emperor Diocletian, whose new wife has accused his adult son, Florentine, of trying to rape her. Over the course of seven nights and days (each called a "process" in the Middle English versions), the Empress tells a tale to convince Diocletian to execute his son, and a different sage counters

---

[43] Peter Brooks, "Law and Humanities: Two Attempts," *Boston University Law Review* 93 (2013): p. 1454.

with a tale of his own, urging the Emperor to spare him.[44] Nico Kunkel has observed that the Sages are clearly engaging in a legally informed defense of the son.[45] Alongside the Emperor, the reader is invited to compare the lessons of each tale and see which is more convincing.

These tales are exempla of justice being done—meant to be applied to the situation at hand by analogy—rather than stories of Florentine himself. In order to compare the tales, the reader must not only judge but also reflect on the reasons for the judgment. On the fifth night, the Empress tells the story of the traitorous Virgilius, who as a prince caused the emperor's very young son to break a mirror that provided guard to the city of Rome. The emperor is unable to punish his own son for this disaster, and so is soon shamed and destroyed, and the rule falls to Virgilius. In describing Emperor Virgilius's eventual downfall, the Empress emphasizes that the satisfaction of the justice is in its symmetry, its poetic nature:

> For he let falle the myrour
> For couetyse of tresour ...
> Thus for golde and tresour
> The Emperor was slawe
> Withouten any proses of lawe. (ll. 2060–1; 2073–5)

> For he let fall the mirror
> For covetise of treasure ...
> Thus for gold and treasure
> The Emperor was slain
> Without any process of law.[46]

The Empress advocates here for a style of justice that rests on a narrative structure (symmetry) to the exclusion of the law ("Withouten any proses of lawe"). This is not her only argument; she also compares the power-hungry

---

[44] Most of the scholarship on *The Seven Sages* focuses on the misogynistic foundation of the tales: Nico Kunkel's "Misogyny, Wisdom, and Legal Practice: On Narrative Flexibility across Different Versions of the Seven Sages of Rome," *Narrative Culture* 7, no. 2 (2020): pp. 181–197; Katya Skow-Obenaus, "The Whole Is the Sum of Its Parts: Misogyny as a Unifying Factor in *Die Sieben weisen Meister*," *Fifteenth-Century Studies* 26 (2001): pp. 169–182; Bea Lundt, "'Sieben weise Meister gegen eine Frau.' Ein populäres Volksbuch aus frauen- und geschlechtergeschichtlicher Perspektive," in G. Klein and A. Treibel (eds.), *Begehren und Entbehren, Bochumer Beiträge zur Geschlechterforschung* (Pfafffenweiler: Centaurus, 1993), pp. 185–206. For a reflection on how these tales briefly made it into Chaucer apocrypha, see Guillemette Bolens, "Narrative Use and the Practice of Fiction in *The Book of Sindibad* and *The Tale of Beryn*," *Poetics Today* 29, no. 2 (2008): pp. 309–351.

[45] Kunkel, "Misogyny, Wisdom, and Legal Practice," pp. 189–190; Allen, "Episodes," p. 193.

[46] Jill Whitlock, ed., *The Seven Sages of Rome (Midland Version)*, Early English Text Society (Oxford: Oxford University Press, 2005).

and manipulative Virgilius to Florentine, suggesting that his motivations are corrupt. But the Sage who responds knows that this slander is not the substance of her plea, which he correctly recognizes as the argument that justice should function like a story without the procedure of the law. In response, the Sage spins his tale on the importance of due process.

The message is that the Empress's stories are a threat to justice not just because she is evil or has nefarious intentions, but because they propose narrative satisfaction as a proper guide to legal action. Thus, an overly literary mind (so goes this critique) might confuse narrative satisfaction for justice and divert the proper course of the law to more closely resemble a story. Likewise, it is the Emperor's prioritization of narrative over his own son that keeps the son in danger. Unlike Sharyar of *One Thousand and One Nights*, who only spares Scheherazade at the end of each night, the Emperor grants a stay of execution *before* each sage delivers his rebuttal, more eager for narrative than justice.

Narrative's threat to justice weighed on Gower's mind. A professional pleader and poet who straddled the two arenas and reflected in writing on both professions, Gower proposes a stylistic solution. A pleader's duty, he writes, is to:

> ... pike
> Hou that he schal hise wordes sette,
> Hou he schal lose, hou he schal knette,
> And in what wise he schal pronounce
> His tale plein withoute frounce. (Book 7, ll. 1590–9)

> ... pick
> How he shall set his words,
> How he shall loose, how he shall knit,
> And in what way he shall pronounce
> His plain tale without frounce.[47]

Disavowing "frounce" is how the pleader produces not only a successful plea, but a righteous one. Gower gives an example of how this ought (and ought not)

---

[47] John Gower, *Confessio Amantis*, vol. 3, eds. Andrew Galloway and Russell Peck (Kalamazoo: Medieval Institute Publications, 2004). Gower never wrote directly for his fellow men of the law, but as Conrad van Dijk puts it, "for Gower, every exemplum is a potential *casus*," or legal case (*John Gower and the Limits of the Law* [Suffolk: Boydell and Brewer, 2013], p. 33). Characters have cases to be proven ("so mai it proven be this cas") and judged ("adiudicauit"), and those subject are compensated (with "amendes") or are put to death ("interfici"). Within these cases, he is able to reflect on the moral issues he faced in his professional practice.

to work in the trial of Catiline for his conspiracy against Rome in the *Confessio Amantis*. In Gower's source, Brunetto Latini's *Tresor*, Caesar rescues a guilty but righteous Catiline from execution for treason with an eloquent plea. For Latini, this is a triumph. But Gower condemns Caesar's fine words.[48] Rather than focusing on the political or moral righteousness of Catiline's actions, he brings our attention to their unlawfulness, which transforms Caesar's eloquent rescue from a triumph of rhetoric over injustice into rhetoric's perversion of the law. It becomes a cautionary demonstration that the emotional power of stories might move us to overlook more sedate goods, like logic and common benefit, and he locates this emotional power in the style with which each pleader moved his audience.

And so Gower advises a plain style for the righteous pleader, though he is clearer on what it is not than on what it is. Caesar's perverting style provides the foil: "the wordes of his sawe/Coloureth in an other weie," ("the words of his saying / He colors in another way," ll. 1624–5). The words he has colored are specifically designed to aim the audience's sympathies rather than to build an argument: they "excite / The jugges," and "sette here hertes to pite" ("excite / The judges," and "set their hearts to pity," ll. 1618–21). Cillenus's effort to speak "plein after the lawe" ("plain after the law," l. 1623), on the other hand, participates in no such perversion. This plainness allows him to testify "to trouthe an as he was beholde / The comun profit forto save" ("to truth as he was beholden / And the common profit to save," ll. 1608–9). Although Gower does not describe Cillenus's style as such, the prepositions here position Cillenus's words as a gear in a larger machine; their connection to the common good sets them into motion, and they engage seamlessly "after" the law and "to" the truth. "Plainness" signifies the truth because—though we cannot identify what it *does* have—it lacks not only color but emotion, the ability to move affectively.

Gower's directive to create a plea without "frounce" belies an anxiety about what he implicitly concedes: that a pleader's work is very similar to that of a tale-teller, and those listening to it might be taken in by the tale's emotional power and ignore its truth value. A tale-teller has to make all the same choices Gower describes as a pleader's duty (picking his words, arranging the events, planning the style of his delivery), and Gower's demand for "plainness" is the only clear way he distinguishes the "tale" (a term he also uses for pleas) of law and the "tale" of literature. As Gower demonstrates in this passage, the problem

---

[48] Ann Astell attributes Gower's contradiction of Latini to his political position on a similar conspiracy by Richard II. Ann Astell, *Political Allegory in Late Medieval England* (Ithaca, NY: Cornell University Press, 2002), p. 87.

with Caesar's words is not the man himself or even his intentions, it is their effect, that they influence the judges to mercy by exciting their hearts. Thus, Gower figures "plainness" as a way to prevent the audience from engaging their literary ears, which in turn protects the law from too-literary expectations.

Chaucer's Man of Law is a literary pleader more comfortable with his audience's literary ears, but less certain that audience can be enticed away from stories by good stylistic choices. As Carolyn Dinshaw puts it, the Man of Law is "a man made up of law."[49] He holds the "caas and doomes alle / That from the tyme of king William were falle" ("case and decisions all / that were decided from the time of William the Conquerer,")—the common law itself—in his head.[50] In his work in the law that prescribed and maintained medieval society, his writing is unimpeachable; "Therto he koude endite and make a thing, / Ther koude no wight pynch at his writing" ("He could compose and write a thing / So that no one could criticize his writing").[51] This makes him a consummate tale-teller; as Anne Middleton observes, Chaucer repeatedly uses both "endite" and "thing" to refer to writing poetry, especially when he is calling attention to the createdness of a literary text.[52] To tell his tale of Custance, therefore, the Man of Law combines tale and plea, embedding in his *historia* of this popular story a legal defense of his heroine.

His tale is a legend popularized by Nicholas Trevet and adapted by both Chaucer and Gower: the blameless and Christian Custance is set upon the water, and in her travels from Rome to Syria and Northumbria she endures many tribulations and injustices. With her innocence and goodness, she passively converts the Sultan of Syria and his men, as well as King Alla of Northumbria and his company. Trevet and Gower focus their stories on her perfect character to establish her as the blameless vessel for Christianity. But for Chaucer's professional pleader, blamelessness is best established as a defense, an exculpation. He builds his tale around false accusations and suspicious deaths so that he (her able *narrator*) can come to her aid, telling the story to her advantage and exonerating her before the reader. And like Gower's Cillenus, the Man of Law also claims the protections of style. He notoriously announces that instead of creating poetry (the medium of emotion), he will

---

[49] Carolyn Dinshaw, "The Law of Man and Its 'Abhomynacions,'" *Exemplaria* 1, no. 1, p. 118.
[50] Chaucer, "General Prologue," ll. 323–4.
[51] Chaucer, "General Prologue," ll. 325–6.
[52] Anne Middleton, "Chaucer's 'New Men' and the Good of Literature in the *Canterbury Tales*," in Edward Said (ed.), *Literature and Society*, English Institute Essays (Baltimore, MD: Johns Hopkins University Press, 1978), pp. 15–56. See also Lynn Staley Johnson, "Chaucer's Tale of the Second Nun and the Strategies of Dissent," *Studies in Philology* 89, no. 4 (1992): pp. 314–333.

"speke in prose," and that his tale will be a simple "hawebake," which Eleanor Johnson argues he uses not literally but as "a designation of truth."[53]

The Man of Law invents two perilous scenarios for Custance, ones in which she would almost certainly be found guilty of murder and hanged in a fourteenth-century felony court. The first is unique to Chaucer's version, and it leads the reader through a scenario in which Custance is both legally and morally innocent. Without suspense or the opportunity to evaluate her innocence ourselves, the audience is encouraged to dwell on the satisfaction of her accuser's punishment instead. A knight in Northumberland—whose advances on Custance were unsuccessful—frames her for the murder of her friend and convert, Hermengyld. The knight sneaks into their room in the night, slits Hermengyld's throat, and lays the bloody knife in Custance's bed. In the morning, he accuses her of the murder, and the case is heavily stacked against her. Custance is found with the bloody knife in her bed, bringing to life the classic shorthand for incontrovertible guilt; as Bracton says: "if a person has been captured over a dead body with a bloody knife … there is no need of other proof."[54] The amiable and welcomed Custance is, quite literally, Chaucer's "smylere with the knyf."

When the knight swears on a book of the Gospels, God intervenes to smite him with a blow to the neck that bursts his eyes out of his head. For the internal audience, this proves Custance's innocence. But for the external one, the divine intervention is merely satisfying retribution for the knight's false accusation, not proof of her innocence. When the false accusation comes, the Man of Law arranges the narrative of the murder around his argument for an already-sympathetic audience. He establishes the knight's premeditation ("And for despit he compassed in his thought," | "for malice he plotted in his mind," l. 591) and his stealth ("Al softely is to the bed ygo," | "so softly went to the bed," l. 598), both important to a felony characterization. The act is vicious and followed neatly by the frame-up: he "kitte the throte of Hermengyld atwo, / And

---

[53] Chaucer, "Man of Law's Tale," ll. 95–96, hereafter cited parenthetically in the text. Since he goes on to tell a tale in verse anyway, this claim has been the subject of much debate, and Eleanor Johnson argues convincingly that he uses the label "prose" because it was gaining traction as the preferred form for histories. Eleanor Johnson, "English Law and the Man of Law's 'Prose' Tale," *Journal of English and Germanic Philology* 114, no. 4 (2015): pp. 504–525, p. 524. Trevisa, in arguing that prose was the best form for his *Polychronicon*, sets it in contrast to a picture of rhetorical ornament that sounds a lot like Gower's "frounce:" a history should have "nought sotilte of sentence, nother faire florischynge of wordes" ("nothing subtle of sentence, nor other fair flourishing of words," John Trevisa, *Polychronicon*, ed. Churchill Babington and Joseph Lumby, Rolls Series [London: Longman, 1886], p. 15). Another popular suggestion is that "prose" was meant to refer to the Tale of Melibee (Alfred David, "The Man of Law vs. Chaucer: A Case in Poetics," *PMLA* 82, no. 2 [1967]: pp. 217–225, p. 217).

[54] "cum quis capt fuerit super mortuu cum cultello cruentato … in quo casu non est opus alia probatione" (Woodbine, *Bracton*, vol. 2, pp. 403–404).

leyde the blody knyf by dame Custance" ("cut the throat of Hermengyld in two / And laid the bloody knife by Dame Custance" ll. 600–1). Throughout, the Man of Law repeatedly calls our attention to the falseness of the parties and the evidence before us; her accuser is the "false knight, that hath this tresoun wroght" ("false knight, that hath this treason wrought," l. 619). A reader primed for repetition and association would recognize all the parts of a felonious murder and a false accusation. Alla has just begun to set up a trial procedure ("yet wol we us avyse / Whom that we wole that shal been oure justise" | "we will think carefully about / Whom we desire to be our justice" ll. 664–5). We might be satisfied by the punishment, but the Man of Law's jury—his audience—has already exonerated her.

We are left to reflect on that certainty when a murkier case emerges, with no internal audience. Custance is attacked while alone on her boat with her infant son, and the reader is the only witness who could bring a case against her. A man boards her boat as it drifts in the Strait of Gibraltar and attempts to rape her. Custance resists, "struggling well and mightily," (l. 921) in a scene that offers, as Jill Mann notes, "the only instance ... in Chaucer, of a woman fending off rape by her own physical efforts."[55] The man then falls off the boat to his death. In his competing version, Gower (perhaps balking at such a violent Custance) removed all possibility that she was involved in the death. Brendan O'Connell concludes that Chaucer tailored his version to fall neatly into the category of self-defense, and that when he "shortens the timeframe in which the attack takes place, (he renders) physical resistance the only possible response."[56] O'Connell recognizes the legal argument and sees in it a case for a "killing (that) is non-felonious because it is committed in self-defense."[57]

But a professional pleader like the Man of Law would have understood that a self-defense claim that required a pardon (and all the reputational and physical damage the wait for such a pardon would necessitate) would be an imperfect outcome; a perfect one would prevent a homicide conviction in the first place. Therefore, his wording around the death of the would-be rapist scrupulously avoids making Custance's hand the one by which he dies:

> For with hir struglyng wel and myghtily,
> The theef fil over bord al sodeynly,
> And in the see he dreynte for vengeance (ll. 921–3).

---

[55] Jill Mann, *Feminizing Chaucer* (Woodbridge: Boydell and Brewer, 2002), p. 107.
[56] Brendan O'Connell, "Struglyng Wel and Myghtily: Resisting Rape in the Man of Law's Tale," *Medium Aevum* 84, no. 1 (2015): pp. 16–39, p. 35.
[57] O'Connell, "Struglyng Wel and Myghtily," p. 32. Judicial comment from a few decades later detailed the necessary elements of a "self-defense" argument; see Chapter 1, note 15.

> For with her struggling well and mightily
> The thief fell overboard all suddenly,
> And in the sea he drowned for vengeance.

"The thief fell" and "he drowned"; Custance is merely present at the scene.

And yet, if we peer just barely around this delicate construction in which "she struggled" and "he fell," we easily perceive it to be a derivation of "she struggled and *therefore* he fell," and not a very distant one.[58] She killed him, we must see. A medieval reader especially would perceive the echoes of other accounts behind Chaucer's version; Trevet has Custance kill the man in unapologetic self-defense. Revealing this to us is a choice: Chaucer could have removed her from all suspicion, as Gower does. Instead, he preserves the transparency of his own lie, allowing us to see both his skillful story and the truth behind it. In the first scene, Custance's factual and essential innocences align; she is both innocent of this murder and innocent in general. When we read of her framing, accusation, and trial, we are able to stay comfortably ahead of the internal audience. This allows us to experience the pleasing coincidence of factual *and* narrative satisfaction. But this second scene asks us to reflect back on those satisfactions; if we had to choose, which did we prefer?

Chaucer stages that narrative threat to the law which the author of *The Seven Sages* and Gower both fear: a believable lie. And yet, by preserving both the truth and the lie for the reader, he demonstrates that the fault of this deception lies not with the narrative, but with the reader's desires. We can see that she pushed him. But between our long sympathy for her and our desire to see the story finish happily, we are content to adopt the believable lie and ignore what is in front of us. That is, Chaucer demonstrates that it is not the lie that tricks us, it is we who chose to believe it, who find the truth undesirable. Thus, Chaucer's Man of Law poses belief in untrue stories not as the threat that literary thinking poses to the law, but as a problem of the law that literature reveals.

Reading Hugh

These literary pleaders seem to believe that the danger of narrative to the law is that it might make one believe untrue things and thus turn one away from justice. Even if Chaucer conceives of this turning as a choice, he still recognizes

---

[58] I am indebted to conversations with my students in my ENGL315: Chaucer course of Spring 2022 at California State University, Fullerton for this observation, in particular Vincent Gomez and Leah Hernandez.

the mechanism: the good story turns us away from the truth. We might expect this critique to be even stronger in legal texts. And yet, in the most-discussed scene in the *Placita Corone*, an emotional and troubling exchange, it is the law that has turned away from justice, and narrative that sets it right. In it, Hugh de M is brought up on charges of horse-thievery, and the justice tricks the hapless man into confessing. The case is one of three seamlessly woven together in a single scene of dialogue between one justice and various parties, without the intervention of the narrator. John testifies that Hugh took a dark-colored mare valued at 20s. from a field, brought it home with him, and kept it for a while, telling his neighbors that it was lent to him. Sometime later, he took it to the market and sold it for a mere half mark.

We can already see that this is not an ordinary tale of horse-thievery; the extremely low price suggests that Hugh was not accustomed to owning a horse and did not know its value. His own plea confirms his longstanding "poverty and distress."[59] Unsurprisingly, he is representing himself. But he demonstrates immediately that he is aware of his own ignorance and knows that it will have consequences:

"Sir, by God, I am a simple man and am not used to making pleas, so I know I cannot defend myself properly, and for this reason, sir, I beg you to let me be advised by some learned man (*prodhomme*) as to how I can best defend myself in this case."

The justice responds:

"What, Hugh? That would be clearly against the law of the land and against right, for who can better certify your deed than yourself? Do as a gentleman (*prodhomme*), and as a good and lawful man; keep God before you and tell us the truth of this matter, and we shall be as merciful as we can, according to the law."[60]

Hugh might be illiterate, but he understands the nature of the law well enough. He knows that he is about to embark on a form he does not know how to

---

[59] Kaye, *Placita Corone*, p. 17.
[60] In the manuscripts this exchange is rendered as a single block of text without indication of who is speaking, like this, from the Bodleian Christ Church MS. 103, f. 145r–v: "Sire pur deu Je su un simples homs et nynt ay geres use playe de terre paront Je me say meyns suffisaument defender et pur ce vous pri je sire ke je puisse estres consille de aukun prodhomme coment jeo me puisse meus defender en ceo cas. Coment Hue. Ce sereyt une deverie apertement encontre ley de terre et encontre dreyture kar ky nous porra meuz certifier de vostre fet demeine ke vous memes. Mes fetes com prodhomme et com bon et leaus et eyez deu devant vous et reconnussez al verite de ceste chose et lem vous serra asez merciable solom dreyture" (Kaye, *Placita Corone*, p. 17).

navigate. When the justice scolds him for this (correct) assessment, he tries to convince Hugh there is no special knowledge to pleading, no craft. He attempts to shift Hugh back from his correct but nascent sense of pleading as an intentional creation, replacing Hugh's "prodhomme" (by which Hugh clearly means a *narrator* even if he does not know the technical term) with his own, meaning simply "gentleman" or "upright person." The justice's argument powerfully recalls Gower's exhortation to "plain style," and reveals that this advice does not just associate lack of craft with truth, it also implies that expertise in this craft is unnecessary in a court of law, an implication so obviously false that it calls into question the intent of the advice itself.

Having been tricked into thinking that the form he seeks does not exist, Hugh turns to an institutional narrative form that he does know: the confession. His confession is dramatic and sad. Hugh speaks of unbearable poverty, ignorance, temptation by the Devil, a first offense, and deep remorse. In a religious confession, each part of the narrative—character, context, act—all matter to the ultimate penance and restitution, and Hugh notes many circumstances which would have been mitigating in a confessional. John Mirk's *Instructions for Parish Priests* reminds confessors that

> fyrst þow moste þys mynne,
> What he ys þat doth þe synne
>
> ...
>
> Pore or ryche, or in offys (ll. 1405–9)
>
> first you must mind this:
> What he is who does sin
>
> ...
>
> Poor or rich, or in (church) office.[61]

and Thomas de Chobham's *Summa Confessorum* adds that "the sin is diminished for he who steals from the anguish of hunger."[62] Chobham also notes that sins committed out of impulse must be counted as less serious, and Hugh makes a point of noting that he had never done such a thing before when the idea to steal the horse came into his head.[63]

---

[61] John Mirk, *Instructions for Parish Priests*, ed. Edward Peacock (London: Early English Text Society, 1868), p. 44.

[62] "si quis furetur pre angustia famis diminuitur peccatum" (Thomas Chobham, *Summa Confessorum*, ed. F. Broomfield [Paris: Louvain, 1968], p. 47).

[63] Chobham, *Summa Confessorum*, p. 56.

The justice recognizes that Hugh thinks he is standing before a priest and seizes the advantage, joining him in the form of the confession, hinting at mercy, until he extracts an admittance of guilt. He advises Hugh to keep God before him and mentions mercy until Hugh tells him the whole story. As soon as he does, the justice has no more use for the confessional, shedding his priestly disguise and returning abruptly to legal ground. He taunts Hugh for his misunderstanding with a cold, "May God forgive you, if it pleases Him," and orders the bailiff to hang him.[64] By denying the truth of pleading—that it is a construction—the justice has tricked Hugh and then hung him for his gullibility.

It is hard to read this as historically representative and not agree with Bellamy's assessment of the scene, that judicial conduct was "a mixture of bullying, contempt, and wheedling" that "sneered at the accused's explanations."[65] On the evidence of Hugh's sad case, Kaye argues that "justices regarded a prisoner's defenses or objections to aspects of procedure as irritating obstacles to be overcome by any possible means."[66] Using the same case, Green contends that the medieval justice more generally did not seek "to establish a factual case against the accused, merely to maneuver him into an untenable position."[67] As modern readers we feel immediate contempt for the justice's tactics, sympathy for the perceptive yet helpless Hugh, and disgust for the dishonesty of the whole situation. We might also imagine this to be visible only from our distant vantage point.

However—I do not think that, when we now find this a horrifying scene, we are being anachronistically moved by modern sensibilities. After all, Hugh is described as "deceived" ("et issint fust il deceu"), hardly a noble reflection on the justice.[68] While medieval statutes were unyielding in the letter, in practice the same qualities that Hugh names mitigated sentences in the courtroom as well as in the confessional. Courts frequently reduced punishments in cases of theft driven by poverty (as I will discuss at more length in Chapter 4), as well as for first-time offenses. Bracton advises distinguishing between those who steal entire herds and those who lift a single animal, and as Kamali notes, "even where a theft exceeded the felonious floor of twelve pence, it is unlikely that jurors felt that capital punishment was warranted in any but the most serious of cases."[69] Moreover, a medieval reader encountering Hugh would have known

---

[64] "Deu le vos pardomt, si li plest ... Baillif, fetes ly aver le prestre" (Kaye, *Placita Corone*, p. 17).
[65] Bellamy, *The Criminal Trial in Later Medieval England*, p. 110.
[66] Kaye, *Placita Corone*, p. xxxvi.
[67] Kaye, *Placita Corone*, p. xxxvi; Green, *A Crisis of Truth*, p. 131.
[68] Kaye, *Placita Corone*, p. 17.
[69] Bracton, vol. 2, p. 299; Kamali, *Felony and the Guilty Mind*, p. 229.

that the justice was offering incorrect advice about the role of a professional pleader, would have recognized the religious tenor of Hugh's confession, and thus might also have found the justice's punchline ("May God forgive you, if it pleases him") in poor taste.

If we take a broader view of this scene as part of a larger, created narrative, we might begin to sort through what the scene communicates about the law. First, Chaucer's example of preserving both the story and the truth for the reader provides a place to begin with the most pressing question of the justice's conduct. As with Custance, we can see both Hugh's guilt and his innocence. We can see the justice's easy rectitude and his injustice. This careful preservation of both layers in the two men leads me to believe that the reader's allegiance to the justice is not predetermined here. In the rest of the text, the justice and the narrator seem closely aligned; here the narrator has dropped away entirely, freeing us from loyalty to the justice. That is, I think we are free to see him as a character, one who sometimes bests and is sometimes bested, who is navigating the scene motivated by his own flawed interests.

Second, we can see that Hugh's case is only the first part of a longer, unbroken piece of dialogue that incorporates two additional defendants with the same justice. The justice who urged a plea free from invention to Hugh is clearly the same one who attacks his next defendant's style: "Thomas, you have greatly embellished your tale and colored your defense."[70] The reader of the justice as a character will feel some satisfaction when Thomas is proven correct; a jury inquest corroborates his version of events, and the justice is forced to request a pardon on his behalf. But the real satisfaction for the reader comes with the other defendant in this triptych, Nicholas. Caught in a similar charge and with similarly meager resources, Nicholas is Hugh's foil. Like Hugh, Nicholas represents himself, but unlike Hugh, he understands both the createdness of the plea and the justice's attempts to hide it.

Up until this moment, the justice has remained in charge of terms and fictions as well as their interpretation. But Nicholas reveals that it is the justice who has depended on the defendants' willingness to allow terms to go undefined and uninterrogated, like Hugh's "prodhomme." Instead of answering the justice's questions, Nicholas turns to the legal terms the justice uses and dissects them, revealing both that they have specialized meanings in the law and that the justice has been unwilling to admit that. The justice demands he reply to the charge of cattle-stealing, of which "les bone genz del pays se pleynent" ("the good people of this district complain"). Rather than responding to the

[70] Kaye, *Placita Corone*, p. 18.

charge, he asks "if there is any man willing to make suit against me," taking the legal term "bone genz," which meant reputation or complaint in a collective sense, and understanding it as an actual collection of men.[71]

The justice, stymied, becomes cagier. Rather than returning to the charge, he introduces a legal fiction, perhaps hoping Nicholas will be intimidated enough to stop dissecting and answer the charge. The justice points out that since he is under indictment, there *is* a man proceeding against him: the king. But Nicholas stays the course, excavating this legal fiction and revealing its createdness. If the king is making suit against me, he says, then "I am ready to defend by my body."[72] The justice is forced to say that the king does not wish to do battle, because he cannot say that this is simply a fiction that allows an indictment (which has no appellor) to be treated procedurally like an appeal. In other words, Nicholas demonstrates what Lon Fuller warns about legal fictions: "A fiction taken seriously, i.e., 'believed', becomes dangerous and loses its utility."[73]

Nicholas's triumph stages an interruption in the justice's power, an interruption so pleasingly symmetrical that perhaps the Empress of *The Seven Sages* would approve. He targets the very mechanism with which the justice tricked Hugh—the technical and colloquial meanings of words—to outsmart the justice, and punishes him for his abuse. That is, when we see the treatise as calling upon our literary instincts to create associations and continuity wherever we can, we can see the character of this justice—clever, deceptive, and a little cruel—and experience both his artful transgression and fitting comeuppance. This is precisely the enjoyment the author of *The Seven Sages* and Gower feared for the law, but the *Placita Corone* does not seem to share this anxiety. Perhaps Gower would have found it irresponsible, and perhaps the author of the procedural manual was not quite as worried about the ethics of it all, but it seems to me that the book openly revels in narrative, in its demands and its satisfactions.

*

In this chapter, I have suggested that the attraction of the *Placita Corone* lay in its ability to demonstrate, manipulate, and teach the demands of narrative satisfaction. Thus, it might tell us that not only was narrative recognized as part

---

[71] "si il i yet nul homme ke voile pursiwre vers moi," (Kaye, *Placita Corone*, p. 18). This phrase does not refer to witnesses or oathworthy men, either. As chapter 7 of Ian Forrest's *Trustworthy Men* shows, the collective "bon genz" represented the communal will rather than referring to the various individual "trustworthy men," who were called upon to give testimony and serve on juries.

[72] "je suy prest a defendre" (Kaye, *Placita Corone*, p. 18).

[73] Lon Fuller, *Legal Fictions* (Palo Alto: Stanford University Press, 1967), p. 7.

of the business of pleading, it was seen as a craft that required guidance and pedagogy. If most professional lawmen found criminal pleading boring and without need of elucidation, perhaps its procedure needed no guidance.[74] But an understanding of narrative satisfaction apparently did. If we read the *Placita Corone* in this light, it becomes a far more interesting text, demonstrating that law and literature both attended to audience abilities and expectations, and arguing that literature's work training an attentive and engaged reader benefited the pleader as well as the poet. It also seems to suggest that the text did not share literature's anxiety about the dangers of a good story to justice. Perhaps this is naivete about stories, perhaps it is optimism. Whatever the case, what I find most interesting is that this legal treatise that has seemed so dull and hapless to a legal reader comes alive for a literary one.

Part of the work of this chapter has been to encourage further study of the *Placita Corone* that accounts for its literary engagement. There is much work left to be done; though the text is thin, I have only been able to engage with a small percentage of its many cases. Its prologue, for example, takes many shapes and many attitudes across the manuscripts, and would offer a good place to consider the types of readers this text attracted across its lifetime. There is also a fascinating appeal brought by a woman who claims her husband died in her arms. The phrase "in her arms" reflects a requirement in some prescriptive sources that a woman's husband must have died "in her arms" for her to bring an appeal for his death.[75] In practice, this phrase was generally taken to be metaphorical, implying that the wife had been present at her husband's death. But the plea in the *Placita Corone* describes the scene; is the text's literalization of this metaphor a misunderstanding of the law or a demonstration of how best to tell a story that meets the audience's expectations of a grieving wife?

If this has been a triumphant story of narrative's good deeds, the next chapter tempers that optimism. The plea was just one voice in the procedure of criminal law; the far more pervasive one was that of the oathworthy witness, which could enter at almost any step, from coroner's inquest to the trial itself. As we know from Hugh's story, certain narratives are condemned not because they are untrue, or even inelegant, but because of the mouth that speaks them. In the next chapter, I turn to the creation of reputation in the law by the oathworthy witness and his cross-jurisdictional, pervasive power in medieval society.

---

[74] Bellamy, *The Criminal Trial in Later Medieval England*, p. 13.
[75] For this formulation in appeals, see for example TNA, JUST 1/643, m. 4, and KB 27/313 Rex, m. 22d. For discussions of this requirement in judicial treatises, see: Hall, *Glanvill*, XIV c. 3, and Woodbine, *Bracton*, vol. 2, pp. 388, 397.

Chapter 3
Testimony

The Pistil of Swete Susan and the Oathworthy Witness

In Chapter 1 I discussed the fantasy that evidence might come to life and explain itself. The next chapter argued that this fantasy is connected to another: that all information might deliver itself to the law, as *St. Erkenwald's* judge does, as a story. In this chapter, I examine what I see as a collision of this desire for narrative—a desire that elevated testimony above all other forms of evidence—with growing unease about how that narrative came to the court and in particular, the cross-jurisdictional power of the "oathworthy" witness. Recent scholarship in law and literature—in particular that of Emma Lipton and Ian Forrest—has explored the central role of witnessing in creating and sustaining medieval communities.[1] This reliance naturally came with strong warnings against false witnessing, but it is more difficult to locate contemporary articulations of the critique that came later—that the testimonial system itself overlapped so neatly with economic and social power that it was inherently vulnerable to corruption.

I argue that this critique took some of its first shapes in legal-minded literature, where the perversion of talk is a central figure, especially in texts that figure talk as evidence. I focus on the example of the Middle English *Pistil of Swete Susan*, which transposes the Book of Daniel's Susannah and the Elders—the archetypal tale of false witnessing—into fourteenth-century England. In the biblical story, the virtuous Susannah rebuffs the sexual advances of two lecherous Elders, who take revenge on her by accusing her of adultery with an invented lover. Based on their testimony, the community seems ready to

---

[1] Forrest explores the social contexts and identities of the *viri fidedigni* in the canon court system, demonstrating how they were intertwined with other forms of power within communities in *Trustworthy Men: How Inequality and Faith Made the Medieval Church* (Princeton, NJ: Princeton University Press, 2020). In Lipton's *Cultures of Witnessing: Law and the York Plays* (Philadelphia, PA: University of Pennsylvania Press, 2022), she argues that the York Mystery Plays inculcated a sense of responsibility and communal identity by modeling witnessing practices for their audiences, a topic I discuss in more detail in Chapter 5. Previously, Susan Phillips's *Transforming Talk: The Problem of Gossip in Late Medieval England* (University Park, PA: Pennsylvania State Press, 2010) explored the concept of "janglyng" in Middle English literature and argued that while gossip was believed to corrupt, it also structured a variety of social relationships.

execute her. A young Daniel intervenes, asking each Elder separately under which tree he saw Susannah with her lover. Each gives a different answer, and Susannah is spared. For penitential literature, the story provided a demonstration of the evil of false witnessing, and for legal procedure, it suggested a straightforward solution. But the fourteenth-century English version is less interested in Daniel's elegant solution than in what trapped Susannah in first place: the system's structural vulnerability to the corruption and interests of its foundation, the "oathworthy" witness, whose power across various court systems forecloses all the avenues of relief Susannah might seek. This critique, I suggest, can also help us identify some attempts in the legal record to articulate how the testimonial system was vulnerable to abuse, anticipating a conversation about hearsay and laws of evidence that is generally understood to have begun centuries later.

Both canon and common law systems depended heavily on the testimony of "proper witnesses." Canon law focused on the witness's proximity to the event, stipulating that firsthand, sensory knowledge was what made a witness reliable. But English common law lay the stress on "proper," privileging the quality of the source rather than the directness of his information. According to Glanvill, oathworthy witnesses might speak to "what they know about the matter from what they themselves have seen and heard." But he continues: they might also testify to knowledge that "they are bound to believe *as if* they had seen or heard it themselves."[2] This "as if" became the far more standard form of testimony; as Charles Donahue and others have demonstrated, witnesses to criminal cases most often testified to "matters of which they (had) no personal knowledge," but instead were the "common knowledge" of social consensus.[3] The right witness, properly sworn, spoke for the collective as well as himself.

The probative weight of common knowledge delivered by oathworthy men in medieval procedure has seemed especially heavy from the perspective of later centuries, in which laws of evidence attempted to edge out hearsay and reputation. This has left us with both a progressive narrative about the trusted

---

[2] G.D.G. Hall, ed., *The Treatise on the Laws and Customs of the Realm of England Commonly Called Glanvill* (Oxford: Clarendon Press, 1994), II.17, p. 35.

[3] Charles Donahue, Jr., "Proof by Witnesses in the Church Courts of Medieval England: An Imperfect Reception of the Learned Law," in Morris S. Arnold, Thomas A. Green, Sally Scully, and Stephen White (eds.), *On the Laws and Customs of England: Essays in Honor of Samuel E. Thorne* (Chapel Hill: North Carolina University Press, 1981), p. 143. According to Paul Brand, testimonial evidence to general consensus was already "a regular and accepted feature" of the common law by the thirteenth century ("Dower Ex Assensu and Trial by Jury and Trial by Witnesses in the English Medieval Common Law," *Journal of Legal History* 42, no. 2 [2021]: p. 147). Thelma Fenster and Daniel Lord Smail's introduction to their edited volume on *fama* discusses the distinctions and overlap between *fama*, talk, and reputation: *Fama: The Politics of Talk and Reputation in Medieval Europe* (Ithaca, NY: Cornell University Press, 2018), pp. 1–14.

witness in the law—that Anglo-American law eventually rejected its muddled evidentiary value in the name of empiricism and fairness—and a roughly epistemological one—that its role was specific to a moment in which the "local" in "local knowledge" was so circumscribed that what reliable neighbors said tended to be true. Extensive legal historical work established criminal procedure's heavy reliance on testimony to common opinion, the type of men who were trusted to deliver it, and the role of witnessing in creating an ethical and responsible society.[4] But a lack of structural critique in contemporary legal literature combined with the reliance of the proof procedure on elements of "common knowledge" deep into the sixteenth century has made it seem as though medieval legal thinkers themselves saw little danger in this testimonial system, or at least none to outweigh its benefits.

But of course, talk and its catastrophic effects are main characters in Middle English poetry. As Susan Phillips points out, the Prologue to Chaucer's "The Canon's Yeoman's Tale"—in which the Yeoman is gradually coaxed into the pleasures of gossip—is a cautionary tale about the damage even true talk can do when entered into the record.[5] Susannah and the Elders was the classic tale of false talk, and figures as both story and reference in many literary scenes of gossip. Unlike much of the literature I discuss in this book, both legal and literary sources always recognized its direct utility to the law. Penitential literature valued the story for demonstrating so well the consequences of false witnessing; as Chaucer's Parson warns, "Certes, for fals witnessyng was Susanna in ful gret sorwe and peyne, and many another mo" ("Surely, for false witnessing Susannah was in full great sorrow and pain, and many other more,").[6] For canon law, it provided unusually direct guidance for witness procedure (in order to guard against false testimony, one must interview each witness separately), guidance that was at least mentioned in common law as best practice, whether or not it was often followed. As a medieval Latin adaptation of the story puts it, "Henceforth this was how the judge examined all witnesses."[7]

---

[4] In addition to Lipton's, Forrest's, and Phillips's work cited above, see also Marjorie Keniston McIntosh, "Finding Language for Misconduct: Jurors in Fifteenth-Century Local Courts," in Barbara Hanawalt and David Wallace (eds.), *Bodies and Disciplines: Intersections of Literature and History in Fifteenth-Century England* (Minneapolis: University of Minnesota Press, 1996), pp. 87–122; Shannon McSheffrey, "Jurors, Respectable Masculinity, and Christian Morality: A Comment on Marjorie McIntosh's *Controlling Misbehavior*," *Journal of British Studies* 37, no. 3 (1998): pp. 269–278; Barbara Shapiro, *A Culture of Fact: England, 1550–1720* (Ithaca, NY: Cornell University Press, 2000).
[5] Phillips, *Transforming Talk*.
[6] Chaucer, "The Parson's Tale," in *The Riverside Chaucer*, p. 315, l. 796.
[7] "Hinc erat ut iudex testes examinet omnes." The text is extant in Harley MS 2851, and I have cited it here from Alan of Melsa, *Tractatus metricus de Susanna per fratrem Alanum monachum de Melsa de Beverlaco*, ed. J.H. Mozley, as published in J.H. Mozley, "Susannah and the Elders in Three Medieval Poems," *Studi Medievali* 3 (1930): p. 34, l. 403. Lynn Staley argues that the Melsa version's deep focus

The Middle English version, *The Pistil of Swete Susan*, combines the moment's literary interest in talk's pervasive power with a sophisticated legal critique of the mechanisms that trapped Susannah in the first place. The poem updates not just the legal actions but the legal logic of the story to the fourteenth century. Susannah's inner purity that protects her in Daniel is translated into a spotless reputation, the fourteenth-century's version of legal truth, and the Elders are transformed from religious leaders to oathworthy witnesses. The poem demonstrates that, in its legal context, this extends their power, rather than diminishing it. The results of this adaptation are dark; while the circumstances of the sexual advance, false accusation, and procedural rescue remain mostly the same, Joachim publicly abandons Susannah, the people do not rise up against the Elders, and it is unclear whether Susannah's reputation recovers. The biblically triumphant tale of false witnessing thwarted, when transposed into the medieval English legal context, becomes a more cynical story about the inability of the proof procedure to escape powerful men even when their corruption is known and their word shown to be false.

I will begin with a conspiracy case from Northampton—in which the court is unable to escape the power of men known to be corrupt—to outline the relationship between trusted witnesses and local power structures in criminal procedure. Then I will turn to *The Pistil of Swete Susan* to identify its critical analysis of this system. Finally, I will turn back to the case to demonstrate how the poem can deepen our understanding of its dynamics and how the critique it mounts can help us locate its same threads in other cases that address local abuses of power. I build here on the work of Jamie Taylor and Lynn Staley, whose work on Susanna as a model of the female witness comprises the most recent scholarship on the poem, to highlight that in addition to its legal themes, it is also making a legal argument about the testimonial system in fourteenth-century England.[8] For legal history, I hope that pointing out a medieval discourse that locates the roots of common opinion in contingent power structures rather than in truth helps us recognize a medieval initiation of the (long, slow) turn away from reputation and toward rules of evidence that took place over the following two centuries.

---

on the law and extensive description of Joachim's gardens makes it a likely source for *The Pistil of Swete Susan* ("Susanna and English Communities," *Traditio* 62 [2007]: pp. 25–58, pp. 26–27).

[8] Taylor, *Fictions of Witnessing*; Staley, "Susanna and English Communities."

Oathworthy Witnesses

In 1329, a group of men in Northampton entered the house of Walter Pateshull, local coroner, dragged him by his hair into the street, and beat and trampled on him. Having done this, they took him to the local guildhall and forced him to abjure the office of coroner and any other office in the future ("li ousterent de son offitz de coroner et lui firent faire serment qe mes ne serreit en offitz de la ville").[9] The eyre roll records that the men were indicted before Chief Justice Scrope, who delivered a surprisingly candid piece of advice:

> At the opening of the eyre we promised you that we would be gracious in matters that fell within our discretion, saving our position as justices. We are still of that mind. Consider, therefore, whether you may wish to pay a fine. For it would be better to pay a fine than to make a dozen jurors perjure themselves or await the peril of their decision.[10]

As other cases in the eyre demonstrate, Scrope is capable of a well-turned threat. But his tone here is altogether different. Almost deferential, he recommends a fine—not the typical consequence for assault on an officer of the king—and says the quiet part loud: clearly, men who can unilaterally remove a coroner from office in broad daylight can also rig a jury in their favor in that same community. So, he offers his professional opinion that it is easier to pay a fine than to rely on the delicate (and probably more expensive) task of forcing twelve men to perjure themselves. Scrope's transparency about the power balance is striking; he seems to have reason to believe intimidation will not work with these men, and takes a gamble on forthrightness.

The dialogue of this case brings to life the familiar power struggle between local representatives and the crown that played out in the eyre courts. But it also gestures toward some aspects of the struggle that are more difficult to get at, opening an array of questions. The first facet is the hidden third party to this power struggle—the local victims. Walter Pateshull, for obvious reasons, did not bring an appeal directly; his case was brought by presentment,

---

[9] Donald Sutherland, ed. *The Eyre of Northamptonshire 3–4 Edward II*, vol. 1 (London: Selden Society, 1983), pp. 194.
[10] "En le commencement del eyre nous vous promismes de faire grace de ceo qe a nous appendoit, sauue nostre estat. Et en tiele volunte sumes nous vncore. Par quei auisez vous si vous veulletz faire fin. Qe vaut mieultz de faire fin qe de faire vn dozeine destre pariurs ou dattendre le peril de .xij." The eyre record is printed in Sutherland, *The Eyre of Northamptonshire 3–4 Edward II*, vol. 1, pp. 194–195. But the enrollment created at the eyre (as opposed to the one that was collected and edited for dissemination and the maintenance of common law), which I will discuss later, is at TNA, JUST 1/635, m. 74–75.

which allowed community members to present bills to the justice anonymously. What can we know about their experience of the case and their interest in bringing it? Second, the record highlights the role of the testimonial system in this power struggle. Scrope is clear that he is painted into a corner because the jury is easily (or already) captured by these men. What does this case identify in the structure of the testimonial system—in which a set of local men were trusted to deliver information about their communities to the courts—that supported and maintained defendants such as these? This case outlines this matrix with unusual clarity, and I will treat each part in turn.

Because much of the information we have about local abuses of power is available through the crown's objections to them, it has seemed more logical to conceptualize these trials as part of the larger negotiation of the balance of power between local and royal forces, making it harder to identify the agency of the local victims of this abuse. But communal forms of indictment can express a voice less often heard—that of the direct victims of local abuses.[11] Presentment allowed anyone (or multiple people) to bring a complaint directly to a judge, who would ask a jury to investigate and either dismiss the accusation or endorse it as a "true bill" (*billa vera*).[12] Presentment and clamour, had the dual benefit of relieving individual accusers of the cost of an appeal and shielding them from retribution through the indictment's communal attribution.[13] This case was probably suggested to the justice by one or some of the many who witnessed the assault, and even though we do not have the text of that presentment, we are reading it because of the risk they took.

The headaches that feuding and disloyal lords caused the crown is well known. But from the perspective of the local communities, these powers might be better understood as—for want of a better word—local big men. There were

---

[11] In her book, *Literature and Complaint*, Scase has demonstrated the range of voices we can hear in the various communal forms of indictment that were under development in the late medieval period, including *pleinte, querela*, the *libellus*, the *bill*, and *clamour*.

[12] There is no contemporary description of the procedure for presentment, but in 1286 a judge incidentally offered a description of the procedure to defend himself against a complaint of corruption (namely, that he had written a false bill in his own hand and given it to a jury for their verification). He asserted that he acted "according to law and custom" (*secundum legem et consuetudinem*), which allows that "any one of the people may present such a bill to a major or minor justice and that same justice must receive it, and hand it over to the twelve jurors, so that if what is contained in it is true they will present it in their verdict, and if it is not true they will deny the bill" ("quicumque de populo huiusmodi billam optulerit cuicumque iusticiario maiori vel minori idem iusticiarius illam billam debet recipere, et tradere eam duodenis iuratoribus ad capitula corone, ita quod si verum sit quod in ea continetur ipsi presentant illud in veredicto suo, et si non sit verum quod deniant illam billam"). Cited from Hilda Johnstone and T.F. Tout, eds. *State Trials of the Reign of Edward the First, 1289–1293* (London: Royal Historical Society, 1906), p. 69. This corroborates the procedure as described in another case from 1442, in which jurors were dismissed for not agreeing with the rest of the jury of presentment (Exeter College MS. 115, f. 33).

[13] Bellamy discusses this benefit in relation to presentment in *The Criminal Trial*, p. 22.

the infamous Folville brothers, who found themselves in felony records up and down the fourteenth century for harassing and murdering the tenants of other lords. Sir John Molyns feuded for years with Gerard Braybrooke, sending his men to assault Braybrooke's people, "ride night and day through the country," and attack Braybrooke's tenants such that "no work could be done on his lands."[14] And there was Thomas de Lisle, who burned down the houses of Blanche of Lancaster's people and, when ordered to pay damages, had her servants murdered instead. In all of these struggles for local power, the violence fell on the tenants and servants. It is no wonder that in the dream allegory *Piers Plowman*, Wrong is an abusive local who terrorizes both his neighbors and those dependent upon them. According to Peace, who brings suit against him,

> He maynteneth hise men to murthere myne hewen,
> Forstalleth my feires and fighteth in my chepyng,
> And breketh up my berne dores and bereth awey my whete
>
> He maintains his men to murder servants
> Forestalls my fairs and fights in my marketplace
> And breaks open my barn doors and bears away my wheat.

leaving his victims without the money to bring pleas against him.[15] The abuses of these men ranged from petty, everyday corruption that lined the pockets of local officials to outright terror, in which they used their clout to rig juries, plunder their inferiors, and wage war on their equals.

This is power enough. And yet, as a second record of the Northampton charge reflects, part of the influence these men wielded was that they were precisely the type who, in another case, would have been asked to offer sworn testimony to a jury or serve on it themselves. The case record that provided local documentation gives more detailed information than the version in the edited eyre record, which condensed and arranged cases to serve as precedent across the country.[16] The eyre roll only cites "treis hommes," ("three men")

---

[14] Natalie Fryde, "A Medieval Robber Baron: Sir John Molyns of Stoke Poges, Buckinghamshire," in R.F. Hunnisett and J.B. Post (eds.), *Medieval Legal Records* (London: H.M. Stationery Office, 1978), p. 201.

[15] William Langland, *Piers Plowman: A Parallel Text Edition of the A, B, C and Z versions*, ed. A.V.C. Schmidt (Kalamazoo, MI: Medieval Institute Publications, 2008), B 4.55–7, hereafter cited parenthetically in the text. The poem even refers to the Folville brothers by name, calling the practice of settling a dispute by brute force, "Folvyles lawes" (B 19.248). There is a tendency in scholarship to see these men as part of a tradition of noble outlawry, resisting royal overreach, but the term casts them as villains.

[16] As Sutherland says in his edition, the eyre records were clearly widely disseminated, and the twenty-two contemporary manuscripts that remain "are evidently the survivors of what were once

but the case record lists eleven men, their names, and their professions. Some seem like career criminals (one was already being held for the theft of two dozen pairs of shoes), but the first named is Simon of Laushull, the former mayor, who appears repeatedly on jury lists for other felony cases and coroners' inquests from Northampton, as do two other men on the list, William Elys and Adam of Naylesworth. Lest we think Simon the only consequential man on the list, there is also Richard of Stratford, who produces a royal pardon "for all homicides, felonies, robberies, thefts, and trespasses committed against the peace of Edward II."[17] Anyone might apply for a pardon for a single offense, like killing in self-defense, but to procure such a blanket pardon suggests purchase or connections. His son is also allowed to remain in exigence for unspecified reasons.

Obvious bad behavior did not preclude one from remaining an oathworthy man, a status that seems to have been more invincible than one's criminal record. While references to "oathworthy" men abound, as Nancy Bradbury notes, there is little direct discussion of exactly what made one oathworthy.[18] A variety of medieval disputes rested their epistemology on oathworthy men, from property disputes at local guildhalls to marriage cases at ecclesiastical courts. As all such witnesses followed the same oath, drawn from Gratian's *Decretum*, many men served this same function in multiple institutions, and some of these institutions are more forthcoming on what made one "oathworthy." In canon law courts, they were called *viri fidedigni* (trustworthy men), and Forrest's careful work on the identities and social standing of these men has revealed that, as very local elites, they "were defined by gender, age, family, and wealth, but also by the relationships they formed with authority."[19] Specifically, local office-holding—like mayor—was "perhaps the surest route toward unassailable trustworthy status."[20] Thomas de Lisle was Bishop of Ely. The Folville brothers often served on juries and in local office, as did John Molyns, who fell in and out of the service of the king throughout his life.[21]

---

many, many, copies, for none of them derives from any of the others" (*The Eyre of Northamptonshire*, vol. 1, p. lix). The case record is at TNA, JUST 1/635, m. 74–75.

[17] TNA, JUST 1/635, m. 74

[18] Nancy Bradbury, "The Erosion of Oath-Based Relationships: A Cultural Context for 'Athelston,'" *Medium Aevum* 73, no. 2 (2004): p. 192.

[19] Forrest, *Trustworthy Men*, p. 157.

[20] Forrest, *Trustworthy Men*, p. 156.

[21] Fryde, "A Medieval Robber Baron," p. 204; E.L.G. Stones, "The Folvilles of Ashby-Folville, Leicestershire, and Their Associates in Crime, 1326–1347," *Transactions of the Royal Historical Society* 7 (1957): p. 118.

In *Piers Plowman,* the character Peace brings his suit directly to the King. During this time, the crown began to cultivate more legal avenues to bring local abuses of power directly to royal authority. These avenues usually cut their way through felony procedure, because felony charges fell under the purview of the royal courts. The Commissions of Trailbaston, for example, sent royal courts to the countryside to seek presentments of felonies and select trespasses (like extortion and bribes) in order to root out violent opposition to the crown.[22] The relatively new charge of conspiracy took aim at legal abuses by targeting the "malicious procurement of pleas" and other attempts to create or support false indictments.[23] Some crimes that were normally not felonies could also be reclassified as felonies for the purpose of redirecting them to royal courts; for example, the right of purveyance (the practice of acquiring provisions for the sovereign's use at a lower-than-market level) was often abused by local officials, so some justices charged it as robbery—a felony—rather than as false purveyance.[24] But of course, if the mechanisms of procedure themselves—the testimonial system—are captured by local power, there is a limit to what such maneuvers can achieve.

In this context, we can see more clearly why Scrope's authority is precarious, and that he is aware of having to conserve it for cases in which he will be able to pursue the king's interests more directly. It explains why the defendants only end up paying between 20 shillings and 1 mark in total, hardly the typical outcome for assault and tampering with a crown office under a sworn alliance. We can also see Forrest's argument about his *viri fidedigni* in action; trustworthy men were not chosen because they were the most honest Christians, but because their status would ensure that their word would not be contradicted. But the very existence of such a record, with its scrupulous documentation

---

[22] Amy Phelan's excellent article on the first commissions demonstrates that these circuits were attempts to wrangle as many violent crimes as possible under the purview of the crown in order to address disorder: "Trailbaston and Attempts to Control Violence in the Reign of Edward I," in Richard Kaeuper (ed.), *Violence in Medieval Society* (Woodbridge: Boydell and Brewer, 2011), pp. 129–143.

[23] The "De Conspiritoribus Ordinatio," 12 Edw. I (1293) that established the crime of conspiracy reads in part: "De illis qui conqueri voluerint de Conspiratoribus in patria placita maliciose mover procurantibus, ut contumelie braciatoribus placita illa et contumelias ut campipartem vel aliquod aliud commodum inde habeant maliciose manutenentibus et sustinentibus, veniant de cetero coram justic' ad placita Domini Regis assignatis, et ibi in-veniant securitatem de Querela sua prosequend'" ("Those who want to complain about the Conspirators in the country maliciously trying to procure pleas, so as to injure by those pleas and injuries, and those who maliciously maintain and support them in order to have a part of the profits or some other advantage therefrom, let them come before the justices assigned to the pleas of the Lord King, and therein let them come to pursue their complaints. Cited from *The Statutes of the Realm,* 11 vols. [London: HMSO, 1810–1828]).

[24] Alan Harding discusses how this attempt to address false pleas led to the charge of conspiracy: "The Origins of the Crime of Conspiracy," *Transactions of the Royal Historical Society* 33 (1983): pp. 89–108.

of the failure of the court to hold the men accountable, the tense negotiations of the compromise, and the insolence of the lie and the initial offer of half a shilling, opens more questions. What did the unnamed person(s) hope to achieve with this presentment, knowing these men? Does this record simply showcase the hubris of these defendants and the steep climb Scrope faced, or does it mount a more systemic critique of the nature of this encounter? If so, where does it locate its flaws? In the next section, I will turn to *The Pistil of Swete Susan* to see what a poetic account of local big men who abuse the testimonial system can reveal about these questions.

The *Pistil of Swete Susan*

It is easy to see why a story of corrupt, powerful men brought low by their own lies might appeal in such a moment. The legal critique I want to identify in *The Pistil of Swete Susan* lies in its confrontation between the tale's standard interpretive pathway and the one offered by the poem, each of which tells a different story about the law. In the usual legal and penitential interpretive tradition of the tale, comprising the Vulgate and Middle English translations as well as Latin poetic adaptations, the villains are a few false witnesses motivated by sin. In this version, the Elders' clout is extralegal and therefore defeated by the assertion of proper legal procedure; Susannah's freedom is a celebration of the ability of the law to reveal the truth in the face of corrupt power. But the poem traces another interpretive pathway. By making Susannah's best defense her reputation rather than her chastity, and by making the Elders oathworthy witnesses to that reputation, it suggests the more cynical but technically correct interpretation that the law lay with the Elders, and that it is Daniel's intervention that is the aberration. In fact, the poem asserts, the scrupulous pursuit of the law would have had Susannah die by the Elders' false accusation. The poem moves back and forth between these readings, torn between the story's longstanding and celebratory interpretive tradition and its acute sense of what might have happened to an English Susannah.

The traditional interpretation of the tale as the triumph of procedure over the aberrations of bad actors is made possible by its clearly religious jurisdiction. Within it, the Elders are not just witnesses or accusers, they are judges and trusted figures in the community, capable of swaying public opinion violently against Susannah. In the Wycliffite translation, when the Elders have told their story, the audience participates in condemning her: "The multitude bileuede to hem, as to the eldre men and iugis of the puple, and condempneden hir to deth." ("The multitude believed them, as the elder men and judges of the people, and condemned her to death,").[25] The religious jurisdiction also made Susannah's defense spiritual rather than legal. When she is brought in, she does not speak, turning instead away from the earthly proceedings to the judge Himself: "And sche wepte, and bihelde to heuene, and hir herte hadde trist in the Lord" ("And she wept, and looked to heaven, and her heart had trust in the Lord,").[26] Jerome argues that her ability to resist this judgment was "because of the greatness of the chastity with which she called out to the Lord," and Augustine portrays Susanna as a kind of ambassador for chastity: "Susanna too gave them something and didn't send them away empty-handed, if they had been willing to take her advice about chastity."[27] Susannah's inner purity is her best defense; she leaves the legal proceedings to Daniel.

In this way, it falls squarely into the tradition of cautionary tales of false witnessing. The dangers of false witnessing in a testimonial system were evident to both legal and penitential thinkers, but they were generally thought of as an isolated threat that was easily remedied by the law. Penitential treatments are full of warnings against the spiritual consequences of false witnessing, and they connect their warnings to legal consequences. Dan Michel's *Ayenbite of Inwit* specifically warned against bearing false witness in "leawede cort" (common law court) and "cristene cort" (ecclesiastical court), and the confessional manual *Handlyng Synne* connected these sins to their dire consequences in law:

> Wyl men swere falsly a sawe,
> And bere wytnes of swyche a fals
> To make a man hang be the hals.[28]

> Men will falsely swear a saying,
> And bear witness of such a falsehood
> To make a man be hung by the neck.

In most cases, false witnessing was tied to sin and personal animosity, like Bracton's "one neighbor who accuses another through hatred and the like," or the false witness in *The Book of Vices and Virtues* who lies out of envy.[29] There

---

[25] Daniel 13:41, in Conrad Lindberg, ed., *The Earlier Version of the Wycliffite Bible* (Stockholm: Almqvist and Wiksell, 1973), pp. 172–173.
[26] Daniel 13:35.
[27] *Sermons 359*:3, trans. Edmund Hill, in Augstine, *The Works of St. Augustine: Sermons*, ed. John E. Rotelle (New York: New City, 1995).
[28] Morris and Gradon, *Dan Michel's Ayenbite of Inwyt*; Robert of Brunne, *Handlyng Synne*, vol. 1, p. 95, ll. 2686–8.
[29] Woodbine, *Bracton*, vol. 2, p. 404.

are plenty of harsh condemnations for the motivations of false witnesses, who (as Chaucer's Parson warns) lie "for ire, or for meede, or for envye" ("for anger, or for money, or for envy,").[30] But most of the suggested remedies for this danger turned back to the foundations of the system. In fact, Bracton's only test for whether hearsay is reliable is seek out the standing of the source. If one comes to "some low and worthless fellow, one in whom no trust must be in any way reposed," then one can be sure the information is false.[31] Daniel's *deus ex machina* therefore demonstrates the power of legal procedure to reveal truth, a steady thing that abides even when a few bad actors try to conceal it. The story is so firmly pinned to its epistemological coordinates that it makes Daniel's procedural solution seem like a natural consequence.

The Pistil of Swete Susan appears in two major manuscripts from the period (the Vernon and the Simeon), indicating a significant readership. Russell Peck's argument that it draws upon the Wycliffite Bible translations of Daniel as its source suggests a partly Wycliffite audience.[32] But it departs starkly from the translation in the characters it builds and the legal system it constructs for them, and in doing so, it changes the mechanisms by which Susannah is protected and made vulnerable. First, the poem updates Joachim and Susannah to recognizable late fourteenth-century English types. Joachim is a proper English lord, whose aristocracy and lineage is established by fifty lines on his beautiful English gardens (nearly a fifth of the poem), in which "The rose ragged on rys, richest on rone, / I-theuwed with the thorn trinaunt to sene" ("The rose thorny-branched, richest in thicket / Cultivated with hawthorne, flourishing to see,").[33] His orchards are low, his cottages are high, and "alle riches that renke arayed he was riht" ("he was arrayed correctly with all the riches of rank," l. 4). Susannah is "sotil and sage" ("subtle and wise," l. 14), "tristi and trewe," ("trusty and true," l. 187) and just as importantly, she is "lovelich and lilie whit" ("lovely and lilywhite, ," l. 16).

Second, the poem updates the legal structure in which Susannah exists. The *Pistil* is bursting with fourteenth-century legal procedural language: the Elders bring an "apele" against her with "poyntes to preve," she is brought to the "barre," and Daniel brings a "proces apert" to "disprove this apele" (ll. 160, 189, 294). Unlike in the Vulgate and Wyclif versions, she is put in a dungeon to await trial (l. 174). When the Elders present their plaint, they refer directly

---

[30] Chaucer, "The Parson's Tale," l. 795.
[31] Woodbine, *Bracton*, vol. 2, p. 404.
[32] Russell Peck, ed., *Heroic Women from the Old Testament in Middle English Verse* (Kalamazoo, MI: Medieval Institute Publications, 1991), p. 100.
[33] Peck, ed., *Heroic Women*, ll. 72–73. Hereafter cited parenthetically in the text.

to the duties of the English first finder (a person who witnesses a crime or finds a body) to apprehend the suspect, saying that they could not carry out this duty because their dress prevented them ("ur copes weore cumberous and cundelet us care" l. 224). The setting is also clearly town or rural, rather than city; though most trials in medieval poetry (like the trials of Mede in Langland's *Piers Plowman*, the knight in Chaucer's "The Wife of Bath's Tale," and the hero in Marie de France's *Lanval*) take place in royal court, *The Pistil*'s Elders haul Susannah to a guildhall, the center of English town life.

The poem emphasizes Susannah's literacy and deep study of the law: "They taught her the letter of that language ... Thus they taught her the law" ("Thei lerned hire lettrure of that langage ... Thus thei lerne hire the lawe," lines 18 and 23). She fits the emerging class of literate and learned English gentlewomen who valued vernacular religious literature like this poem. Peck and A.I. Doyle have suggested that the Simeon manuscript in which this poem is found might have been held or commissioned by Joan Bohun, a prominent and pious widow for whom Thomas Hoccleve translated the verse Complaint of the Virgin, and the poem might have been selected because this Susannah so elegantly reflected her audience.[34] As a result, the English Susannah is more active; she attempts to start her own legal proceedings, speaking on her own behalf. Taylor argues that Susanna's "careful cri" (line 153) in the face of the Elders' aggression is a response to Glanvill's demand that rape victims produce an "open cry," and "soon after the deed is done ... show to trustworthy men the injury done to her."[35] This makes sense with the legal education that the poem invents for her. She also testifies at her trial: she "asked merci with mouth in this mischeve: / 'I am sakeles of syn'" ("asked mercy with her mouth in this mishap: / 'I am guiltless of sin'", ll. 239–40).

But this update is not just procedural; the characterization of a fourteenth-century appeal would be incomplete without the reputations of those parties. From the very first lines, we learn that not only is Susannah married, faithful to her husband and God, and chaste, she is also *known* to be so. Her chastity itself is her protection in the patristic commentaries, but for the English Susannah, this protection comes from outward *fama* rather than inward purity: she is "safe" because she has a prominent husband, famous beauty, and a spotless reputation. Meanwhile, though the Elders are "preostes and presidens preised

---

[34] A.I. Doyle, ed., *The Vernon Manuscript: A Facsimile of Bodleian Library, Oxford, MS. Eng. Poet. a.1*, (Cambridge: D.S. Brewer, 1987), pp. 15–16. For a discussion of BL MS Additional 10596, which contains the stand-alone *Pistel*, see Mary C. Erler, *Women, Reading, and Piety in Late Medieval England* (Cambridge: Cambridge University Press, 2002), p. 4.

[35] Taylor, *Fictions of Witnessing*, pp. 83–85. Hall, *Glanvill*, XLV, p. 6.

als peere" ("praised as peers of priests and governors," l. 33) they were also "dredde" because of their

> wikkednes [that] comes
> Of the wrongwys domes
> That thei have gyve to gomes (ll. 36–8).

> wickedness [that] comes
> From the perverse judgments
> That they have given to people."

In a major departure from the Vulgate, the Elders of the poem are already known to be corrupt before they encounter Susannah. And this reputation continues even after the accusation. In the Vulgate, "the many believed them as elders and judges of the people; and they condemned her to death."[36] But *The Pistil* is less clear on the community's involvement, posing them as an audience to her condemnation rather than condemners themselves: "Nou heo is dampned on deis; with deol thaugh hir deve" ("Now she is condemned on the dais, they deafen her with grief," l. 235).

Under the common understanding of *fama*, this disparity should have provided powerful protection. In furnishing its characters with a fourteenth-century reputation, the poem actually stacks the decks in Susannah's favor; public opinion toward her is spotless, while her opponents are already feared and known to be corrupt. English common law treatises provide no direct definition of "common opinion" (*fama*). As Daniel Lord Smail has shown, in canon law, justices sometimes quizzed witnesses on its meaning to confirm that they understood the concept before they spoke to it. "It's what people say," offered one witness. That is, *fama*'s medium was speech and was possessed in common, which made it a good basis for community decisions. In Chapter 1, *fama* provided the coroner with the backstory of the "old quarrel" between Amicia and Robert, the man killed with a knife in the street. Well into the fourteenth century, *fama* alone could be the basis for arrest in a procedure called *inquisicio de fama et gestu*. At the plea and trial stages, one's reputation for criminality was provided by *fama*, and as Carol Elder has calculated and as I will discuss in Chapter 4, this could be powerful; language of afforcement (like "notorious thief" or "known robber") significantly raised conviction rates.[37]

---

[36] "Credidit eis multitudo quasi senibus et judicibus populi, et condemnaverunt eam ad mortem," Daniel 13:41.
[37] Carol Elder, *Gaol Delivery in the Southwestern Counties, 1416–1430* (MA Thesis, Carleton University, 1983), pp. 168, 275–278.

But another witness fine-tuned this definition of *fama*. In order to emphasize the generality of the information, he turned the phrase around: "It's what is commonly said." This passive construction gestures at a perilous part of *fama*; it leaves little trace of who is doing the saying, and how that saying makes its way to us. And indeed, there were some attempts in the thirteenth to fourteenth centuries to mitigate the power of *fama* had within the system to bring someone the full distance from good standing to conviction. If *fama* delivered someone to gaol, he must be presented at the next sheriff's tourn. At that point, it would be asked "if anyone wanted to indict him," and if the answer was no, he would be released.[38] Some justices objected to this practice as early as the late thirteenth century, arguing that a person should not be held on "general suspicion" without a specific charge, and justices repeatedly warned juries that they must not convict a man on rumor alone. But this warning seems to have been often ignored, not just because it was inconvenient, but because it contradicted the purpose of the jury itself. As Karl Shoemaker has argued, criminal juries in medieval England were chosen locally because they were asked to testify to the accused's status in the community, in a kind of holdover from ordeal juries that might decide who ought to undergo an ordeal.[39] How could this be done without asking witnesses to speak to "what people say"?

The medieval legal system's strong belief in the epistemological value of *fama* has been well-documented, and the poem does not challenge that belief; Susannah and the Elders' reputations are accurate. And yet, they are not sufficient. When these reputations are carried through the testimonial system to the law, Susannah fares worse. Where the biblical Elders lose first their reputations and then their heads for their offenses, the Elders of *The Pistil* merely lose their positions as judges, and it is unclear if Susannah's reputation—her most important possession as a lady—is ever repaired. The triumph of the story has been woefully depreciated, and it is clear this depreciation takes place in the testimonial system: in the work of the Elders as witnesses and in the system that receives their testimony. Thus, part of the poem's horror lies in the fact that Susannah, prior to this event, was as protected as it was possible to be as a woman. As the poem demonstrates, *fama* was not equally protective for all; a woman's sexual reputation was particularly and perpetually fragile. Hanawalt argues in her work on reputation in criminal procedure that "gender, class, social status, wealth, connections, bribes, friends, and community all

---

[38] Bellamy, *The Criminal Trial*, p. 105.
[39] Karl Shoemaker, "Criminal Procedure in Medieval European Law: A Comparison between English and Roman-Canonical Developments after the IV Lateran Council," *Zeitschrift der Savigny-Stiftung für Rechtsgeschichte, kanonistische Abteilung*, 85, no. 1 (1999), p. 184.

played a role in how quickly or how permanently a person's reputation could be damaged."[40] But within the argument of the poem, Susannah's supposedly protected status also invites us to consider—if common opinion is both true and powerful within the law—why we do not expect her to triumph.

For a poem so specific about its legal actions, it is remarkably fuzzy about its jurisdiction. Part of that is the crime at issue: adultery was normally a matter for a church court, but as Caroline Dunn has shown, because adultery could have ramifications for inheritance, it could be brought under the jurisdiction of common law courts as a matter of theft and charged as *raptus*, a felony.[41] That is certainly what the language of "appeal" would seem to suggest (only felony could be brought by appeal), but then again, the guildhall setting indicates local arbitration, another possible forum to charge adultery.[42] This jurisdictional vagueness might reflect an imperfect understanding of legal procedure, or it might reflect the ambiguity of actual practice. But it also aptly illustrates another shift the poem makes. In Daniel, the Elders act as both accusers and judges in Susannah's case; in the Vulgate the men are *iudices*, which the Wyclif translates to *iugis*. But in *The Pistil*, while they are known to be judges ("two domes of that lawe," l. 32), in Susannah's case the judge is separate, and they are merely trusted witnesses called to testify against her.

This turns out to be an elevation—rather than a diminution—of their power. The poem lingers repeatedly on the mouths of the Elders, calling them "maisterful men with mouthes" (l. 288). Taylor connects references to Susannah's mouth to the mouth of Philomela, which Tereus mutilates after raping her, arguing that her mouth represents her ability to testify.[43] If we apply that logic to the Elders as well, we can see a comparison not of ability to testify but of one's testimonial power. The only time Susannah speaks in the court, "heo asked merci with mouth" ("she asked mercy with her mouth," l. 239) and when

---

[40] Barbara Hanawalt, *"Of Good and Ill Repute": Gender and Social Control in Medieval England* (Oxford: Oxford University Press, 1998), p. 1. Marie Kelleher also discusses the intersections that could affect one's reputation as a woman in "Later Medieval Law in Community Context," in Judith M. Bennett and Ruth Mazo Karras (eds.), *The Oxford Handbook of Women and Gender in Medieval Europe* (Oxford: Oxford University Press, 2013), pp. 133–147.

[41] As she says, this overlap reminds us that even when it comes to family law, medieval jurisdiction cannot be cleanly divided between church and crown: *Stolen Women*, p. 131. For issues of jurisdiction with common law marriage, see Robert Palmer, "Contexts of Marriage in Medieval England: Evidence from the King's Court circa 1300," *Speculum* 59, no. 1 (1984): pp. 42–67.

[42] Adultery might be tried through local arbitration, as a London case from the period demonstrates. In 1414 in London, Richard Fawcett and Robert Fuller entered into an arbitration to resolve a matter of adultery between Richard and Robert's wife. The two men each chose equal numbers of a panel to work as their arbiters, and each promised forty shillings if they did not abide by the *laudo*, or judgment, of their arbitration. Twenty shillings was agreed upon to be paid by Richard to Robert, as well as a declaration of faith, probably a public one that might restore Robert's good name. London Metropolitan Archives, DL/C/B/043/MS09064/003, f. 72r.

[43] Taylor, *Fictions of Witnessing*, p. 72.

she accepts Joachim's departure from her side, she says, "I ne dar disparage thi mouth" ("I do not dare disparage your mouth," l. 253) suggesting that it is his oathworthiness she does not want to taint, as a damned woman. The Elders themselves characterize their testimony with their physical mouths: "this word we witness for ay, / With tonge and with toth" ("this word we witness affirmatively / With tongue and with tooth," ll. 220–1). Their voices are unusually strong; the Elders in the Vulgate and in several other adaptations have voices weakened by their lust. But in *The Pistil*, "the rethly cherl ruydely rored" ("the fierce churl rudely roared," l. 341) his accusation. In some ways, their actions fit the crime of conspiracy, which targeted the "malicious procurement of pleas" and required that multiple people plan from the beginning to abuse the legal system.[44] In Daniel, the elders catch sight of Susannah separately, and make their separate plans because they are too ashamed to reveal themselves to one another ("erubescebant enim indicare sibi concupiscentiam suam"). In *The Pistil* their confederacy is set from the beginning, and they approach her in the first-person plural: "Wolt thu, ladi, for love on ure lay lerne, / And under this lorere ben ur lemmone?" ("Will you, lady, learn our law for love, / And under this laurel be our lover?" ll. 135–6).

Thus, the jurisdictional slipperiness of Susannah's trial pulls our attention to the cross-jurisdictional power of the oathworthy mouth, and how it forecloses every avenue of relief Susannah might seek. The Elders' voices subsume not only Susannah's, they subsume the testimony in the court and the narrative of the poem itself, conquering and altering it in startling ways. We are forced to spend three times as many lines on their testimony as on the poem's narration of the event. Unlike the biblical Elders who shamefacedly hide their intentions from one another until found out, they boldly conspire together from the beginning. They also play their roles as trusted witnesses well, giving the reader information about *fama*; their testimony is how we learn of her reputation as "tristi and trewe" (l. 187). This narrative power also has physical implications: they are allowed to touch her at trial in a way that they were not allowed to before.

In this way, the poem demonstrates that the position of the trusted witness enables an attack that began outside the law to continue within it. Peck remarks that *The Pistel* is "not as energetic or as skillfully narrated as *Patience*" or other

---

[44] As a case from 1350 demonstrates, conspiracy must involve preplanning with multiple others but does not need to be executed by multiple people: YB Mich. 24 Edw. 3.34, f. 34b (Seipp 1350.147), published in *Year Books; Or Reports in the Following Reigns, with Notes to Brooke and Fitzherbert's Abridgments* (commonly called the Vulgate edition), 11 vols. (London: George Sawbridge, 1678). See also: Given-Wilson et al., *The Parliament Rolls*, vol. 1, 96a.

biblical narratives, but it is at its subtle best when characterizing the elders' exercise of this power. As they both ruin her reputation and sanctimoniously mourn its loss ("We schul presenten this pleint, hou thou ever be paied, / And sei sadliche the soth, right as we have sene" | "We shall present this plaint, how you sought pleasure, / And say sadly the truth, just as we have seen" ll. 203–4), they use the trappings of the institution to humiliate her further. Her appearance in court is obligatory, but they drag her to the bar half-naked, "sengeliche arrayed / In a selken schert" ("singly arrayed, / In a silken shirt," ll. 196–7) with her shoulders bare. As they announced their plaint, they "homliche on hir heved heor hondes thei leyed, / And heo wepte for wo" ("familiarly laid their hands on her head, / And she wept for woe," ll. 200–1). The scene of their performative sorrow, with their hands upon her head as she weeps, half-naked, expresses their sexual pleasure at being able to arrange her body for their enjoyment and to touch her at last.

The poem reveals that the nightmare of the story is its ordinariness. Lust and lying, the focus of the biblical version and other adaptions, are harmful but deeply quotidian. The poem instead reserves its attention for how such sins explode far out of proportion to their original harm in the testimonial system. In this context, Bracton's only suggestion for how to detect false witness—to see if the rumor originated with "some low and worthless fellow"—seems either flippant or hopelessly naïve. The Elders might be known to be corrupt, but they are able to testify because they are neither low nor worthless, and their sin does not make them so. The slope from their first sight of her to her ruin is precipitous, taking place in a tight three lines:

> And whon thei seigh Susan, semelich of hewe,
> Thei weor so set uppon hire, might thei non sese.
> Thei wolde enchaunte that child—hou schold heo eschewe?
> (ll. 44–46)

> And when they saw Susannah, seemly of color
> They were so set upon her, they would not cease.
> They would enchant that child—how could she escape?"

The standard misogynistic framing—that the woman's beauty provokes the abuse—is still present, but it is subsumed under the activity of the men: "they saw," "they were so set," "they would not cease," "they would enchant." She is likewise subsumed; the question of how she might escape is so faint it is barely rhetorical. Where the biblical tale has a fantasy of full vengeance, the poem downgrades this to the hope that they might at least lose their positions. It would be hard to miss the warning in this sadly diminished fantasy: Daniel was the exception, and he is not coming to save you.

In carrying the story and its characters into the fourteenth century, the poem sets up the contemporary scene and then allows the pieces to fall as they most likely would, inviting us to attend to the structures that direct this sequence of events, as well as our own expectations of how Susannah and her accusers would likely fare. These alterations direct us to the mechanisms that connected such people in such a case to the law; reputation, talk, and the testimonial system. In doing so, it guides us to a complicated critique, one that does not doubt the epistemological value of "common opinion" but recognizes that in its identification, articulation, and conveyance to the court comprise a system deeply entwined with corrupted and corrupting power. In its caricature of the evil Elders, the poem maintains a sense that the false accusation was the result of individual bad actors. But their merely partial defeat sustains their threat over Susannah's community, and articulates a lingering and troubling vulnerability that lurks in the procedure itself.

*

The poem makes a final departure from its sources, so small and curious it almost seems like a mistake. In Daniel, one Elder claims to have seen Susannah and her lover under a mastic (*sub schino*) tree, and the other says he saw them under an evergreen oak (*sub prino*). The specific species are rarely exactly duplicated in adaptations, since their difference, not their identity, is the point. *The Pistil of Swete Susan* seems to aim for sonic similarity to the Vulgate: the trees are a hawthorne (cyne) and an evergreen oak (prine). But the poem includes a detail absent from other versions; when the Elders first approach Susanna, they threaten to say, "we saw you with a lover / Under this laurel tree." In fact, they mention the laurel three times throughout the poem. In other words, the procedure Daniel so cleverly invents should not work at all; they already have their story straight.

This aberration recalls a provocative exchange in the Northampton case. When asked how they plead, the men say not guilty to assault and the sworn alliance, and they add that "as for his swearing not to hold office again, he did that of his own free will (*par son bon volunte*)."[45] It is a lie that does not attempt credibility. It is the equivalent of sneering, "That black eye? He tripped over

---

[45] "Et qant al serment qil fist, il le fist par son bon volunte" (Sutherland, *The Eyre of Northamptonshire*, vol. 1, p. 194).

his own feet." The goading continues in the negotiation; it is clear Scrope is doing them a favor by allowing them to pay a fine, and yet when asked what they propose, they offer half a shilling, an amount so low Scrope could not possibly have taken it even if he wanted to. They eventually come to terms, but it is a long process. Why, when Scrope clearly offers them a quick resolution, do they not simply offer a story and an amount the court can reasonably accept, and go on with their lives? I see more than insolence in the refusal to put a narrative to their position, even when doing so would painlessly forward their own interests.

This strange parallel—of refusing or forgetting to tell the truth even when it would benefit you—brings into focus the critique both texts mount of a proof procedure so deeply imbricated with local power structures. This inconsistency demonstrates that when the Elders threaten to "telle trewely" (l. 141) their lie, it is hardly a misrepresentation; what they say will *become* true in a legal sense: they will tell it into truth. Perhaps their "telling truly" has in fact encroached on their own experience, and the Elders simply did not remember what they had threatened. Likewise, the refusal of Simon of Laushull and his men to meet the court halfway with a plausible narrative is both the insolence of power and an understanding that political and social power is narrative as well. The poem's more obvious mistake demonstrates that in both cases, this narrative power guarantees a kind of unmooring from the coordinates of reality. Why bother to pin actual events in your mind if your word is verification itself?

This brings me back to my original intention for this chapter: to identify a shared critique of the testimonial system in both the poem and the case record. In both cases, the texts are dealing with a story whose ending is fixed from the start. One cannot convict the former mayor any more than one can change the ending to a biblical story. But in both cases, the text mounts its critique by refusing to smooth out these failures, to rationalize them or celebrate them. These texts, while vivid, both strike the reader as uneven, out of tune, perhaps. That is, they have ended the way they had to, but along the way they have preserved the tension between the attempt to say something different and the requirement not to. When the Elders forget their laurel, we suddenly see that their corruption is far deeper than their attempt to entrap Susannah; they are so comfortable with their power that any truth—even truth that would help them—seems irrelevant.

As I mentioned in the Introduction, cases like the Northampton one are often cited as evidence of the struggle between local communities and royal power. But with the help of *The Pistil* and the perspective of oathworthy power, we can see that this story has three parties. There are the local authorities (Simon, William, Adam, Richard, and their company), and there is the crown (represented by Chief Justice Scrope), but there is also the person (or people) who brought the presentment to the justice. In fact, this text exists because of them, presumably brought at considerable risk. These men will not lose their lives, positions, or even much money. But in the lines of the court record, they could at least lose their hold over the story. What the anonymous presenters and Scrope seem to hope for is to do what *The Pistil* does: transform a story of acquittal into one of warning. Scrope's forceful transparency and the anonymous presenters' bolder action fashions a story with powerful characters and emotional and political resonances. It cannot "tell truly" into the world the way that powerful men can, but it does lay before us the system that allowed this to happen.

Chapter 4
The Records

Roberd the Robbere and Documentary Technology

The previous two chapters of this book have explored the voices—accuser's, witness's, defendant's—that filled the courtroom with stories. Finding these stories has meant treating the records of felony procedure as though they obscure more than they illuminate, and cobbling together what traces of human voice we can excavate from beneath their colorless and partial language. Single plea or gaol delivery records generally resist this work, and so finding these stories has meant reading against the purposes for which the records were designed. In this chapter, I turn toward this design to examine the documentary technology of these records themselves. With cases rarely longer than a few lines, this archive hardly seems to comprise the "key texts for the instantiation of history" that Emily Steiner describes in her book on legal documents in English literature.[1] In general, they hew to a formulaic standard because they were created to produce the common law, and therefore are coded for a reading practice that had to quickly and efficiently scour a large archive. Unlike modern felony cases, the vast majority of charges did not result in convictions, whether redirected by flight, settlement, or acquittal. Most estimates put felony conviction rates between 8–19 percent.[2] And so the vast majority of these records hold a story of an accusation that was never confirmed.

In this chapter, I consider the strangeness of this move—to keep returning to a story of failure again and again, without a sign of pursuing a different answer. It is a habit far more literary than legal. To better understand it, I turn

---

[1] Emily Steiner, *Documentary Culture and the Making of Middle English Literature* (Cambridge: Cambridge University Press, 2003), p. 94.

[2] For example, in Essex sessions of the peace between 1377–1379, only 18.7 percent of those accused of robbery were convicted, and Kathleen Garay estimates the felony conviction rate in English counties as a whole between 1388 and 1399 to have been about 14 percent. *Essex Sessions of the Peace, 1377—1379*, ed. E.C. Furber (Essex: Essex Archaeological Society Occasional Papers 3, Colchester, 1953), pp. 59–60; K.E. Garay, "'No Peace Nor Love in England': An Examination of Crime and Punishment in the English Counties, 1388–1409" (PhD dissertation, University of Toronto, 1977), pp. 338–339. Bellamy offers a thorough summary of the statistical studies of conviction rates in *The Criminal Trial*, pp. 96–98.

to the felon who plagues the main character of William Langland's *Piers Plowman*: the Good Thief, the robber who was crucified beside Christ and was first among the saved. In the dream vision, the Good Thief—a "feloun" who "lyved al his lyf with lesynges and with thefte" yet "was sonnere ysaved than Seynt Johan Baptiste" ("felon" who "lived all his life with lying and with theft" yet "was sooner saved than Saint John the Baptist," B 10.411–14)—is framed as an insoluble theological problem; his unearned acquittal cannot be reconciled with the facts of his life.[3] The poem revisits the story four times, and each time the parable gradually expands, filling longer lines and more of them, blooming into true preoccupation. Yet the effort is bound to a fixed ending; Langland cannot actually damn a man Christ has already saved. Each episode is forced to end in a lamented acquittal. Eleanor Johnson argues that the poem offers "accretive and echoic opportunities" to think through the problems it places before the reader, and I suggest that here its repetition of the unpunishable robber helps us think through what else this self-consciously interconnected archive might have sought to achieve besides conviction.[4]

Most scholarship on the poem has treated the four appearances of the Good Thief in the poem as unrelated episodes, and has focused on the parable's "exegetically eccentric" theological implications.[5] David Allen, Alexander Gabrovsky, Pamela Gradon, and Ralph Hanna have written most directly on the passages, and they have all noted that its conclusions are pointedly "out of tune" (as Gradon puts it) with other theological discussions in the poem.[6] But what if we consider these episodes and their plainly legal language as part of one episode, and believe Langland when he says he is talking about a felon? It is after all Roberd the Robbere who first mentions the Good Thief, in a defense by precedent designed for the courtroom. Perhaps Langland, with his intimate

---

[3] All quotations of *Piers Plowman* are from the B version and cited from William Langland, *Piers Plowman: A Parallel Text Edition of the A, B, C and Z versions*, ed. A.V.C. Schmidt (Kalamazoo: Medieval Institute Publications, 2008). All modern English translations are mine.

[4] Eleanor Johnson, "*Reddere* and Refrain: A Meditation on Poetic Procedure in *Piers Plowman*," *Yearbook of Langland Studies* 30: p. 4.

[5] Alexander Gabrovsky, "The Good, the Bad, and the Penitent Thief: Langlandian Extremes, the Edge of Salvation, and the Problem of Trajan and Dismas in *Piers Plowman*," *Marginalia* 12 (2011): p. 3.

[6] David Allen, "The Dismas *Distinctio* and the Forms of Piers Plowman B.10–13," *Yearbook of Langland Studies* 3 (1989): pp. 31–48; Pamela Gradon, "Trajanus Redivivus: Another Look at Trajan in Piers Plowman," in *Middle English Studies: Presented to Norman Davis in Honour of his Seventieth Birthday* (Oxford: University of Oxford Press, 1983), p. 106; Gabrovsky, "The Good, the Bad, and the Penitent Thief"; Ralph Hanna III, "Robert the Ruyflare," in Richard G. Newhauser and John A. Alford (eds.), *Literature and Religion in the Later Middle Ages: Philological Studies in Honor of Siegfried Wenzel* (Binghamton, NY: Center of Medieval and Early Renaissance Studies, 1995), p. 93. See also Robert Frank, *Piers Plowman and the Scheme of Salvation: An Interpretation of Dowel, Dobet, and Dobest* (New Haven, CT: Yale University Press, 1957), p. 58.

knowledge of the law, looks at this theological triumph and can only see a legal failure: a robber set free.

Placed next to the story of fourteenth-century robbery, we can see that the parable's failure as criminal justice is constitutive of the landscape Langland is trying to understand. Indeed, he must have watched this scene, of a canny villain who escapes both punishment and repentance, play out again and again. Robbery attracted a great deal of attention in parliament rolls, statutes, and judicial comment. It seemed to provide a helpfully explicit distillation of the antisocial attitudes of the "undeserving poor," those villains of fourteenth-century poetry who withheld their industry from society and yet demanded its support. And yet, generally low conviction rates meant that criminal juries repeatedly hauled suspects before the court and into their records, only to release almost all of them. With the help of Langland's Thief, we can see the unpunished robbers of the fourteenth century as a set story to which appellants and juries kept returning. In doing so, they could register all the things that fixed ending might have meant—its social valences, its context, what guilt and innocence were. Though we know these records were routinely accessed and cross-referenced, what was gained by this referencing for the law beyond the single case? And how did they together build the larger theorization of a crime? In this way, the argument of this chapter takes a similar form as that of Chapter 1; I seek to understand what the literary can tell us of legal movements too obscure to have been recorded in the documents of the law themselves.

If, as so many have contended, this uniquely legal poem and legal texts more generally shared a way of thinking and writing about the law, then they might also have shared an attitude toward the law's less significant documents: how they ought to be produced and preserved, the manners in which they ought to be retrieved and read, and to what purposes they ought to be put. I will begin by considering the attitude the law took toward the production and preservation of records before considering two cases of robbery, each of which seem to tell a different story about that attitude. I turn to the parable of the Good Thief in *Piers Plowman* to argue that its repetitions of the story model a legal practice that built its definition of crimes like robbery through the accretion of cases. By providing an example of this technology in motion, it demonstrates how the theorization of a crime and the law's own response (or in this case, nonresponse) to it might build over time, even in cases not significant enough for collection or judicial comment. Finally, I turn back to my example cases to demonstrate that this form allows both Langland and the legal records to expose and preserve contradictions in the way felonies were theorized and punished.

The Theories of Robbery

The definition of robbery was clear—it was theft by violence—and judicial comment on robbery offers such a damning picture that it is hard to imagine that anyone who had committed, attempted to commit, or stumbled into a robbery would escape punishment. And yet we know this not to have been the case; a robber was much more likely to safely flee, abjure the realm, claim benefit of clergy, turn approver, or simply be acquitted than hang. While conviction rates do not offer a full picture of this circuitous path, they do indicate that, despite death having long been the only official end of guilty robbers, it took all the right conditions and a considerable amount of bad luck to find oneself at the end of a rope. Yet indictments remained high, and as Bellamy wrote, in social records "robbery was possessed of what we might now call a 'high profile.'"[7] In other words, robbery was clearly defined, roundly condemned, and hardly ever punished. In this section, I will discuss its theorization in comparison to related crimes like theft, and then I will consider two cases that, in the language of their records, tangle with these contradictions.

Modern scholars have observed that robbery seems to have constituted the line between less and more grave felonies; Thomas Green pointed out that jury nullification, a practice of leniency, was more likely to take place in cases less serious than robbery, like "unplanned homicides and thefts that did not involve violence or housebreaking."[8] Simple theft, usually classed as a trespass rather than a felony, had been distinguished sharply from robbery's open violence since at least the early eighth century. The theft of small amounts in secret was often linked to poverty and therefore to the many robust medieval theorizations of need, and its prosecution recognized a spectrum in severity and consequences.[9] On the one hand, as Aquinas notes, its offense is double: the

---

[7] Bellamy, *The Criminal Trial*, p. 77.
[8] Thomas A. Green, *Verdict According to Conscience: Perspectives on the English Criminal Trial Jury, 1200–1800* (Chicago: University of Chicago Press, 1985), p. xv.
[9] "Leges Inae 10," in F. Liebermann, ed., *Die Gesetze der Angelsachsen*, vol. 1 (Tübingen: Halle a.S. Max Niemeyer, 1898–1916), p. 95. Bellamy's study of the criminal trial's procedures notes that "the history of robbery from the thirteenth to the fifteenth centuries poses fewer problems than burglary" and other forms of theft like larceny (*The Criminal Trial*, p. 76). John Hudson's work on English common law uses robbery as an example of how other crimes that involved violence would have been treated (*The Formation of English Common Law: Law and Society in England from King Alfred to Magna Carta*

act of taking offends justice, but its secrecy (or darkness, drawing on Isidore's assertion that *fur* derives from *furvus*) also betrays a liar.[10] On the other hand, most recognized that necessity could play a role, and that, as the *Roman de la Rose* puts it, "Senseless Poverty / brought her son, Larceny, / who runs to the gallows / to help his mother and / gets himself hanged there."[11] Over the twelfth and thirteenth centuries, we can see this concern in a widening distance between theft that involved goods over a certain sum (usually twelve pence) and was punishable by mutilation or death, and lesser theft, which involved less valuable items and could be punished by a fine or pillory.[12] This distinction was so important that *The Mirror of Justices* tells us that Edward I himself ordered that no one be sentenced to death if he stole less than twelve pence.[13]

But whatever motivated robbers, medieval men and women were quite sure it was not necessity. Where the definition of theft and its punishments were subject to ever-finer distinctions, judicial comment sought to emphasize robbery's seriousness by repeatedly expanding the limits of its definition (perhaps to the point of overstating its breadth). An incomplete attempt to commit the crime seems to have been sufficient, as Chief Justice William Gascoigne argues: "if a man lie thus in wait with intent to rob me, and I am stronger than he, and

[Abingdon: Routledge Press, 2018], p. 48). Kamali's book does not take robbery as the primary focus, but because the crime was so well-documented many of the groundbreaking conclusions she draws about the essentially intent-based definition of felony are based on data drawn from robbery cases, and she covers admirably broad ground in her summary of the history of robbery's statutory and penitential history (*Felony and the Guilty Mind*). Valérie Toureille's work focuses on robber bands in France, but she makes a few insightful comparisons to the English system and argues that the two legal systems underwent parallel conceptual evolutions after the decline of the ordeal (*Vol et brigandage de môyen Âge* [Paris: Presses Universitaires de France, 2006]).

[10] Thomas Aquinas, *Summa theologica*, trans. Fathers of the Dominican Province (Benziger Bros., 1947), IIaIIae 66; and "On Theft and Robbery," X.106.

[11] "Povreté qui point de sens n'a, / Larrecin son filz amena, / Qui s'en vet au gibet le cors/Por faire à sa mere secors / Et fait aucune fois pendre." (Guillaume de Lorris and Jean de Meun, *Roman de la Rose*, ed. Félix Lecoy, vol. 3 [Paris: Champion, 1965], ll. 9511–9514).

[12] Legal treatises, including *Britton* and *Fleta*, comment substantially on the matter and agree that larceny that deprives the victim of less than twelve pence ought to be treated as an amendable offense (that is, one in which "medicinal" punishments are recommended for the first several offenses in hopes of rehabilitation). Jean le Breton, *Summa de legibus Angliae que vocatur Bretone*, ed. Francis Nichols, 2 vols. (Oxford: Clarendon Press, 1865); H.G. Richardson and G.O. Sayles, eds., *Fleta* (London: Bernard Quaritch for the Selden Society, 1955).

[13] W.J. Whittaker, ed., *The Mirror of Justices* (Cambridge: Selden Society by the Belknap Press of Harvard University Press, 1895), pp. 28; 141. Other similar crimes against property received less attention. Burglary, or breaking into a house or other building for the purpose of stealing, received less and less mention toward the end of the fourteenth century, possibly because burglaries could often be considered robberies, especially if the burglar was discovered in the act. In two burglary cases from the early fourteenth century, the poverty of the accused is mentioned in his acquittal. See Walter Guisborough, *The Chronicle of Walter of Guisborough*, ed. H. Rothwell (London: Camden Society, 1957), pp. 361–362.

take him, so that he does not rob me ... it will be adjudged as felony."[14] But sufficient also was committing it (or almost committing it) without planning. In 1353, a guest at an inn attempted to steal linen and other goods without force and was discovered by the innkeeper. The thief reacted violently, and he was quickly overpowered and did not harm the innkeeper. Nevertheless, Chief Justice William Shareshull commented that a man should be convicted of robbery even if he did not intend force, hurt no one, and took nothing at all.[15] And yet we know that, statistically, both of these justices were far more likely to acquit robbery suspects than to send them to hang.

This contradiction is reflected in the images of robbery we can draw from other social records. One version is that of the vagrant-turned-robber out of laziness and malice. In the final decades of Edward III, years marked by a flurry of labor laws meant to restrict labor mobility, bargaining for wages, and begging, bills seeking to control vagrancy consistently framed robbery as the natural end of an idle workforce. In 1376, a bill begins with a familiar complaint against wandering laborers, but it goes on to detail their lives after they leave their homes, including their motives, associations, and inherently treasonous character:

> (Wandering laborers) are strong of body, and could well ease the community with their labor and service, if they would serve. And many of them become vagrants, and lead also an idle life, and together rob the common people in simple villages, by two, three, or four together, and maliciously cause suffering in their malice. And the greater part of said wandering servants become altogether strong robbers, and increase their robberies and felonies by day on all sides, in destruction of the aforesaid realm.[16]

This robber archetype speculatively creates a class of criminals united by demographics. The essential malice of robbery becomes a biography; first

---

[14] "si home gist issint *in praedando* al entent de moy robber, et jeo suy pluis fort que luy, et luy preigne, issint qu'il ne moy robba pas, ... il serra adjudge come felony" (YB Mich. 13 Hen. 4.20, f. 7b. [Seipp 1411.069]). In *Year Books; Or Reports in the Following Reigns, with Notes to Brooke and Fitzherbert's Abridgments* (commonly called the Vulgate edition), 11 vols. (London: George Sawbridge, 1678).

[15] John Maynard, eds. and trans., *Year Books, Liber Assissarum*, vol. 5 (London: G. Sawbridge, W. Rawlins, and S. Roycroft, 1678–1680), pl. 29.

[16] "(Les laboreres corores) sont fort de corps, et bien purroient eser la commune pur vivre sour lour labour et service, si ils voudroient servir. Et plousours de eux devenent stafstrikers, et mesnent auxint ocious vie, et communement desrobent la pitaille en symple villages, par deux, troys ou quatre emsemble, et malement sont soeffert en lour malice. Et la greyndre partie des ditz servantz corores devenent communement fortes larounes, et encrecent de eux roberies et felonies de jour en altre, par touz partz, en destruccion du roialme avantdit." "Edward III: April 1376," in C. Given-Wilson, et al. (eds.), *The Parliament Rolls of Medieval England.*

he rejects work, which leads him to wander and beg, then he becomes indigent, and finally, he unites in conspiracy with others like himself to rob "the common people in simple villages." The vague but leading language in the bill ("a greater part" "commonly become") suggests that the connection was backed by a strong intuitive association but rather less rationalizing effort. The language also escalates ominously; "many" become "a greater part," and the increase in criminality is exponential, not linear ("[the crimes] increase from one day to another on all sides"). With its continuously proliferating criminality, this description recalls the terrorism of a highwaymen's ambush, encircling the commons as they travel on a dark, isolated road in the woods, glancing anxiously into the trees.

And yet, the most common social valence of robbery—in this case, preserved in penitential handbooks, commons complaints, and the records of actually convicted robbers—was that it stemmed from the abuses of the powerful. In penitential literature, robbery is a side effect of strife among the mighty. Evil lords, not indigent malefactors, commit the robbery of Avarice in the *Ayenbite of Inwit*, in a section absent from its source, the *Somme le roi*. According to the *Ayenbite of Inwit*, robbery's roots lie in the strength of "the greate princes other barounes ... and the other riche men" ("the great princes or barons ... and other rich men") who rob their underlings and weaker neighbors of "londes/vines/other othre thinges" ("lands/vines/and other things") and who, like wolves, "ureteth the ssep" ("devour the sheep").[17] That lordly robbery is a "bough" of Avarice seems to have been Dan Michel's invention, but another contemporary translation of the same source perceived abuse of power in the passage as well, warning that robbery befalls villages as a result of "werre bitwen tweie grete lords" ("a war between two great lords").[18] Robbery, in the social imagination, was the natural byproduct of the strife of the mighty, rather than the recalcitrance of the low.

When we turn to commons complaints, we can see where this impression came from. John Molyns, one of the local big men of the last chapter, was said to have harassed his neighbors with "a continuous campaign of robbery."[19] Either of the penitential accounts above might as well be talking about Sir Hugh Eland, a knight robber. In 1381, he had recruited his household to rob a neighbor, Robert de Burton, of goblets, gold spoons, clasps, and gold rings

[17] Dan Michel's *Ayenbite of Inwyt or Remorse of Conscience: Richard Morris's transcription now newly collated with the unique manuscript British Museum MS. Arundel 57*, ed. Pamela Gradon (Oxford: Oxford University Press, 1965), vol. 1, p. 39.
[18] W. Nelson Francis, ed. *The Book of Vices and Virtues: A 14th Century English Translation of the "Somme Le Roi" of Lorens d'Orléans* (Oxford: Oxford University Press, 1942), p. 26.
[19] Stones, "The Folvilles of Ashby-Folville"; Fryde, "A Medieval Robber Baron."

to the tune of forty pounds, despite being a man of considerable means and standing himself. By the time He was finally convicted for these offenses, his terrorism was well-documented. The men who robbed Geoffrey Chaucer (on the very road his pilgrims took to Canterbury) were no vagrants; the appeal lists a goldsmith, a clerk, and a man wealthy enough to have a household of servants that he involved in the plunder.[20] A different kind of robber slips the noose here, one who paints the law not as insufficiently punitive, but insufficiently powerful, unable to reach the most prominent wrongdoers and protect the less powerful from them.

As we can see in the care they took with cases of theft, whether juries saw robbery as a proliferating disease born of laziness or an abuse of the powerful might matter a great deal to the outcome they chose. Yet left without a consistent theorization, juries were required to build their own. As Thomas Green has shown in his work on jury nullification and Maureen Mulholland in her work on manorial courts, juries had their own definitions of crimes, and were willing to modify the facts and the record in order to make the crime fit the law.[21] In the following cases, we can watch two different juries engage in this extralegal modification. But, perhaps unsure of their footing in the landscape of robbery's social consequences, they also preserve evidence of these modifications. In doing so, they bring to the record the tension in the theorization of the crime itself, retaining it without resolving it.

My first example comes from an acquittal, which stands in a long list of similar summary judgments:

Richard Taylor says William Turner assaulted Richard in order to rob him. William comes and says Richard does not name the day or hour and no one was present, therefore etc. This notwithstanding, Richard is not guilty of false appeal.[22]

---

[20] Martin M. Crow and Clair C. Olson, eds., *Chaucer Life-Records*, from Materials Compiled by John M. Manly and Edith Rickert, with the Assistance of Lilian J. Redstone and Others. (Oxford: Clarendon, 1966), p. 481.

[21] Thomas Green demonstrated that juries often assessed the defendant's act on their own terms, sometimes making humane distinctions (such as between types of homicide) that the law did not. They then modified the interpretation of evidence to accord with the verdict they believed was deserved: "Societal Concepts of Criminal Liability and Jury Nullification of the Law in the Thirteenth and Fourteenth Centuries," in *Verdict According to Conscience*, pp. 28–64; Maureen Mulholland, "Trials in Manorial Courts in Late Medieval England," in Maureen Mulholland and Brian Pullan (eds.), *Judicial Tribunals in England and Europe: The Trial in History, Volume I* (Manchester: Manchester University Press, 2003).

[22] "Ricardus Taylur dicit Willelmus Turner ipsum Ricardum insultavit ad furandum. Willelmus venit et dicit Ric' non dicit diem neque horam et nul' praesente ideo etc. hoc non obstante Ricardus n' culp' mend' appell'." TNA, KB 27/695, m. 3d.

Richard comes with an appeal about an assault with the intent to rob, in an accusation that would seem to accord perfectly with Gascoigne's definition of the felony. In his defense, William brings up a fairly common but effective point of procedure; Richard cannot say when this supposed assault took place, and there were no witnesses. The "therefore" is in the voice of the jurors; therefore, William is acquitted. However, the last sentence takes an unexpected turn. Generally, if a person was acquitted of an appeal that touched their reputation, the court could issue a harsh penalty on the appellor for making a false appeal. In 1341, a false appeal of homicide earned the liar a year's imprisonment.[23] Yet the jurors specify here that, the dismissal notwithstanding, Richard is not guilty of making a false appeal. So, which is it, a false appeal or a true one? This judgment betrays a bit of unease. William Turner's issue of procedure carries the day, but the jurors and their recordkeeper temper this victory by allowing it to be recorded that William has been called a robber and was not allowed to reverse this serious (if he were actually innocent) slander. Leaving a claim like this unanswered was also a kind of judgment, one that contradicted the official end of the case.

In the second case, another William comes before the court and is not so lucky. But the record shows a similar interest in preserving both the facts and judgment of the case, even when they were at odds:

> William le Just de Clyda taken for suspicion of robbery committed against Eli de Sintone comes and denies everything, etc., and for good and ill puts himself on the country. The jurors say under oath that he is not guilty of that robbery but of many others. Therefore, etc. His chattels are 9 pence for which the sheriff will answer.[24]

It seems that William had a reputation, well-known to the jury or to witnesses. He is convicted for this reputation, but *fama* does not entirely win the day. The jury split their primary inquiry (guilty or not guilty) into two questions. The one for which he hanged (confirmed by an S for *suspensus* in the margins) was, "Is this man a robber?" They decided that yes, he was, "Therefore, etc." But though they could have, especially in records such as these,

---

[23] Luke Owen Pike, ed., *Year Books of the Reign of King Edward the Third: Years XIV and XV*, vol. 5 (London: Eyre and Spottiswoode, 1889), Rolls Series no. 31, part B, pp. 366–367.

[24] My emphasis. "Willelmus le Just de Clyda captus pro suspicione roberie facte Elye de Sintone venit et defendit totum etc. et de bono et malo ponit se super patriam. Juratores dicunt super sacramentum suum quod non est culp' de illa roberia set de pluribus aliis' Ideo etc. Cat' eius ix d unde vic' r." TNA, JUST 1/664, m. 37; my emphasis.

the jury does not abandon the factual question: "Did this man commit this robbery?" The answer to this, they specify, is no: he is "not guilty of that robbery." The reference to many other robberies, Richard's unusual testimony, and the outcome suggest that this conviction was long coming, and that perhaps the community had tolerated William's behavior for some time. Yet even in this success the record scrupulously documents the jury's failure on the facts, undermining its own purpose, a dynamic more at home in literature than in legal recordkeeping.

The preservation of uncertainty in the records that lead up to trial—the coroners' rolls, the plea, witness accounts—makes sense for the proof procedure; any information that might better inform an eventual decision has good reason to be retained. And yet these rolls, which record an already-accomplished conclusion, betray *more* equivocation than, say, the coroners' inquest on Robert Curteys's death in Chapter 1. What were the purposes of preserving these contradictory findings in the jury decisions? And then, what was the effect of that preservation on movements of the larger archive? If these cases were designed to contribute to the creation of common law, one might expect more certainty, not less. Does this uncertainty relate to the contradictions in the way robbery's social context was perceived, as the work of both the lazy vagrant and the abusive lord? In the next section, I argue that Piers Plowman's treatment of a robber, and its method of allowing returning again and again to the same problem, can help us identify the kind of theoretical work that might have taken place in these documents.

The Robber of *Piers Plowman*

It is Roberd the Robbere, fittingly, who first introduces the Good Thief, as an unearthed precedent, a document Roberd digs up in his own defense. But rather than denying the case's applicability or directly countering Roberd's transparent bad faith, the poem takes the story seriously. Medieval biblical commentaries instructed their audiences to celebrate the common criminal who was first among the saved as a promise that grace can erase the sins of any life. "The thief came to the cross by guilt," Gregory exults of the Good Thief, "but behold how he leaves it by grace."[25] But in *Piers Plowman*, this story

---

[25] "illi qui talis ad crucem venit ex culpa, ecce qualis a cruce recedit ex gratia" (Gregory, *Moralia in Iob*, in *Corpus Christianorum, Series Latina* 76, ed. M. Adriaen [Turnhout: Brepols, 1979], 143A: 929–30). Aquinas makes the same comparison to other saints that Will does but for him, as for most medieval readers, the story of the Good Thief gave cause to rejoice in the comparison: "The demand

undermines the very formula the dreamer seeks—the good life that will ensure salvation—by offering the shocking story of a bad life that led to the first salvation, a story that the poem returns to four times, each version longer and less scripturally tenable. By the time it gets to the final version, the poem has managed to force some (nonscriptural) punishment into the story; the character Imaginatif closes his version with a grandiose but theologically impotent warning: "For he that is ones a thef is evermore in daungere,/And as lawe lyketh, to lyve or to deye:/*De peccato propiciato noli esse sine metu*" ("For he that is once a thief is evermore in danger,/And as the law likes, to live or to die:/*Be not without fear for a sin propitiated*," B 12.206–7).[26]

This version comes dangerously close to denying scripture; as David Allen has pointed out, the suggestion that the Thief remains in spiritual peril in heaven "wreaks havoc on (an interpretive) tradition Langland almost certainly knew."[27] It also willfully misreads the text itself, since (as Langland notes offhandedly almost ten passus later) the thief was in fact punished; he was crucified, and only saved after death. One could hardly say he went unpunished. And yet, Langland's Will insists on seeing only his salvation. And for what? As Augustine cautioned, the Good Thief's personal relationship to Christ and his presence at the crucifixion make him a good saint but a poor exemplar.[28] From a narrative standpoint, the introduction of the Good Thief is maddening: the poem is fairly plagued by unavenged wrongdoing, but Langland welcomes yet another repeat offender to the poem, this one who seems to Langland scripturally unpunishable.

Anne Middleton argued that *Piers Plowman* is an episodic poem that doubles back to provide its own "accounting" of the project.[29] This means that

for punishment is satisfied and the exiles are recalled to the kingdom. And so it was that Jesus at once said to the thief on the cross, 'Today shalt thou be with me in paradise.' This was not said formerly. This was not said to Adam, nor to Abraham, nor to David; but today when the gate was opened, the thief sought grace" ("expiata est pena, exules ad regnum reuocantur. Et inde est quod statim latroni dixit 'hodie mecum eris in paradiso.' Hoc non dictum est olim, hoc non dictum est Ade, non Abrahe, non Dauid; sed hodie quando aperta est ianua, latro ueniam petit"). I use both the Latin and the translation from: Aquinas, *The Sermon-Conferences of St. Thomas Aquinas on the Apostles' Creed*, Leonine Edition, ed. and trans. Nicholas Ayo (Notre Dame, IN: University of Notre Dame Press, 1988), pp. 70–71. Bonaventure went further when he cast Christ himself as "the good thief, who lay in ambush for the devil, so that he might carry off his possessions" (Bonaventure, *St. Bonaventure's Commentary on the Gospel of Luke*, ed. and trans. Robert Karris [New York, Franciscan Institute Publications, 2004], vol. 3, p. 2147).

[26] The quotation is from Sirach 5:5, but clearly refers to sins unpropitiated during life, not after salvation.

[27] Allen, "The Dismas *distinctio*," p. 33.

[28] Augustine, *The Retractations*, trans. Mary Inez Bogan, vol. 60 (Washington, DC: Catholic University of America, 1968), p. 83.

[29] Anne Middleton, "Narration and the Invention of Experience: Episodic Form in *Piers Plowman*," in Larry D. Benson and Siegfried Wenzel (eds.), *The Wisdom of Poetry: Essays in Early English Literature in Honor of Morton Bloomfield* (Kalamazoo, MI: Medieval Institute Publications, 1982), pp.

repetitions in *Piers Plowman* do not simply reiterate or intensify a subject, they offer opportunities for continuing to think through it in different ways, reflecting on both a subject's past iterations and the way in which they were iterated. In this section, I argue that Langland treats the Good Thief like a legal record, one that can only be revisited through preservation and addition, and that this movement can help us see that the documents of any given legal question were tightly woven together by a common readership and a legal practice that continually cross-referenced its own collection. This poetic case demonstrates how the preservation and indexation of these routine documents could allow a conversation between them to build, such that each new record could tap into a larger context of the accused's history and into what other cases have indicated about the identification, proof procedures, and social context of the crime.

When the Good Thief first appears, Repentence has been attempting to confess the Deadly Sins. It has not gone well. He has faced, with mounting exasperation, a slew of bad faith efforts by the personification of the Deadly Sins to evade restitution (Envy claims to be sorry—that he cannot get revenge, Covetise "confuses" rifling through someone's bags with restitution, and Sloth falls asleep during his confession because repenting is very tiring).[30] Repentence calls for a return to order by explaining the sacrament of penance one more time:

> "Til thow make restitucion' quod Repentaunce, 'and rekene with hem alle
> And sithen that Reson rolle it in the Registre of hevene
> That thow hast maad ech man good, I may thee noght assoille"
> (B 5.271–73)

> "Until you make restitution' said Repentance, 'and have a reckoning with them all;
> And until Reason records it in the register of heaven
> That you've made every man good, I may not absolve you,'"

But Roberd, who brings up the rear in this procession of Sins, is not an allegorical figure. He is the only named character in a parade of personifications,

---

91–122. See also Eleanor Johnson, "Reddere and Refrain: A Meditation on Poetic Procedure in *Piers Plowman*," *Yearbook of Langland Studies* 30 (2016): pp. 3–27.

[30] Envy: "I am sori, I am but selde other, / And that maketh me so mat, for I ne may me venge" (B 5.128–129); Covetise: "I wende ryfliynge were restitucioun, for I lerned nevere rede on boke, / And I can no Frenche" (B 5.235–236); Sloth: "He bigan Benedicite with a bolk, and his brest knokked. / Raxed and rored—and rutte at the laste. / 'What, awake, renk!' quod Repentaunce, 'and rape thee to shryfte!'" (B 5.391–393).

and his sudden appearance corrupts their allegorical register. And his response moves the conversation from the lofty ground of penance to the courtroom, a space of negotiation with which he was probably more familiar. He has listened carefully to Repentance's speech, but he knows records are not so univocal as all that, and sees Repentence's interest in recordkeeping as an opportunity to present an alternative text:

> "Crist, that on Calvarie upon the cros deidest,
> Tho Dysmas my brother bisoughte thee of grace,
> And haddest mercy on that man for *Memento* sake;
> So rewe on this Rober(d) that *Reddere* ne have ..." (B 5.463–7)

> "Christ, who on Calvary upon the cross died,
> There Dysmas my brother sought grace
> You had mercy on that man for *Memento*'s sake;
> So have mercy on this robber(d) who has no *Reddere*."

He begins by reading ("looked on *reddite*"), and when he cannot meet those terms he turns to another key text, also retrieved by its keyword: *memento*. He is referring here to the Good Thief's only words to Christ, according to Luke: "Remember me (*memento mei*) when thou shalt come into thy kingdom."[31] He is using a familiar practice of recalling and indexing passages by their incipits. But in nominalizing the incipit, he transforms it into the text *for which* the Thief was saved, an exchange to replace the restitution demanded by Repentence. He finishes with tight precedential logic; "So rewe on *this* Roberd." As a defense, his argument is very neat; the Good Thief who was crucified next to Christ was also a *latro* or "robber"—closer to a highwayman than a common pickpocket—yet was the first upon whom Christ's mercy fell.

Like William's quibble over Richard's timekeeping, this is clearly a bad faith point of procedure, but it is a knowledgeable one. Cynthia Neville has demonstrated that those brought up on gaol delivery often wielded impressive legal knowledge for their level of education and literacy. She cites some 725 individuals between 1354 and 1460 who successfully challenged the legal validity of the charges against them, sometimes based on very recent changes in statute, jurisdiction, and precedent.[32] One might imagine that for veterans of the court like William and Roberd, such information was one of the resources of the

---

[31] "Et dicebat ad Jesum: Domine, memento mei cum veneris in regnum tuum" (Luke 23:42).
[32] C.J. Neville, "Common Knowledge of the Common Law in Later Medieval England," *Canadian Journal of History* 29, no. 3 (1994): pp. 461–478.

profession, meticulously passed among practitioners, and this detail marks Roberd as the worst kind of robber—professional, inveterate. From a spiritual perspective, Roberd's defense here is very thin; he is no Good Thief.

And yet Langland seems to honor the point of procedure. Roberd disappears, but the poem quickly picks the precedent again, literally expanding the record; the three lines in Roberd's version become eight in Will's account, and eight become thirty-two for Imaginatif. In this dilation, Langland treats each return not as a separate episode but as additions to an ongoing account, where each mention of the Good Thief picks up where the last had left off, despite the intervention of whole dreams, major episodes, and hundreds of lines. Five passus after Roberd submits his defense, Will "finds" it ("On Good Friday I fynde, a felon was ysaued," | "On Good Friday I find, a felon was saved," B 10.413) and extrapolates on its logic, which leads him to believe that salvation is essentially random. This thought is so disturbing that it cuts off the conversation he has been having with Scripture and drives him further into sleep, into a dream within his dream and into the arms of Recklessness, where he squanders a lifetime in rootless pleasure. Though Roberd's troublemaking self is gone, his record continues to wreak havoc on the narrative of the poem.

When Imaginatif, one of the dreamer's guides, picks up the case two passus later, he responds as though Will had just finished speaking ("The thef that hadde grace of God on Good Fryday as thow speke" | "The thief that had grace of God on Good Friday as you spoke," B 12.191), addressing Will's concern over the unfavorable comparison between the Thief and John the Baptist. He preserves Will and Roberd's records within his own, even when it requires him to perform some interpretive acrobatics. Despite scolding Will for bad readings, he does not set aside Roberd's disingenuous reading of the parable's justice and return it to its original framework of grace's forgetting power, though this surely would have been a simpler solution, and though Roberd himself has now fallen seven passus in the past. Instead, Imaginatif takes on the far more compromising task of attempting to reconcile Roberd's framing and Will's extrapolation without revising either of them.

He accepts Roberd's (exegetically untenable) frame that the Good Thief gained salvation by works, but he also accepts Will's concerns. In order to bring the two into better balance, he invents details to mitigate the Thief's sins and to dampen his reward. Since he cannot change the premise, he adds a penitential apparatus to the Thief's credit, complete with contrition and confession, quite unlike his scriptural original, who merely asks to be remembered:

"Ac though that theef hadde hevene, he hadde noon heigh blisse,
As Seint Johan and othere seintes that deserved hadde bettre.
Right as som man yeve me mete and sette me amydde the floor:
I hadde mete moore than ynough. ac noght so muche worshipe
As tho that seten at the syde table or with the sovereynes of the halle,
But sete as a beggere bordlees by myself on the grounde." (B 12.196–201)

"But though that thief had heaven, he had no high bliss,
Such as Saint John and other saints who had deserved better.
Just as some man might give me food and set me in the middle of the floor;
I would have more than enough meat, but not so much honor
As those that sat at the side table or held sway in the hall,
But like a beggar, not at the board, but by myself on the ground."

Imaginatif's version invents sincere penitence for the Good Thief, and argues that he had grace because of ("was for") it, a purchase Imaginatif points out is open to anyone "that buxomliche biddeth it, and ben in wille to amenden hem" ("that eagerly seeks it, and has a will to amend himself," B 12.194). Furthermore, he adds, the "reward" that follows is calibrated to the greater reward of those around him; he had "no high bliss," and those "that deserved it had better." Even these additions only partially offset his life of felony, so to keep with the principle of exchange, the Thief is left with "more than enough" but not the fullest salvation, because he is relegated to loneliness on the floor of heaven.

Parables, like all genres in which the end is known from the beginning, find their narrative momentum in the process of connecting two known points. But the momentum of this logic cannot take hold if one already actively grieves the ending. Will's outrage for the unjust reward prevents him from imagining what it might mean to get what he wants, a subversion of the ending, or to realize that the Thief is actually punished after all. Imaginatif, rather than moving toward either or these resolutions, allows Will's dissatisfaction to limit his own work. In fact, baldly offering a subverted ending—say, one in which the Good Thief is damned by his sins despite Christ's will—might have repelled Will back into the arms of the parable's standard message. Instead, Imaginatif simply accepts Will's logic: "And for to serven a seint and swich a thef togideres— / It were neither reson ne right to rewarde both yliche" ("And to serve a saint and such a thief together— / It would be neither reasonable nor right to reward both alike, ," B 12.208–9); once a thief, always a thief. Imaginatif's final words on the case demonstrate that his "yes, and" approach to Will's argument is an inherent effect of building a concept by accruing records indefinitely: "For he that is ones a thef is evermore in daungere, / And as lawe lyketh, to lyve or to deye" ("For he that is once a thief is evermore in danger, / And as the law likes, to live or to die,", B 12.206–7).

Michelle Karnes argues that the character Imaginatif dramatizes the labor of making "proper, spiritual use" of what Will encounters.[33] As a spiritual guide, his work here is dubious. But as a juror, facing a case where guilt is clear but punishment is not possible or not desired, his moves are familiar, and even responsible. We can see some work worthy of Imaginatif in the careful balance the jury struck in the matter of William Turner. Let us say he did rob Richard, but the jury either could not (because of corruption or threats) or would not (because they believed hanging too harsh) convict him. Neither of their two options seemed to accord with the circumstances, so they mitigated his acquittal by letting the accusation stand, layering the damage to his reputation on top of the preservation of his life.

The Unresolved Robber

The inescapable probability that a robber will go free is a fixed ending. But for literature, especially medieval literature that so often rewrote old material, fixed endings do not preclude new directions. As Andrew Cole put it, one facet of Langland's intertextuality is that he takes on the priorities of the forms he engages and "inscribes within his poem (the) genre's working obsession."[34] With this wider notion of the literary, Langland demonstrates how he can—without revising or discarding any previous version of the story—change the significance of the Thief's salvation. Langland helps us see how the individual cases might build their own conversation, one that could not change the crime's definition or punishment but could nevertheless build its own working dossier, not only of each particular case, but of the crimes themselves, preserving and building their social significances.

If we return to the bill that framed robbery as a fundamentally antisocial attitude that proliferated alarmingly and was never satisfactorily punished, we can see that this version of robbery is an allegorical connection masquerading as a

---

[33] Michelle Karnes, *Imagination, Meditation, and Cognition in the Middle Ages* (Chicago, IL: University of Chicago Press, 2017), p. 179.

[34] Andrew Cole, "Scribal Hermeneutics and the Genres of Social Organization in Piers Plowman," in Kellie Robertson and Michael Uebel (eds.), *The Middle Ages at Work* (New York: Palgrave Macmillan, 2004), p. 180.

causal one. For one thing, this image matched effortlessly with what landowners and employers already thought of "wasters," those who could work but did not.[35] After all, robbers are a convenient literalization of the malice famously associated with wasting; while the fact that idle laborers "might well ease the community" implies that withholding their labor deprives others, robbers—in a helpfully literal way—simply take. Where the lack of civic feeling which John Gower famously deplored in the post-plague labor force implies a kind of social violence ("they are vagabond laborers / who see the world in need / of their services and labor, / and there are so few of them / for this they are arrogant"), robbers engage in actual violence.[36] In a poem whose most prominent episodes worry over the problems of labor in society, it is easy to see how the acquittal of the Good Thief might have also taken on the weight of the unpunished wasters.[37] This version of robbery levels an argument about vagrancy more than it does about robbery: it proposes that the fault of the law is that it is insufficiently punitive toward the lesser crime of vagrancy, and its leniency has allowed the problem to metastasize to something worse.

It seems clear that the language of proliferation in the bill probably did not come from the way robbery worked, but from the way its documentation did.

---

[35] For some of the effects and enforcement of the flurry of labor legislation that responded to this concept, see: Chris Given-Wilson, "Service, Serfdom and English Labour Legislation, 1350–1500," in A. Curry and E. Matthew (eds.), *Concepts and Patterns of Service in the Later Middle Ages* (Woodbridge: Boydell and Brewer, 2000), pp. 21–37, pp. 21–22, on restrictions of worker mobility in the labor statutes; Christopher Dyer, in his essay "*Piers Plowman* and Plowmen: A Historical Perspective," *Yearbook of Langland Studies* 8 (1994): p. 168, notes the role of prosperous peasants in enforcing the statutes, while Miri Rubin, in *Charity and Community in Medieval Cambridge* (Cambridge: Cambridge University Press, 2002), pp. 32–33, describes a "new class of substantial tenants" who enforced the labor statutes.

[36] "Ly labourer qui sont truant / Voiont le siècle busoignant / De leur service et leur labour, / Et que poy sont le remenant, / Pour ce s'en von ten orguillant" (John Gower, "Mirour de l'Omme," in *The Complete Works of John Gower*, ed. G.C. Macaulay, vol. 1 [Oxford: Clarendon Press, 1899–1902], p. 293).

[37] On the vast and fruitful subject of *Piers Plowman* and labor regulations, see: Anne Middleton, "Acts of Vagrancy: The C Version Autobiography and the Statute of 1388," in Steven Justice and Kathryn Kerby-Fulton (eds.), *Written Work: Langland, Labor, and Authorship* (Philadelphia: University of Pennsylvania Press, 1997), pp. 208–317; Lawrence Clopper, "Need Men and Women Labor? Langland's Wanderer and the Labor Ordinances," in Barbara A. Hanawalt (ed.), *Chaucer's England: Literature in Historical Context* (Minneapolis: University of Minnesota Press, 1992), pp. 110–129; Britton J. Harwood, "The Plot of Piers Plowman and the Contradictions of Feudalism," in Allen J. Frantzen (ed.), *Speaking Two Languages: Traditional Disciplines and Contemporary Theory in Medieval Studies* (Albany: State University of New York Press, 1991), pp. 91–114; Kellie Robertson and Michael Uebel, eds. *The Middle Ages at Work: Practicing Labor in Late Medieval England* (New York, NY: Palgrave Macmillan, 2004); Kellie Robertson, "Branding and the Technologies of Labor Regulation," in *The Middle Ages at Work: Practicing Labor in Late Medieval England* (New York, NY: Palgrave Macmillan, 2004), pp. 133–155; Kellie Robertson, *The Laborer's Two Bodies: Literary and Legal Productions in Britain, 1350–1500* (Basingstoke: Palgrave Macmillan, 2005); Kate Crassons, *Claims of Poverty: Literature, Culture, and Ideology in Late Medieval England* (Notre Dame, IN: University of Notre Dame Press, 2010); Micah Goodrich, "Lolling and the Suspension of Salvation in Piers Plowman," *Yearbook of Langland Studies* 33 (2019): pp. 13–42.

Felony records, in particular of robbery (with its high profile and social significance), often indexed previous iterations, either of the same case or similar ones, with what Bellamy has called the "language of afforcement." As we can see from the way that common knowledge was brought to bear in William le Just de Clyda's case, one purpose of the many records of acquittal was to eventually lead to a conviction. Even if you could not locate a previous case, language that emphasized the severity of the crime, the certainty of the indicting jury, or the crime's effect on the community implied previous cases. In the robbery and murder of Sir William Cantilupe in 1375, for example, the indictment that claimed that two of his servants "with seditious premeditation" (*sedicione precogitate*) set about to plot their crime and committed it "out of malice" (*ex malicio*) gestured towards a failed first indictment.[38]

Strong language in bills of indictment for robbery most often referred to the robber's notoriety or specific individuals whom the robber had been known to harass (like specifying that a robbery was committed "at night" or by a "known robber"). That is, they hinted at previous cases by focusing on the effect of the crime in the community. Writing in 1514, Anthony Fitzherbert mentions a case where Chief Justice Tresilian told petty jurors that because they had acquitted a man whom the indictment had described as a "common" robber, they would be responsible for his good behavior in the village. As a result, they changed their verdict to guilty.[39] Almost no consistent factors seem to correlate with higher conviction rates save this one: Edward Powell has found that bills for felony offenses that include language of afforcement raised the conviction rate from one in eight to one in three.[40] In this way, we can imagine the cases of William Turner and de Clyda as the beginning and ending of the same story of language of afforcement, one the source of such language and one the product.

The records of robbery proliferated in another way; robbery was a naturally conspiratorial crime, and for this reason robbers were often pressured to turn approver, or king's evidence. Approval had been encouraged since the twelfth century in exchange for unspecified leniency, and A.J. Musson points out that it was one of the few ways the Crown took an active role in seeking

---

[38] Rosamond Sillem, *Records of Some Sessions of the Peace in Lincolnshire, 1360–1375* (Hereford: Lincoln Record Society, 1936), p. 142.

[39] Anthony Fitzherbert, *La Graunde Abridgement* (London: John Rastell and Wynkyn de Worde, 1516), f. 250r. A recent study found that 60 percent of those called "common" felons in some manner were indicted for more than one felony; "common" offenders comprised a quarter of all accused. C. Elder, *Gaol Delivery in the Southwestern Counties, 1390–1416* (PhD dissertation, Carleton University, 2014).

[40] J.S. Cockburn and Thomas A. Green, eds., *Twelve Good Men and True: The Criminal Trial Jury in England, 1200–1800* (Princeton, NJ: Princeton University Press, 2014).

out prosecution of local crime.[41] Thus, robbery did not just increase, it was a proliferating source of information, spawning approval after approval. The testimony of Richard Breyerly, one of Chaucer's robbers, detailed nine other robberies and named fifteen other persons, some of whom went on to turn king's evidence themselves.[42] The fact that approval could result in a delay of one's own trial may have encouraged approvers to appeal multiple people, the farther away the better. John Kyroun of Norfolk, for example, sent the king's men on a wild goose chase across the country: two years later, the sheriff had to acknowledge that the people and places in Kyroun's appeal were fictitious.[43]

Sir Hugh, our knight robber, was eventually caught and held at Newgate. In fact, we know so much about him because he wrote a petition to the king on behalf of the gaol's prisoners, complaining about the filthy conditions and the long delays before trial. He found a better way out than trial and turned a sort of professional approver, spending the rest of his years tracking down his old compatriots and collecting gossip among the criminal classes to bring back to the sheriff. Thus, the impression of proliferation contained in that bill might not have come from the sense that robbers tended to recruit or swell their numbers, but from the fact that anyone, once caught, could provide access to an almost endless network of information.

The example of *Piers Plowman*'s robber might also help us understand the nature of creating self-contradictory records. It is unsurprising that juries sought to assert and record their own resentment over these abuses, even when they—for whatever reason—could not or chose not to convict. We can see some of this resentment in the way Imaginatif attempts to punish the unpunishable Thief: the Thief might have been personally brought to heaven by Christ, and no amount of wishing can convict him at this point. But once he is there, Imaginatif sits him back on the ground. In order to preserve both the Good Thief's salvation and some semblance of consequences, Imaginatif has speculated a robber identity that transcends the barriers of judgment, punishment, and reward, whether criminal or spiritual. In doing this, he demonstrates one way in which the records of robbery coped with the contradiction between robbery's unwaveringly harsh representation in statutes and judicial treatises

---

[41] Musson surmises that repeated attempts to reduce the torture of approvers suggest that coercion to turn approver was still widespread: "Turning King's Evidence: The Prosecution of Crime in Late Medieval England," *Oxford Journal of Legal Studies* 19, no. 3 (1999): pp. 467–470. Approvers (and their mistreatment) had become so widespread by the early fourteenth century that in 1327, the government gave justices of assize powers to investigate complaints about the making of appeals, and in 1340, the Ordinance of Conspirators further specified that if it was found that a prisoner was forced to turn approver through duress, the gaoler would be liable.

[42] Crow and Olson, eds., *Chaucer Life-Records*, p. 481.

[43] The manuscript of the original trial record is at TNA, JUST 3/48, m. 20d.

and the infrequency with which that representation played out in reality. By leaving the robber "evermore in danger," the records could leverage some of the power the law could not. Sir Hugh Eland might not have been properly punished for his abuses, but his neighbors knew he was a robber, and thanks to the documents, so do we.

The idea that a person remains in peril of their soul after salvation is a scripturally untenable position. But as a legal failsafe, it makes practical sense. A note from the middle of the same eyre I cited earlier demonstrates how a preserved record might keep a thief "evermore in danger." A man was arraigned for robbery, for which he claimed to have been previously acquitted. The record was searched and, in a stroke of enviable archival luck his acquittal was found, with the further exonerating detail that he had not fled before trial. But the documents take a sudden turn: "this notwithstanding, his chattels were forfeit because it was found in the coroner's roll that he had fled on account of the felony."[44] With no name and no specifics, this note was clearly not meant to function as a case record, but rather as instruction for the usefulness of records in preserving a threat to those acquitted but at least partly guilty. Preserving Richard's accusation meant that if William ever stepped out of line again, it would be known—in writing—that he was a robber, which would make it much less likely he could slip the noose twice.

Likewise, recordkeeping that keeps a thief "evermore in danger" might explain the case of William le Just de Clyda, the innocent but guilty robber. If we imagine that this was not his first brush with the law, then this accusation is merely the final record of many. The phrase "but of many others" collects all his previous encounters with the law within itself, justifying the jury's explicitly counterfactual decision as a comprehensive, final account of a thick case file. The quick turn of the last line works like Imaginatif's warning to all thieves despite the Thief's salvation, a statement that goes against the grain of the facts but in favor of what the community has long known to be true.

Like the note on the robber who fled, both Imaginatif and the juries of the two Williams instruct on why and in what way to preserve records, even of acquittals and cases that may never be picked up again. Documentation usually served to reinforce medieval memory, but in this case, it was critical that the collection of documents also behaved like memory, such that even when one impression has been proffered, more can surface if one repeats the search. As Albertus Magnus describes it, memory is not just recollection but repeated

---

[44] "Hoc non obstante, ses chateus furunt forfetz pur ceo qe troue fu par role de coroner qil se fui par resone de la felonie" (TNA, JUST 1/635 m. 3d).

recollection, a practice that becomes a habit that forms the mind.[45] It was important that the record of an accused's interaction with the law not only be preserved for recollection, but that it also admit variety and heterogeneity in those impressions, so that each recollection is an opportunity to yield more than the sum of its parts. Preservation of the record, just as it is (rather than rewriting the parable from scratch), allows Langland to keep adding to the story's archive so that it might never entirely end.

*

The final addition to the Good Thief's record comes in passing in the C version, when Langland seems to suddenly realize that the Thief *was* punished after all—he was crucified. Therefore, a second punishment might not be legal: "Hit is nat vsed on erthe to hangen eny felones / Oftur then ones" ("It is not custom on earth to hang any felon / More often than once," C 20.421–2) no matter what they did, and if he had already been punished "a thief tholie sholde deth other iewyse, / Lawe wolde he goue hym lyf" ("a thief who would suffer death or other justice / The law would give him life," C 20.423–4). In this final thought, Langland manages to wrench the scriptural story into better harmony with the law. There have been costs along the way; all of Will's suffering, Imaginatif's heterodox theories about punishment in heaven, and the consequences of this "solution" (since surely it suggests that all felons put to death ought to be saved). That Langland nevertheless continues to work on this case suggests its importance, both to the narrative and to Langland's theories of justice.

Clearly, Langland hopes to find an accord between spiritual and legal justice. But he takes the most difficult path, sticking to the form of a legal precedent which, once unearthed, cannot be discarded and proceeds to influence all future cases on the same matter. In doing so, he expresses a worry that procedures that pursue documentation as a way to circumvent the usual story risk the procedure's relationship to factual proof. If we return to Roberd, we can see that he triumphs *through* his literalness, his adherence to procedure. Taking Repentence at his word, Roberd says that he has already lost what he once had gained through his theft, and so cannot literally return it. With his willingness to document, Roberd puts pressure on Repentence's own documentary impulse. This impulse arises out of Repentence's anxiety over unjust dealings, but Roberd reveals that it is also what makes his logic vulnerable

---

[45] Albertus Magnus, "De Partibus Prudentia," trans. Mary Carruthers in *The Book of Memory: A Study of Memory in Medieval Culture* (Cambridge: Cambridge University Press, 2008), p. 268.

to the Dysmas story, and indeed, to many possible accounts of reward and punishment in scripture.

And with this perspective, we can see that his worries were borne out in the records. When William le Just de Clyda was hanged (not for the particular robbery at hand, but for being known to be a robber), we can imagine the strain on this relationship through the eyes of the jury. They were given an opportunity to confirm the nature of criminal procedure; does it value factual proof or the right answer? We can glean from the short record that it must have been satisfying to those who knew William's reputation as a robber that this case managed to finally send him to trial. It would seem right to convict him. But there does not seem to have been enough evidence—factual proof—to do that. There were probably no eyewitnesses, and he declined to confess. Thus, it would also seem right to acquit him. So, the jury chose both innocence and guilt, stipulating his innocence in the record (he was "not guilty of that robbery") and confirming his guilt in the sentence ("but of many others"). In this way, they managed to document not only their own knowledge (that he was a robber) but also the knowledge produced by the procedure (that he did not commit this robbery). In the end, the jury chose a compromise that recognized the value of documentation. A clever and sophisticated move, but they must have recognized the precarity of this choice, and how easily it could fall prey to bad actors.

It makes sense, then, that Langland's final word on Roberd is to decline a final word: "What bifel of this feloun I can noughte faire schewe" ("What befell that felon I cannot fairly show," B 5.501). Unable or unwilling to choose between fact and truth, all he can offer his dreamer is the promise of nonresolution. It seems to me that Langland's increasingly cramped efforts to fix the problem of the Good Thief in *Piers Plowman* get us to the heart of what we want criminal justice to do and what we are afraid it cannot. We might imagine procedural attention springs from a sense of injustice that seeks resolution. But the poem's outrage over the Good Thief pointedly avoids resolution, and it exposes a more troublesome version of this project: where does a feeling of injustice that refuses to be dispelled lead us? Outrage at a system one finds unjust has a natural place in law, but outrage that lingers after "good justice" threatens to expose a drama central to criminal punishment and its reform: that it is motivated by an affect it might not be able to resolve.

Piers' frustrated attempt to "amaistren" ("master") the wasters of the Half-Acre Scene is betrayed by a burst of honesty when he cries, "al in pure tene ... 'I shal apeyre yow alle'" ("all in pure fury ... I shall avenge you all," B.4.170–1). Langland's furious focus on the Good Thief's punishment (rather than his salvation) traps him in repetitive attempts to "amaistren" the robber. His increasingly procedural bids to resolve a case that cannot be resolved show that the impulse toward the rationalization of criminal process is driven not by a desire for order but by lingering feelings of resentment, powerlessness, and fear. Like the child in Freud's *Beyond the Pleasure Principle* who throws his favorite toy away from his crib again and again in order to work through the distressing experience of loss, the poem repeatedly returns to the story of the Good Thief to confront an unjust experience of justice. By refusing to either reject or surrender to the conclusion that has already been written, Langland accesses the only narrative in which judgment is avoidable—one where the ending is already known but the middle refuses to proceed toward it.

Chapter 5
Standing Mute

Silence and Consent in Law and Literature

The triumphal story of the English jury trial goes like this: when the Fourth Lateran Council (1215) called for an end of priest involvement in trials which put people to death, it effectively ended trial by ordeal for serious crimes. In the ordeal, the accused would be put to a physical trial—like holding a hot iron for some paces or plunging their hand into boiling water—the outcome of which would presumably be interpreted by a priest. In determining whether or not the wound had healed sufficiently, the ordeal was thought to channel God's judgment. When the priest and the church setting could no longer provide that conduit, felony courts had to find another way to determine guilt. The European continent turned to the confession of the accused, and often torture to produce it. But England turned to the jury trial—the rational inquiry by a panel of trustworthy men—making confession and torture unnecessary.

This origin story spun into two axioms about the development of English law. The first was that the jury trial initiated a long but inexorable turn toward a rational and centralized legal system grounded in disinterested proof. Karl Shoemaker, Paul Hyams, and Thomas A. Green have all proven the overbearing simplicity—not to mention inaccuracy—of this teleological narrative, especially the idea that the ordeal in England left no trace of its own logic behind in subsequent procedure.[1] But, as Emma Lipton observes, it stubbornly remains a "truism" in histories of English law and especially in our longue durée understanding of Anglo-American law's development.[2]

---

[1] Shoemaker has argued for the continuity in procedure between the trial of ordeal and trial by jury; both involved a kind of grand jury that decided if the person should be put to trial, and both devolved most of the control over the procedure and decision to local juries ("Criminal Procedure in Medieval European Law: A Comparison Between English and Roman-Canonical Developments After the IV Lateran Council," *Zeitschrift der Savigny-Stiftung für Rechtsgeschichte, Kanonistische Abteilung*, vol. 85, no. 1 [1999], pp. 174–202). See also: Paul Hyams, *Rancour and Reconciliation in Medieval England* (Ithaca: Cornell University Press, 2003); Thomas A. Green, *Verdict According to Conscience: Perspectives on the English Criminal Trial Jury 1200–1800* (Chicago: University of Chicago Press, 1985).
[2] Emma Lipton, *Cultures of Witnessing: Law and the York Plays* (Philadelphia: University of Pennsylvania Press, 2022), p. 14.

The second axiom is that, from the end of the ordeal onward, English law fully rejected judicial torture and viewed it, in the words of Lord Chief Justice Fortescue, as "a Practice so inhuman, (it) deserves not indeed to be called a Law, but the high Road to Hell."[3] Although both the continental and insular systems were Christian, English literary depictions of judicial torture often associated it with Jewish or Muslim authority, further distancing the practice from English shores and souls.[4] These two beliefs intertwine; distaste for torture has seemed to motivate rational procedure, and the elegance of an evidence-based proof procedure has appeared to make torture distasteful.[5] That is, according to this story, the procedure with which this book is concerned was what brought judicial torture to an end.

But of course, the problem for both this legend and this book is that English felony procedure continued to torture. And here I am not speaking of the exceptional villains—king-killers or heretics—that spring to mind, thanks to Michel Foucault's famous scenes in *Discipline and Punish*.[6] I mean more ordinary defendants. At the start of each felony trial, the justice asked this question, "How do you wish to acquit yourself?" and although the prescribed answers were "guilty" or "not guilty," the question was not about guilt but rather about consent of the accused to be tried by jury. By asking the accused to consent to the jury trial, the court distributed responsibility for the outcome; whatever happened, at least everyone had agreed to take part. As Chaucer's Host reminds the pleader before the "Man of Law's Tale," the tale-telling game is like a trial, and "Ye been submytted, thrugh youre free assent / To stonden in this cas at my juggement" ("You have submitted, through your free assent / To stand in this case at my judgement," ll. 35–6). Most often, this was a rote question to which one could expect an answer. But when the accused did not answer, when consent was not forthcoming, the trial could not continue. In order to prevent a breakdown in the process, those who refused to enter a plea could be put to *prison* or *peine forte et dure*, a procedure that could range from being put on a starvation diet to being gradually pressed beneath heavy stones

---

[3] John Fortescue, *De Laudibus Legum Angliae*, ed. Stanley Chrimes (Cambridge University Press, 2011), p. 69.

[4] See below, and also Sara Butler's exploration of this issue using a variety of literary sources: *Pain, Penance, and Protest: Peine Forte et Dure in Medieval England* (Cambridge University Press, 2022), pp. 338–345.

[5] This was a commonplace so widespread it is difficult to trace to any single origin. One influential source was probably Pollack and Maitland's claim that English common law had no need for torture because it accepted evidence outside of confession and eyewitness accounts in determining guilt (Frederick Pollack and Frederic W. Maitland, *The History of English Law, 2nd ed.* [Cambridge, 1898], vol. II, pp. 659–660). John Baker's standard textbook, *An Introduction to English Legal History*, 5th ed., repeats the claim almost exactly (Oxford: Oxford University Press, 2019), p. 548.

[6] Michel Foucault, *Surveiller et punir: Naissance de la prison* (Paris: Gallimard, 1975).

until the accused relented or was crushed.[7] Perhaps the English jury trial could accommodate a lack of confession, but clearly, it could not abide silence.

In the story of Anglo-American law—our law—*peine forte et dure* has been, as Sara Butler puts it, "a piece of the puzzle that just did not fit."[8] Perhaps as a result, most overviews of English legal history spend little time on it; William Holdsworth's multivolume reference spends less than a paragraph on the subject in its 500 pages on the medieval period, and Paul Brand's popular text does not mention it at all.[9] Medieval legal historians have more recently focused on the obvious hypocrisy around the torture specifically: how did a legal system that proudly condemned torture meant to extract confessions find itself condoning torture meant to extract consent?[10] The contradiction seems to still engender palpable outrage in scholarship: William Blackstone's declaration that it was "a monument of savage rapacity" is echoed as recently as 2020 in references to the practice as a "barbarous moment" in English law.[11] Butler's field-defining book from 2022 takes up the question of torture and this contradiction, and persuasively argues that the law justified the practice as penance, rather than torture.[12]

But in approaching from the perspective of literature—where "saying nothing" and "saying something" are more or less all we talk about—I am most interested in the silence itself. What kind of silence was saying nothing? What

---

[7] The procedure of pressing was described vividly by Thomas Smith in *De Republica Anglorum*: "If he will not aunswere, or not aunsere directly guiltie or not guiltie, after he hath been once or twise so interrogated, he is judged mute, that is dumme by contumacie, and his condemnation is to be pressed to death, which is one of the cruellest deathes that may be: he is layd upon a table, and an other uppon him, and so much weight of stones or lead laide uppon that table, while as his bodie be crushed, and his life by that violence taken from him" (ed. L. Alston [Cambridge: Cambridge University Press, 1906], p. 97).

[8] Butler, *Pain, Penance, and Protest*, p. 190.

[9] William Holdsworth, *A History of English Law*, 7th ed., ed. A.L. Goodhart and H.G. Hanbury; with an introductory essay and additions by S.B. Chrimes, 17 vols. (Mytholmroyd: Sweet & Maxwell Ltd., 1956–1966). Paul Brand, *The Making of the Common Law* (New York, NY: Bloomsbury Academic, 1992).

[10] John Langbein has focused on the relationship between torture and proof across continental and insular systems, and puts the practice in the context of a long turn away from the routine use of judicial torture (*Torture and the Law of Proof: Europe and England in the Ancien Régime* [Chicago: University of Chicago Press, 2012]). James Masschaele has asked what could have been so crucial in the request for consent to merit torture (*Jury, State, and Society in Medieval England* [London: Palgrave Macmillan, 2008]). K.J. Kesselring, in focusing on felony forfeiture, noted that *peine forte et dure* as torture was sometimes also aimed to preventing felons from preserving their property for their heirs, as a convicted felon forfeited his chattels to the crown ("Felony Forfeiture in England, c.1170–1870," *Journal of Legal History* 30, no. 3 [2009]: pp. 201–226).

[11] William Blackstone, *Commentaries on the Laws of England in Four Volumes*, vol. 4 (Philadelphia, PA: Lippincott Company, 1893), p. 371; Miranda Beven, David Ormerod, and Samantha Magor, "Time to Dispense with the Mute of Malice Procedure," *Criminal Law Review* 10 (2020): pp. 912–930.

[12] Butler, *Pain, Penance, and Protest*. The capacious book covers almost all aspects of the procedure, from the demographics of those who stood mute, to the variations in practice of *peine forte et dure*, to standing mute's uses in religious and political protest.

valences did it have for the audience: justice, jurors, and onlookers? What effect did it have on the courtroom dynamic, and—if that effect was not positive for the authority of the law—why did felony procedure allow it? Silence is tricky to talk about; even the usual formulations for standing mute, "nihil dicit" or "rien dit" (says nothing) struggle to record silence as anything other than "saying," even if it is "nothing" where it should be something. The parameters of silence as part of religious or chivalric conduct are well-sketched in medieval literature. But this silence is lifework, and does not necessarily help us understand a single silence, one that disrupts a space in which speech is the rule. In this case, a procedure has demanded speech at a specific juncture, required it with such urgency that the whole process could collapse were it not provided. What can we learn about the silence of non-provision, then, the silence that constitutes an individual's refusal to give a procedure what it requires to function?

I have argued throughout the book that felony was theorized in its practice, mostly by people untrained in the law, who were guided by cultural concepts rather than legal theory. I end the book with a consideration of a practice unique to felony, one that overlaps especially clearly with the purview of literature, to explore the edges of these consequences. In trying to understand this silence, we might turn not just to texts that discussed not speaking or holding one's tongue, but to ones that gave silence a physical form by putting it on stage or making it a character, analogues to the silent presence of the accused. I turn to literary sources to understand this silence, not only because I believe they provided guidance in the gaps the law left, but also because the devices available to literature, in this case dramatic staging and allegorical personification, are best able to help us make sense of this silence's aesthetic and ethical ramifications.

After introducing the practice and its context, I will consider two possible paradigms for understanding the silent defendant. The most familiar image of standing mute for most people would have been Christ's silence in the Corpus Christi Plays. While examples of standing mute in literature (including this one) often associate it with nationalistic protest against foreign influence, the way the play stages the practice cautions us against translating silence into speech too hastily. It deliberately returns our attention to the space that saying nothing creates. Second, I turn to the entrance of Mum in the alliterative poem, *Mum and the Sothsegger* (*Silence and the Truth-Sayer*), in which the personification of saying nothing demonstrates the disruptive power of silence to lay bare the script behind the law. I finish with a final example drawn from legal records to help us apply the perceptual lessons the literary texts have taught us.

Standing Mute

In 1357, Cecily is accused of killing her husband, John de Rygeway. When she comes before the bar, the justice asks her, as he did every felony defendant, "How do you wish to acquit yourself?" She says nothing. The justice asks again, offering several more chances. She says nothing. In response, the justice sends her back to Nottingham jail to endure *prison forte et dure*, strong and hard prison, until she relents or dies. Still, she says nothing. Forty long days later, she is pardoned by the king, having survived "without food and drink by a miracle."[13] When the justice asked, "how do you wish to acquit yourself," this was originally meant to ask defendants in what manner they wished to be tried: by battle, by ordeal, or by jury trial. Battle was never available to a wide variety of people, including women, and as ordeal dwindled, the only real option was trial by jury, to put oneself "on the country" ("super patriam"). And so, in a practical sense, "in what manner" became "whether": a request for consent to the only method available.

Technically, this was meant to be a true choice. A justice in 1330 chided jailers for leaving irons on a felon brought to the bar; one choosing to plead should remain free from coercion.[14] But by hinging the continuance of the trial on this moment, felony procedure backed itself into a corner. Dropping charges on all who remained silent was untenable. And consent felt necessary, for many reasons. As James Masschaele has argued, it was especially important in the precarious shift from proof procedures (like the ordeal or battle) that put the question of guilt to God, to those who directed the question to men.[15] Putting the question to God, as these methods did, seemed likely to produce a reliable result; presumably He knew all the circumstances and so could make a just decision. But a jury trial was not so clear. What if all the circumstances were not discovered? What if a juror was compromised? What if jurors found the right answer but were damned for it? As James Whitman has pointed out, this request for consent was also urgent to the persons of the court; jurors and justices alike worried that if they sent

---

[13] She is put to prison "pro eo quod se tenuit mutam," which suggests "holding" silence rather than a single response of silence. It was standard procedure (described in the next note) to ask more than once. *Calendar of Patent Rolls, Preserved in the Public Record Office and Prepared under the Superintendence of the Deputy Keeper of the Records, 1216–1509*, 55 vols. (London: HMSO, 1891–1916), vol. X (1354–1358), p. 529. This case is also cited by Andrea McKenzie in "'This Death Some Strong and Stout Hearted Man Doth Choose': The Practice of Peine Forte et Dure in Seventeenth- and Eighteenth-Century England," *Law and History Review* 23, no. 2 (2005): pp. 279–313.

[14] TNA, JUST 1/635, m. 17.

[15] Masschaele, *Jury, State, and Society*.

a defendant to his death then their souls might then be in peril (even if he was guilty).[16]

And so the demand for a plea was expressed through coercion that attempted not to seem coercive. This could involve a variety of measures, but the important part was that they be gradual, so that the accused would have ample opportunity to give in. The legal treatise *Britton* described the starvation method; Cecily's pardon describes her receiving no food nor drink for the forty days she survived, but more likely she endured something like this:

> "Let them be put to their penance, until they pray to do it; and let their penance be this, that they be barefooted, ungirt and bareheaded, in the worst place in the prison, upon the bare ground continually night and day, that they eat only bread made of barley or bran, and that they drink not the day they eat, nor eat the day they drink, nor drink anything but water, and that they be put in irons."[17]

By the 1300s, pressing—laying the accused on the ground with a board on top that was gradually loaded with heavy stones—also became standard for *peine forte et dure*. It is important to note that there were practical inheritance reasons for refusing to plead. If convicted of a felony, one's property and chattels reverted to the king and could not be passed to one's heirs. If one felt certain of conviction and therefore hanging anyway, choosing death by pressing was a way to avoid property forfeiture. This is one reason I have chosen women (who generally did not control property) for my exempla; it allows us to focus on the choice to stay silent.

In this chapter, I am interested in how we might understand this "muteness" itself: what kind of silence or "saying nothing" it was, what it achieved, and how it was perceived. What was the nature of this silence, which caused the law to turn to a practice it pronounced antithetical to its core? The scene we can imagine between Cecily and the justice offers some threads with which to begin. First, her saying nothing itself has clearly unsettled the justice. If torture is the high road to hell, then surely the act that merits it must be profoundly evil. And yet, rather than leaping on her silence in righteous fury, the justice does everything he can to coax her out of it, giving her chance after chance to

---

[16] James Whitman, *The Origins of Reasonable Doubt: Theological Roots of the Criminal Trial* (New Haven, CT: Yale University Press, 2008), p. 92.

[17] Francis Morgan Nichols, ed. and trans., *Britton: The French Text Carefully Revised with an English Translation*, vol. 1 (Oxford: Clarendon, 1865), pp. 26–27.

change her mind, a process that is often echoed in other examples of standing mute.[18] We can detect that the justice is treading lightly here, even with a murder suspect. And that the king eventually intervenes to end the stalemate seems an unusual surrender. Does Cecily's silence have valences beyond the procedure of standing mute, of which the justice must be careful?

Second, Cecily's pardon brings about an ending, but even before it, her silence has had a real effect. To state the obvious, whatever the justice is asking for, it is not free consent. If noncompliance results in torture, compliance is not voluntary. And yet, Cecily is able to refuse something substantial, even if at great cost. The trial does not in fact go on. What kind of disruption does this refusal accomplish, and what does it reveal about the law? Finally, this exchange only takes place because Cecily has been accused of a felony. Standing mute's disruptive power was confined to English felony law; other courts happily translated this same silence into legal meaning. In civil and trespass law, it was often entered as a plea of guilty, and in ecclesiastical courts it was usually translated into a failure to appear.[19] This leads to an obvious question: why would felony law in particular make space for its own disruption? In the next few sections, I will take up these questions in turn, beginning with who Cecily's audience most likely saw in her silent performance.

Christ's Silence

The figure at the top of most peoples' minds when they saw any defendant stand mute would have been Christ on trial, specifically the one they witnessed before them in the annual Mystery Plays, biblical stories turned into pageants by townspeople and staged across the major squares of a town or city. Although the plays dealt with all the major events of the Christian timeline, from Creation to the Day of Judgment, they spent a disproportionate amount of time on the last days of Christ's life, including his trials before Herod and Pilate. This association would seem to mount a political critique of felony procedure, one that figured the silent body as a proud martyr to an unjust and clamorous system. But I argue that Christ's figure in the Mystery Plays forms a more complex analogy, one that directs our attention to one's power over one's own speech, and warns us against the tempting ease of translating silence into protest.

---

[18] See my discussion of Isabel of Bury below.
[19] H. Ansgar Kelly, "The Right to Remain Silent: Before and after Joan of Arc," *Speculum* 68, no. 4 (1993): p. 998.

The plays themselves did not just educate the people on biblical stories, they overlaid the town with Jerusalem, and one's neighbors with the shadows of Herod, Pilate, and Christ. As Martin Stevens put it, audiences were made to feel that "the Passion is taking place here and now ... the spectators in the streets gradually recognize that they are really in Jerusalem."[20] All of the cycles contain an extended pageant sequence leading up to the Crucifixion in which they stage the trials of Christ, many of which engage directly in details of contemporary English procedure. In her recent book on the York Cycle—in which she notes that this coincidence of the plays and legal procedure is surprisingly understudied—Lipton argues that the York plays inculcated a practice of "civic witnessing," in which a sense of shared affect and responsibility impart a civic identity onto the audience and train them to be good witnesses before the law.[21]

Christ provides an incarnation of standing mute, and his antagonists an analogue for the court that controls who speaks and when. As Daisy Black argues, the tyrants of the Mystery Plays "are easily identified through their elaborate, self-aggrandizing speeches which demand audience attention, co-operation, and silence."[22] In the four trial plays of the York version, for example, Christ speaks fewer than two percent of the lines, despite being the center of every scene. The trials also explicitly follow felony procedure. For example, sometimes, the justice impaneled an inquest jury to inquire whether the accused was mute by nature or perhaps mad. When John de Dorley was arraigned for a variety of felonies and stood mute, the justice asked a jury to inquire "if he was dumb, or if he could speak if he chose."[23] When Christ refuses to speak in Herod's court, the king first inquires whether he is deaf or mad: "Do carpe on, carle, for I can thee cure, / Say, may thou not here me? Oy, man, arte thou woode?" ("Do say something, man, for I can help you. / Say, can you not hear me? Oy, man, are you mad?").[24] Herod takes the role of a justice facing a mute defendant, and Christ's silence reflects badly on both him and the justice.[25]

---

[20] Martin Stevens, *Four Middle English Mystery Cycles: Textual, Contextual, and Critical Interpretations* (Princeton, NJ: Princeton University Press, 2014), p. 52.

[21] Lipton, *Cultures of Witnessing*, especially pp. 4–5.

[22] Daisy Black, "Commanding Un-empty Space: Silence, Stillness and Scopic Authority in the York 'Christ before Herod,'" in Victoria Blud, Diane Heath, and Einat Klafter (eds.), *Gender in Medieval Places, Space, and Thresholds* (London: University of London Press: 2019), p. 237.

[23] Alfred John Horwood, ed., *Year Books of the Reign of King Edward the First* (London: Longmans, Greens and Roberts, 1863), p. 510.

[24] "Trial before Herod," in Clifford Davidson, ed. *The York Corpus Christi Plays* (Kalamazoo, MI: Medieval Institute Publications, 2011), p. 251, ll. 257–258. Hereafter cited parenthetically in the text.

[25] This practice is a standard feature of Mystery Plays; in the N-Town plays, Herod uses a *peine forte et dure* analogue when he instructs Annas and Caiaphas to beat Christ to force him to speak (Douglas Sugano, ed. *The N-Town Plays* [Kalamazoo, MI: Medieval Institute Publications, 2007], p. 256), and in the Chester version, Herod muses about the possibility that Christ is deaf or dumb or mad (David Mills, ed., *The Chester Mystery Cycle* [East Lansing, MI: Colleagues Press, 1992], p. 277).

This valence—that those who stand mute are Christlike—seems inescapable. Its obvious critique of the practice of forcing those who stand mute to plead is amplified in some versions by a direct critique. In the Cornish Ordinalia, doctors of the law have been brought to tell Pilate what he can legally do:

> by ny heuel dre lagha
>   y coth thotho bos dampnys
> tewel auel vn bobba
>   a wruk pan fue acussys
> nep a tawo yn pow-ma
>   thyrag iug ny fyth iuggys.[26]

> It never appears by law
>   That he ought to be condemned
> Hold his tongue like an idiot
>   He did, when he was accused
> Yet he who is silent in this country
>   Before a judge shall not be tried.

In which country? The superimposition of Jerusalem over Cornwall is particularly intense in this moment. In some ways, the doctors' insistence that Christ cannot be condemned just because he holds his tongue could refer to a nascent sense of protection from self-incrimination that R.H. Helmholz and H. Ansgar Kelly have argued began in the late fourteenth and early fifteenth centuries in canon law.[27] But they also surface what has been submerged under the routinized request for the plea and standard answer: the request for consent. It is easy to forget in the play's chaos of the multiple trials—just as it is easy to forget in trial's rote script—that the law has made a request, and it seems that Christ has said "no." The doctors also articulate another easily forgotten aspect of the procedure, which is that *peine forte et dure* alone does not actually resolve the question; if he continues to be silent, he still cannot be tried.

Although the demand to speak and the imposition of *peine forte et dure* was English, the plays strongly foreground the fact that Christ's justices are not, in order to distance them from him, who was surely meant to seem at least

---

[26] Edwin Norris, ed. *The Ancient Cornish Drama* (Oxford: Oxford University Press, 1859), pp. 412–413, ll. 2383–2388.
[27] R.H. Helmholz, "The Origins of the Privilege against Self-Incrimination: The Role of the European *Ius Commune*," *New York University Law Review* 65 (1990): pp. 962–990; Kelly, "The Right to Remain Silent," pp. 992–1026.

spiritually English. In the York Plays, when Christ stands silent in court, Herod first emphasizes their foreignness to each other, asking "is he king in his kyth where he come froo" ("Is he king in the region he comes from?" l. 230), and the Jewish king repeatedly uses the oath, "be Mahoundes bloode," drawing on the English Christian swear "by Christ's blood" but confusing Herod's Judaism for Islam.[28] In the Ordinalia, "this country" displaces Pilate even from where he currently stands, as though its ways might be unknown to him.

These examples frame standing mute as a virtue defined by both nation and religion. If Cecily's audience saw Christ in her, is this the virtue they saw? Indeed, perhaps the most tempting interpretation of her silence is that she is making a statement of protest, rejecting the authority of the court over her. In her book on *peine forte et dure*, Butler identifies a few places in the rolls where one person stands mute and seems to inspire a cascade of followers. Christina, wife of John Attehil, and her daughter Christina stand mute. Immediately after, so do Beatrice le Say of Brandon and Alice, wife of Nicholas Tascy. The women might have coordinated in prison, but later, men also follow suit: Thomas, son of Geoffrey, Roger, son of Richard Carkeny, and John le Spenser of Besthorpe.[29] Outcomes are not noted in the roll, but if it is unclear what Christina achieved for herself by standing mute, it is obvious she had an effect on others.[30] That standing mute was a contagious act bolsters the sense that it might have signaled protest, perhaps principled and supported by an audience trained to see Christ in the stoic, silent accused.

And we know that some victims of *peine forte et dure* did intend their silence as protest, in a religious context. Margaret Clitherow, probably the most famous female victim of *peine forte et dure*, was arrested for harboring Catholic priests, and she made it very clear that she considered standing mute a protest against Protestant tyranny.[31] Some less notorious victims also translated their standing mute into a kind of informal protest against injustice; an unnamed felon was brought to the bar and refused to speak because he said "that he was in a certain Church" ("que il fuit deins un certein Esglise") and was removed against his will, suggesting that he had claimed sanctuary and

---

[28] This sloppiness regarding the difference between Judaism and Islam was common in English literature dealing with Levantine characters, and as other scholars have noted, it is a typical move in building an English, Christian racial identity against an ill-defined other. Davidson, *The York Corpus Christi Plays*, p. 251.

[29] Butler, *Pain, Penance, and Protest*, p. 14.

[30] TNA, JUST 3/38, m. 27.

[31] Her most recent biography details this produre: Peter Lake and Michael Questier, *The Trials of Margaret Clitherow: Persecution, Martyrdom and the Politics of Sanctity in Elizabethan England* (New York City, NY: Bloomsbury, 2011).

been illegally removed.³² Robert de Kellesay, accused of conspiracy, said that "his enemies have such power in the City" that he knew would not find justice in a trial, and so would not "put himself upon the country" (the standard phrase for consenting to the jury trial).³³

But Cecily does not explain her silence to us, and the silent body in the play complicates any answer we might rush to give. In the York Plays, when Christ is returned from Herod's to Pilate's court, he is again commanded to plead. He finally speaks. But his answer is not a plea, nor does it rail against the power of the court. He has an opportunity to translate his own silence, perhaps into protest, or a denunciation of the injustice of foreign laws, as we might expect. Instead, he muses on the nature of speech itself:

> Every man has a mouthe that made is on molde
> In wele and in woo to welde at his will,
> If he governe it gudly like as God wolde
> For his spirituale speche hym not to spill. ("The Second Trial Before Pilate," ll. 300–3)³⁴

> Every man has a mouth that is made on the earth
> In well-being and in woe to wield at his will,
> If he governs it well like as God wants
> For him not to spill his spiritual speech.

Given an opportunity to tell us about his silence, he says that it is about ... saying nothing. Speech is given by God, but that does not mean that it should always be used; on the contrary, it is better to "govern it" so as "not to spill" it.

The passage draws on the penitential sense that, as Susan Phillips puts it, loose talk "was a disruptive force, blurring categories and crossing boundaries" not only in communities, but within the well-ordered and carefully enumerated divisions of sin.³⁵ The lines echo what Chaucer's Manciple tells us, "be war, and be noon auctour newe / Of tidynges, wheither they been false or trewe" (beware, and be no new author / Of tidings, whether they be false or

---

[32] YB Mich. 8 Hen. IV, p. 3 (Seipp 1406.104). Claiming sanctuary was a technical right, but as studies have shown, it was unevenly enforced not only across territories and jurisdictions, but also between cases within a single system. See: William Chester Jordan, "A Fresh Look at Medieval Sanctuary," in E. Ann Matter, Joel Kaye, and Ruth Mazo Karras (eds.), *Law and the Illicit in Medieval Europe* (Philadelphia: University of Pennsylvania Press, 2008), pp. 17–32.

[33] Helen M. Cam, *Year Books of the Reign of Edward II*, vol. 26, pt. 1: The Eyre of London, vol. 1, 85 SS 44–45 (Seipp 1321.114ss).

[34] Clifford Davidson, ed., *The York Corpus Christi Plays* (Kalamazoo, MI: Medieval Institute Publications, 2011), ll. 300–303.

[35] Phillips, *Transforming Talk*, p. 7.

true").[36] This recalls the ubiquitous penitential warnings about idle talk and unproductive speech.[37] As *The Book of Vices and Virtues* warns its readers, "Men clepen hem idele wordes, but thei beth not ydel, for thei beth wel dere and ful of harm and wel perilous" ("Men call them idle words, but they are not idle, for they are very costly and full of harm and very perilous").[38] In his *Liber Apologeticus de Omni Statu Humanae Naturae*, Thomas Chaundler warns, "let (Man) set a watch before his mouth and door round about his lips, before he brings forth hastily into the light anything about which silence must be kept."[39] The danger of words overflowing might also refer to a sense that the problem with unproductive speech was that it had a tendency to proliferate, accruing "efter telleres" who will spread it further beyond its original bounds.[40]

Loose talk was a sin, but a trial for one's life seems an odd place to go on this tangent. Indeed, the third and fourth lines return the governance of speech to God's will, but the first two lines place speech in the will of the speaker. And not temporarily or in conflict with God's will, but as a permanent state, "in wele and in woo." It proclaims, in a categorical sense, that each man's mouth is his own to govern. While the second half of the speech is a reminder of our responsibility to God's will, the first half is an assertion of a fundamental position—perhaps even right—of the accused. Combined with the Ordinalia's declaration that he who is silent shall not be tried, this speech not only reminds us that the law has asked a question of the accused ("how do you wish to acquit yourself?") but that the question was tied to an immovable control of every person over their own speech.

I argue that by turning our attention back to the not-speaking itself, this strange digression warns against the analogy we might want to make, the analogy that would render Cecily and her forty days without food and water the quintessential English saint, worthy of a legend. Such an association might have made it possible for the king to pardon her; her survival is called a "miracle." But in leaping to translate her, it is helpful to turn back to the text of her trial itself. All we know is that she was asked to speak and chose not to, even after the coercion of starvation. The play's sudden reminder that each person's voice is their own to govern cautions us against the temptation to simply override her governance over her own mouth. Though the intransitive for keeping silent had fallen away by Middle English, in the inheritance of the

---

[36] Chaucer, "The Manciple's Tale," in *The Riverside Chaucer*, ll. 359–360.
[37] Phillips's *Transforming Talk* argues that talk was not just a spiritual problem but a governance one; pastors were continually worried about losing control over their parishioners.
[38] W. Nelson Francis, ed., *The Book of Vices and Virtues*, 55.20–22.
[39] Thomas Chaundler, *Liber Apologeticus de Omni Statu Humanae Naturae*, ed. and trans. D. Enright-Clark Shoukri (Oxford: MHRA Publications, 1974), pp. 59–60.
[40] Morris and Gradon, *Dan Michel's Ayenbite of Inwit*, p. 58.

language, silence was not an absence but a choice. The Old English "swígan" and the Early Middle English "swien" for staying silent are both intransitive and complete in themselves.[41]

Keeping Mum

There was another strong current of thought about keeping quiet when asked to speak, especially in the political context, that associated it with anti-social, even anti-human qualities. Speaking out, speaking truth to power, could be a religious and (especially) political virtue. *Mum and the Sothsegger*, an early fifteenth-century alliterative poem in the *Piers Plowman* tradition, forcefully advocates for this version, identifying the silence of enabling advisors as the source of social and political decay. Keeping mum as a king's advisor may seem a bad fit for standing mute at a felony trial. But the way Mum is characterized— as a recalcitrant and ungrateful obstructor—is a far better match for the way standing mute is described in felony records than the example of Christ is. Chief Justice Gascoigne in 1406 justified his choice to send all defendants of a felony robbery case to pressing because, "when these felons stood mute, they refused every advantage; it was their malice."[42] As a character—a personification of silence where speech is called for—Mum gives us an opportunity to focus on what saying nothing does to those on the side of speech, and what its disruption does.

Those who have the truth are required to speak it, by God and by conscience. The tradition of the preacher's tongue as a plowshare that makes real God's will in the world goes back to before Gregory.[43] This work falls also to friends; Thomas Hoccleve's *Regement of Princes* advised that the best service to one another is to correct errors:

> Of conseil and of help been we dettours,
> Eche to othir, by right of brethirhede;
> For whan a man yfalle into errour is,
> His brothir owith him conseil and rede
> To correcte and amende his wikkid dede.[44]

---

[41] "swígan" in Joseph Bosworth, *An Anglo-Saxon Dictionary* (Oxford: Oxford University Press, 1921), p. 718; "swien" in A.L. Mayhew and W.W. Skeat, *A Concise Dictionary of Middle English from AD 1150 to 1580* (Oxford: Clarendon Press, 1888), p. 231.

[42] "car quant les felons estoient mutes ils refusent chaque avantage, il fuit de leur malice" (YB Mich. 8 Henry 4.2, 1b–2b [Seipp 1406.101]), published in *The Year Books; Or Reports*.

[43] S.A. Barney, "The Ploughshare of the Tongue: The Progress of a Symbol from the Bible to *Piers Plowman*," *Medieval Studies* 35 (1973): pp. 261–292.

[44] Thomas Hoccleve, *The Regiment of Princes*, ed. Charles Blyth (Kalamazoo, MI: Medieval Institute Publications, 1999), ll. 2486–2490.

> Of counsel and of help we are debtors,
> Each to another, by right of brotherhood;
> For when a man has fallen into error,
> His brother owes him counsel and speech
> To correct and amend his wicked deed.

Hoccleve intended to create good advisors to a king, but this passage communicates in a general sense that we are indebted to those around us, and that speaking out to correct one another is a way to discharge that debt.

This charge to speak also came with a sense of inevitability; not only is one required to speak, one is bound to speak in the end. An anonymous political poem from the time confidently asserts:

> And though truthe a while be slayn,
> And doluen depe vnder clay,
> Yut he wole ryse to lyue again
> And al the sothe he wole say.[45]

> And though the truth may be slain for a while
> And buried deep under clay
> Yet he will rise to live again
> And all the truth he will say.

In characterizing the Christ who is slain "a while" but will rise again not as the truth but as a truth-teller, the poem emphasizes that truth cannot rise by itself. It needs a speaker, someone who is alive to say it. After all, in the Old English *Dream of the Rood*, a human being is a "reordberend": one who bears speech.[46] A person is a speaker.

Mum and the Sothsegger is set up to be a debate between personifications of keeping silent and speaking out, but as many scholars have observed, it is no contest: Mum, Silence, is the obvious villain, an insidious force that damages society's most important institutions. Under his reign, poor men are left without an advocate at the law, and the silence of the king's advisors deafens the king to the voice of the people. *Mum* is part of a set of political literature that took aim at what it saw as the decadence of a world in its last days: venality and corruption, perpetual war, a child king (who was later deposed), the rise

---

[45] J. Kail, ed., *Twenty-Six Political and Other Poems* (London: EETS, 1904), pp. 17–18, ll. 101–104.
[46] Michael Swanton, ed., *The Dream of the Rood* (Exeter: University of Exeter, 1987), l. 3.

of dissenters against the church, a peasant uprising, a Great Famine, and the Black Death.

Helen Barr described the authors of this set as "literate members of society who may have been excluded from key positions of sacred or secular authority, but who were keen, in this time of flux and unrest, that their voices be heard."[47] *Mum*'s narrator repeats a saying popular in that literature, "And spare not to speke, spede yf thou mowe," ("And spare not to speak, which will profit you") which John Audelay, the *Mum* poet's contemporary, repeats and associates with literacy specifically: "Yif thou say not, then may won say / That thou art leud and unlerd and letter canste thou non" ("if you speak not, then may one say / that you are illiterate and unlearned and know not your letters").[48] In this world of urgent truth-telling, saying nothing when one ought to say something is not passive; it is an antisocial choice that actively cuts the world off from truth.

In its vilification of keeping mum, perhaps the poem gives us a better sense of what was so intolerable—to the law and to the justice—about silence in the court. The value of personification for our investigation is that Mum is not just how he is described, he is also everything he says and does. For the first part of the poem, the narrator vilifies Mum and his evils in a monologue; Mum has not yet arrived. When he finally does, his entrance is muscular:

> "Nomore of this matiere," cothe Mum thenne,
> "For I mervaille of thy momeling more thenne thou wenys ...
> And thou knowes this by clergie, how cans thou thee excuse
> That thou ne art nycier than a nunne nyne-folde tyme,
> Forto wite that thy wil thy witte shal passe?" (ll. 232–7)

> "No more of this matter," said Mum then,
> "For I marvel at your mumbling more than you know ...
> And you know this by theology/education, how can you excuse yourself,

---

[47] Helen Barr, ed., *The Piers Plowman Tradition: A Critical Edition of Pierce the Ploughman's Crede, Richard the Redeless, Mum and the Sothsegger, and The Crowned King* (Letchworth: J.M. Dent and Sons, 1993), p. 7. See also Edwin Craun, *Ethics and Power in Medieval English Reformist Writing* (Cambridge: Cambridge University Press, 2010), pp. 125–132.

[48] James M. Dean, ed., *Richard the Redeless and Mum and the Sothsegger* (Kalamazoo, MI: Medieval Institute Publications, 2000), l. 86, hereafter cited parenthetically in the text; John the Blind Audelay, "The Counsel of Conscience," l. 424, in *Poems and Carols (Oxford, Bodleian Library MS Douce 302)*, ed. Susanna Fein (Kalamazoo, MI: Medieval Institute Publications, 2009).

> That you are nine times more foolish than a nun,
> For you know that your will to speak surpasses your understanding?"

His entrance helps us clarify what kind of silence he is. Because Mum is a personification, the narrator's characterization of Mum—as an enemy of truth, text, and the quality of personhood—is silence, but Mum's speech, and what it does to this scene, is also silence. Silence, even when speech is called for, can signal many things. Indifference, for one; perhaps the silent person simply does not care enough to answer. It can also signal ignorance or shame, an inability to form the right speech. But this silence is aggressive and condescending: "How can you excuse yourself?" Mum shuts down the proceedings in his very first line ("No more of this matter"). Mum also humiliates the speaker; he breaks the association between speech and knowledge, characterizing the narrator's speech as willful, hasty, and not nearly so clarion as the narrator seems to think. The narrator's impassioned argument is reduced to "mumblings," and he is scolded for mistaking his will for righteousness: "your will to speak surpasses your understanding."

Of course, the irony of personifying silence and having it speak is not just that it makes silence not silent, but that it removes the indeterminacy and illegibility that characterize silence to begin with. This personification seems to limit the interpretive field of the poem; despite the provocative idea of making silence speak, Mum can only be a very particular kind of silence: judgmental, powerful, and silent only because his position has already been spoken into existence by the status quo. Mum's determinacy enables clear readings of the poem. For Stephen Yeager, Mum's instantiation of recalcitrant silence proves the poem the most "literate" of the *Piers Plowman* tradition, and Frank Grady argued that rendering silence as simple inaction makes the poem a "decisive turn away from the dream vision; the answer to the dream's own uncertain calls for reform and for an authoritative, written cultural criticism lies not in visionary poetics but in the documents and instruments of the workaday, wide-awake world."[49]

But if we continue, the rest of the passage does not linger on Mum's arrogance, or his recalcitrance. It focuses instead on the narrator's response, and how Mum's entrance has affected him:

---

[49] Stephen Yeager, *From Lawmen to Plowmen: Anglo-Saxon Legal Tradition and the School of Langland* (Toronto: University of Toronto Press, 2014), p. 260; Frank Grady, "Generation of 1399" in *The Letter of the Law: Legal Practice and Literary Production in Medieval England* (Ithaca, NY: Cornell University Press, 2002), p. 299.

> I blussid for his bablyng and abode stille
> And knytte there a knotte and construed no ferther;
> But yit I thoughte ere he wente, and he wold abide,
> To have a disputeson with hym and spie what he hatte.
> (ll. 239–42)
>
> I blushed for his babbling and stayed still
> And knit there a knot and explained no further;
> But yet I thought before he went, if he would stay,
> That I would have a disputation with him and see what he had.

After the narrator has railed against Mum in absentia for hundreds of lines, the enemy is finally before him. But Mum's interruption extends into disruption; the narrator, clearly taken aback, also lapses into silence. And he stays there, abides there, in contemplation, knitting a knot either literally or mentally. Mum's character has been contagious; the narrator becomes silent. When we encounter his voice again, it has been forced inside, into the narrator's thoughts, and is eager for Mum to stay ("But yet I thought before he went, if he would stay"). Mum's humiliating entrance ended his monologue, so he is forced to search out a different genre—a real disputation.

The focus of the passage seems to be the effect Mum has had on the narrator, which leads me to ask: is Mum aggressive because that is the kind of silence he is, or is he aggressive because silence, when speech is called for, feels aggressive? That is, does Mum personify the silence of a particular person or circumstance, or does Mum personify how silence seems to those who encounter it? It seems to me to be the latter, a reading which has the benefit of retaining the illegibility of silence by making Mum a shell of a personification, only mirroring back what people see in him. Mum is by no means the hero of the story. But his primary misdeed seems to be that he embodies the feeling of asking speech from someone and being refused, an infuriating experience especially if one believes one is entitled to it. His presence mounts a critique of the project of the poem; it is clear his offense as a character lies in the fact that the narrator takes offense to him, not in any primary characteristic of his own. In doing so, he lays bare all the demands and assumptions underlying the primary command to speak.

This version of silence, as opacity and provocation, might help us sketch a broader understanding of the refusal of standing mute that encompassed but was not confined to silence. "Standing mute" could also refer to speaking that did not fit the pattern of a plea; in another case, the king's attorney contended, "it is *as if* (*sicome*) he said nothing, because it is all the same when he pleads a plea which is no answer according to the order of the law, and when he says nothing."[50] Here is an example: in 1321, Isabel of Bury was accused of killing a priest.[51] When she is first brought before the court, she stands mute. The justice admonishes, "you would do better to speak." He explains that if she stays mute and it is found by inquest that she is able to speak, it will go badly for her. Cowed by this, she cries, "Sir, mercy for God's sake!" Pressed again to plea, she says, "Sir, I did it in self-defense." He says, "How do you wish to acquit yourself?" She says, "Sir, I did it in self-defense." With palpable impatience, he says, "Then, do you wish to say that you did not kill him?" She says, "I did it in self-defense." He insists, "You should deny the felony." She does, and is hanged.

We can see more clearly why a reminder that each man's mouth is his (or hers) to govern might be necessary. As Mum reflects the thinness of the narrator's critique of silence, so too does Isabel reflect the absurdity of the demand for speech. Of course, silence was not unwelcome in most parts of the trial. In fact, it was expected. It is only in this very limited moment that speech is demanded, and her sincere attempts to use the moment to communicate expose the demand's disingenuity. Thus, we can see that any answer (silent or spoken) that implied nonconsent or non sequitur truly "said nothing," because it exposed that the request for consent was coercive *and* also a real question to which "no" was a possible answer. It showed that the whole script was underwritten by a compliance that could be assured only by the torture it wished to alienate to outsiders, and that one could refuse this compliance. We can see perhaps why Christina's silence was contagious; once the script is both exposed and subverted, how can it be returned to the darkness of implication and suggestion?

*

This returns us to a question I posed at the outset of this chapter: what did this moment created for speech and silence signify, and why was it unique to felony

---

[50] "sicome il aver rien dit, car tout est un quant il pleda un plee le quel n'est respons solonque l'ordre del ley, & quant il ne parle riens" (YB Trin. 14 Edw 4.10, f. 7a [Seipp 1417.019]), published in *Les Reports des cases en ley que fuerunt argues en temps du roy Edward le Quart. Avec les notations de le tres reverend judges Brook & Fitz-Herbert. Et auter references n'unques devant imprimee. Ovesque un table perfect des choses notables contenus en ycel* (London: George Sawbridge, 1680). Also cited in Butler, *Pain, Penance, and Protest*, p. 85.

[51] Cam, Year Books, vol. 1, 85 SS 73–74. This case is referenced in several texts, including J.J. Jusserand, *English Wayfaring Life in the Middle Ages*, trans. Lucy Toulmin Smith (London: T. Fisher Unwin Ltd., 1889), p. 163, Lydia Stamato, "Presentment of Englishry at the Eyre of Kent, 1313" (Honors Thesis, Syracuse University, 2007), p. 69; Kamali, *Felony and the Guilty Mind*, p. 146, and Butler, *Pain, Penance, and Protest*, pp. 124–125.

procedure? As I mentioned, other forms of law—civil, trespass, ecclesiastical—were perfectly happy to translate an accused's silence into speech. Centuries later, the Criminal Law Act of 1772 (12 Geo. 3 c. 31) brought felony procedure in line with other forms of law. Under its provisions, standing mute became more than a guilty plea: the court "shall thereupon award judgement and execution against such person, in the same manner as if such person (had) been *convicted*."[52] This not only ended *peine forte et dure* but the whole dynamic: the request for consent, the court's dependance on the cooperation of the defendant, and any tension that might have been created by that dependance. But why did the procedure create this dynamic in the first place?

One compelling answer was that the question, "how do you wish to plead," and the reassuring answer that the defendant chose to "put himself on the country" truly did signal consent in a substantive way. Certainly, the existence of *peine forte et dure* while justices openly decried judicial torture suggests that there was something real at stake. This led Masschaele to the question, "why was consent to be tried so highly cherished that even torture was worth accepting to maintain it?"[53] Butler answered that the principle of consent was essential to English law, such that "justices and jurors saw rigorous fasting and even pressing as measures that protected a defendant's right to a fair trial by preventing him from being tried against his will."[54] If the consent conferred in this procedure truly is both substantive and necessary, *peine forte et dure* becomes the unfortunate price for a consent-based judicial proceeding, a price exacted on the defendant. This seems troubling, but not difficult to believe.

But I find it more surprising that the law would allow a price to be exacted on its own authority. Both Cecily and Isabel's justices betray some unease, some desperation in their attempts to make these women speak. When we focus on the silence and disruption itself, we can see that this unease might have stemmed from several simultaneous experiences. The first, as *Mum* reminds us, was that silence when speech is called for feels aggressive: not an affect a justice is accustomed to countenancing from a defendant. The second was probably a recognition that their own authority is made precarious by this request for consent. This experience of precarity was likely heightened by the comparison to Christ that lingered in the minds of the audience. But the experience did not require the analogue. The scene that was revealed by a

---

[52] Danby Pickering, ed. *The Statutes at Large, Anno duodecimo Georgii III. Regis. Being the Fifth Session of the Thirteenth Parliament of Great Britain*, vol. 29, part II (Cambridge: John Archdeacon, Printer to the University, 1772), p. 21; emphasis mine.
[53] Masschaele, *Jury, State, and Society*, p. 82.
[54] Butler, *Pain, Penance, and Protest*, p. 21

defendant's refusal to plead—a felony court asking a defendant's consent to try her—abdicates quite enough responsibility without it.

The landscape upon which the argument of this book depends is one in which crown justices were happy to let much of the practical tasks in the procedure of felony—collecting evidence, finding suspects, determining guilt—fall to ordinary people, who were almost always untrained in the law. As the cases and examples of this book have demonstrated, the people who took up the task of creating felony law approached the work with seriousness and intellectual rigor. They decided what role physical evidence should play in proof, they weighed the value of reputation against the evils of idle talk, and they ruled life and death over their neighbors. Lay people created felony law and the felony court, and so perhaps the court itself ended up having to share the reins over its own order, whether it liked it or not. When the law ceded so much conceptual work, it also ceded some narrative control.

Let us return to Cecily. I suggest that we might be wary of our own impulses to see righteous protest (or anything else) in her. We should remember that her justice also wants to make her speak, to translate her "nothing" into "something." We have no record of the exact exchange between her and her justice, but Isabel's justice offers us an example of what it might have looked like. This justice recalls Cecily's in his repeated attempts to make her speak, to translate this "nothing" into "something." Is she indifferent? He menaces her. Is she saying she cannot comply? A jury can investigate that. Does she not know what to say? He tells her.

But of course, she does not say any of those things. In fact, one of the only things we can be sure of is how hard she worked not to speak. I am inclined to attend to this. Pleading in a felony trial was a rare moment within medieval law—and perhaps society—in which everyone's consent was equally necessary; a woman's consent as necessary as a man's, a shipman's as necessary as a lord's. Isabel wants to communicate something specific; that she acted in fear of her life, but also that she did do it, a more complex concept than is possible in this moment, legally speaking—but perhaps it was the only moment when she could say it.

If we want to translate Cecily, we might imagine that her forty days and nights in starvation might have been meant to communicate something as well. Recall, she is being charged with petty treason: treason against one's petty lord. Her resistance to taking part in a trial might reference abuse, or mitigating circumstances, or self-defense. She is being tried and held among her neighbors, in a world where few people ever left home, a society knit together by the power of gossip. If she had killed her husband in self-defense, surely some in the courtroom audience knew this, possibly even saw this coming, and did not stop it. So, she could be saying that, doing that.

But the Mystery Plays and *Mum* remind us to attend to the disruption itself, rather than smooth it into a clear declaration, as we might be tempted to. Isabel's justice offers her an exculpatory translation: "You should say, not guilty." Even though this does not work out for Isabel, it was not bad advice; around 80 percent of felony trials ended in acquittal.[55] Perhaps Cecily's justice offered her the same. If so, she did not take it. Instead, she understands this request for consent as an opportunity, a moment in which she is allowed to have the floor and have it bear real consequence. One can imagine this might have been an unusual moment for her. Cecily refuses to abdicate it, refuses to say what she does not mean, or does not want to say, even if it costs her her life. Perhaps reading her well means ceding her this space.

---

[55] See my discussion of conviction rates in Chapter 4.

Epilogue

I began my Introduction by observing a conceptual flaw in felony law. In meticulously removing from the felon a future that most of us desire, felony law makes visible what a life worth living means. And yet, the law never defines it. Any parameters we might attribute to its meaning have derived from its practice. The purpose of legal procedure is to make real the law's concepts, but felony moves in the other direction, deriving its reality from its procedure. The chapters of this book have traced how those tasked with felony's practice rose to the occasion, but it has also demonstrated how contingent these practices were, dependent on the specific actors and their prejudices, desires, and interests. This conceptual dynamic—which seems to me to be felony's primary characteristic—deserves more sustained attention.

We might start with its impressive resilience as a category. In US law today, felony remains "as bad a word as you can give to a man or a thing," one which merits the permanent separation of the felon from ordinary life.[1] Felony's gravity has justified an array of collateral consequences from the political (like disenfranchisement) to the personal (like the termination of parental rights).[2] And yet, as Alice Ristroph observes, "there is no uniform principle or logic that explains which criminal conduct is designated as felonious and which is not."[3] It continues to be defined only by its punishment (more than one year in prison), which extends it to crimes that no one would consider particularly

---

[1] *Morissette v. United States*, 342 U.S. 246, 260 (1952), which quotes from Frederick Pollack and Frederic Maitland, *The History of English Law Before the Time of Edward I*, vol. 2 (Cambridge: Cambridge University Press, 1895), p. 465.

[2] For examples of studies of the variety of collateral consequences, see: Claire K. Child and Stephanie A. Clark, "SNAP Judgments: Collateral Consequences of Felony Drug Convictions for Federal Food Assistance," *Berkeley Journal of Criminal Law* 26, no. 2 (2021): pp. 1–26; Nick Sibilla, "Barred from Working: A Nationwide Study of Occupational Licensing Barriers for Ex-Offenders," Publication of the *Institute for Justice*, 2020, https://ij.org/report/barred-from-working/; Lauren N. Hancock, "Another Collateral Consequence: Kicking the Victim When She's Down," *Washington and Lee Review* 77 (2020): pp. 1319-1374; Christopher Uggen and Robert Stewart. "Piling On: Collateral Consequences and Community Supervision," *Minnesota Law Review* 99 (2014): pp. 1871-1920; Sarah Berson, "Beyond the Sentence: Understanding Collateral Consequences," *National Institute of Justice Journal* 25 (2013): pp. 25–28. For a discussion of public opinion on the subject, see: Alexander L. Burton, et al., "Beyond the New Jim Crow: Public Support for Removing and Regulating Collateral Consequences," *Federal Probation Journal* 84 (2020): p. 19.

[3] Alice Ristroph, "Farewell to the Felonry," *Harvard Civil Rights–Civil Liberties Law Review* 54 (2018): p. 613.

villainous, like mail fraud or recordkeeping failures.[4] Far more felonies are committed than can be prosecuted, and so it continues to derive its definition from its practice, which depends heavily on the choices and relationships of local police, district attorneys, and judges. We can perceive the medieval concept of felony preserved, almost in its entirety, in its modern instantiation.

Today, felony's combination of severity and contingency is widely recognized as harmful; scholars have harshly criticized the cruelty and randomness of its collateral consequences and have proven that the classification of felony is central to mass incarceration and has formed a de facto continuation of segregation.[5] And yet, it remains. Why do we retain a concept that is incoherent, vulnerable to abuse and inconsistency, and which we know to contribute to unequal treatment before the law? I am certainly not the first person to ask this. Indeed, some jurisdictions (like those of the UK and Canada) have shifted these crimes onto a spectrum that encompasses all criminal offenses. Based on this possibility, Ristroph argues convincingly for felony's complete abolition in the US system.[6] But if we find this outcome difficult to imagine, perhaps we might ask the question differently—what does this concept do for us that we are reluctant to relinquish?

As the persistence of the term suggests—and as I have attempted to show in this book—felony may not have a legal definition, but it does have a conceptual history. Felony began in both literature and the law as a species of treason, with a definition that told a whole story: the betrayal of one to whom you had pretended to be a friend.[7] This narrative beginning yielded a version of felony that could lurk in the quality of an act. In literature, the term was sometimes used adjectivally ("felon folk") and adverbially ("felonlich").[8] This use—as a quality of action rather than an act—might help us understand the phrase Elizabeth Kamali notes in the legal record: a *felonia felonice facta*, a

---

[4] 18 USC § 3559.
[5] Elena Saxonhouse, "Unequal Protection: Comparing Former Felons' Challenges to Disenfranchisement and Employment Discrimination," *Stanford Law Review* 56, no. 6 (2004): pp. 1597–1639; Margaret Colgate Love, "Deconstructing the New Infamy," *Criminal Justice* 16 (2001): pp. 30–62; Nora V. Demleitner, "Preventing Internal Exile: The Need for Restrictions on Collateral Sentencing Consequences," *Stanford Law & Policy Review* 11 (1999): pp. 153–171.
[6] Ristroph, "Farewell to the Felonry."
[7] See Introduction. *Britton* (the first judicial treatise to use the category as a crime rather than a feudal offense) describes felony as "any mischief, which a man knowingly does, or procures to be done, to one to whom he pretends to be a friend" (Jean le Breton, *Summa de legibus Angliae que vocatur Bretone*, ed. Francis Nichols, 2 vols. [Oxford: Clarendon Press, 1865], vol. 1, p. 40).
[8] "The Trial before Caiaphas and Pilate," l. 16,472 in *Cursor Mundi (The Cursur O the World): A Northumbrian Poem of the XIVth Century in Four Versions*, ed. Richard Morris (London: Published for the EETS by K. Paul, Trench, Trübner & Co., 1874–1893); "Thow (Satan) fettest myne in my place … Falseliche & felounelich," William Langland, *Piers Plowman: A Parallel Text Edition of the A, B, C and Z versions*, ed. A.V.C. Schmidt (Kalamazoo, MI: Medieval Institute Publications, 2008), B 18.349.

felony done feloniously.[9] Such redundant language persisted well into the seventeenth century, where Chief Justice Hobart observes in the case *Weaver v Ward* that accident cannot be felony, because "felony must be done *animo felonico*."[10] As Kamali has observed, this seeming redundancy (can a felony be done nonfeloniously?) suggests that a quality of "feloniousness" is the bar for conviction, not the act itself. On this basis, she has argued that medieval juries had a strong sense of *mens rea*, and it was its presence that distinguished a felony.[11] In his "Parson's Tale," Chaucer bolsters this argument with a fairly clear definition of what this might have looked like; it "comth of felonie of herte avysed and cast biforn, with wikked wil to do vengeance, and therto his resoun consenteth" ("comes of felony of the heart, thought through and planned beforehand, with a wicked will to do vengeance, to which his reason consents").[12] A felony was any act with felonious qualities intended and willed even in the light of reason.

But the most common use of the term was even more obviously indebted to its narrative roots—it could refer to a quality of a person. Judas was the original felon, but literary characters received the label as well; in *Havelok the Dane* (1280), the villainous Godard is "a felon, who plans a full strong treachery, a treason."[13] The pagans in the chanson de geste *Song of Roland* (c.1140–1170) are "felons, deceitful traitors."[14] In these examples, these people are not made felons because they are the antagonists of their stories. In the law, to be a felon was to be categorically different than other people, even other criminals. To return to an example from Chapter 4, theft and robbery might seem to us to exist on a spectrum of the same crime. Theft—a trespass—was punished according to the amount stolen, recidivism, need, and other mitigating factors, with the intention of eventual rehabilitation. A robber, however, was a felon, an entirely different kind of person. If a jury convicted a robber, of however much money and of however much damage, he would hang. James Mudie articulated

---

[9] Elizabeth Kamali, *Felony and the Guilty Mind in Medieval England* (Cambridge: Cambridge University Press, 2019), p. 33.
[10] *Weaver v Ward*, King's Bench (1616) 80 Eng. Rep. 284.
[11] For an example of the argument that *mens rea* did not reach back to the medieval period, see Nicola Lacey, "Psychologizing Jekyll, Demonising Hyde: The Strange Case of Criminal Responsibility," *Criminal Law and Philosophy* 4, no. 2 (2010): pp. 109–133; Kamali, pp. 270–302. Locating felony as the start of a theory of *mens rea* has particularly interesting connotations for present conversations about *mens rea* reform as a way of mitigating statutes seen to be too punitive. See for a summary of the debate: Benjamin Levin, "Mens Rea Reform and Its Discontents," *Journal of Criminal Law and Criminology* 109, no. 3 (2019): pp. 491–558.
[12] "The Parson's Tale," paragraph 35 in Geoffrey Chaucer, *The Riverside Chaucer*, eds. Larry Dean Benson, and F.N Robinson (Boston: Houghton Mifflin, 1987).
[13] William W. Skeat, ed., *The Lay of Havelok the Dane*, EETS e.s. 4 (London: EETS by N. Trübner, 1868), p. 14.
[14] Raoul Mortier, ed., *Les Textes de la Chanson de Roland* (Paris: La Geste Francor, 1940), p. 28.

the permanence of being a felon more directly in 1837: "A convicted felon is unworthy both of future trust and of mingling with and participating in the provident arrangements or the social enjoyments of his former associates and fellow subjects."[15]

In this sense, a felon was always already a felon; the crime simply revealed it. This version of felony—as an act that unmasks the felon behind it—accords with our modern reactions to felony and felons far better than a version in which the act transforms one into a felon, or in which one's motivations make an act a felony. Consider, for example, the charge of felony murder, in which any killing that occurs in the perpetration of a felony is charged as murder, whether the death had been intended or not.[16] If we believed that felony is an action, then only the original felony (say, armed robbery) would be charged as one. If we believed that the felonious mind—the intentions or malice aforethought—made the felony, then an unintended death would not be murder. We would only charge accidental deaths as murder if we believed that the original felony revealed the essential villainy of the perpetrator, such that we could justifiably add the quality of felony to all his actions.

The hypothesis that I forward here—that we treat felony as though we believe it reveals an essential villainy—also makes better sense of the permanence and variety of the collateral consequence regimes in the USA today. Collateral consequences are the permanent consequences for convicted felons, and they apply even to those who do not serve any time at all. These can include permanent disenfranchisement, refusal of social services, ineligibility for professional licensing in a variety of professions, removal of permanent resident status, and even grounds for divorce with cause. They have been harshly criticized for creating a permanent legal underclass (roughly 8 percent of American adults have a felony conviction), and for their apparent capricious cruelty.[17] As consequences for a single act, they make little sense, and they habitually undermine our "commonsense notion ... that punishment ends when the offender is released from prison."[18] But attempts to remove collateral consequences have been met with failure in both legislatures and public perception, because a felon is a villain, not a person who committed a crime.

---

[15] James Mudie, *The Felonry of New South Wales: Being A Faithful Picture of the Real Romance of Life in Botany Bay* (London: Whaley and Co., 1837), p. 21, cited in Ristroph, "Farewell to the Felonry," pp. 579–580.

[16] For a history of the felony murder rule, see Guyora Binder, "The Origins of American Felony Murder Rules," *Stanford Law Review* 57 (2004): pp. 59–208.

[17] Berson, Beyond the Sentence," p. 25.

[18] McCarley Maddock, "Done the Time, Still Being Punished for the Crime: The Irrationality of Collateral Consequences in Occupational Licensing and Fourteenth Amendment Challenges," *Duke Journal of Constitutional Law and Public Policy Sidebar* 18 (2022–2023): pp. 21–46.

I am vividly reminded of *Piers Plowman*'s self-righteous Will and his creative partner, Imaginatif. Unwilling to allow the Good Thief's punishment to end after his crucifixion, Imaginatif attempts to extend it even into heaven:

> For he that is ones a thef is evermore in daungere,
> And as lawe lyketh, to lyve or to deye:
> *De peccato propiciato noli esse sine metu.* (B 12.206–7)

> For he that is once a thief is evermore in danger,
> And as the law likes, to live or to die:
> *Be not without fear for a sin propitiated.*

There is no end to felony. It persists beyond punishment, spiritual rebirth, even the grace of God. In Middle English, the term "felony" and *felonia* traversed legal, literary, and religious contexts, a breadth that has eased the way of this study. Today, "felony" is no longer used in nonlegal speech (in the sense that one would not speak of "felonious" conduct outside of the context of its legal ramifications), but we would be mistaken to believe that in this narrowing it has sloughed off its conceptual history. We treat felons today as though they suffer from a permanent disarrangement of the soul.

If, as it turns out, felony does have a definition, why have we never enshrined this principle in the law? My conclusions here are more tentative, as I am neither a lawyer nor a scholar of the US context. But I believe felony's utility lies in leaving it unarticulated. Felony's lack of definition is not a flaw, it is a conceptual strength that allows it to stand for concepts that we prefer to leave unspecified. Recognizing felony's fundamental incoherence, some have suggested modifications to impose rational boundaries on the category, like excluding from it all crimes that are not violent, sexual, or serious.[19] Likewise, some have suggested excluding those whose capacity for culpability is in question, like juveniles.[20] These measures are framed as reformist, but as Marie Gottschalk has observed, they only reinforce the idea that (once these cases are excluded) there exists a "true crime" to which the category of felony applies.[21] That is, they provide bright lines that make the category appear more rational but always leave the concept untouched, unsaid.

---

[19] Margo Schlanger, "*Plata v. Brown* and Realignment: Jails, Prisons, Courts, and Politics," *Harvard Civil Rights–Civil Liberties Law Review* 48 (2013): p. 185.

[20] See for example: Barry C. Feld, "The Youth Discount: Old Enough to Do the Crime, Too Young to Do the Time," *Ohio State Journal of Criminal Law* 11 (2013): pp. 107–148.

[21] Marie Gottschalk, *Caught: The Prison State and the Lockdown of American Politics* (Princeton, NJ: Princeton University Press, 2015), p. 165.

In the Introduction, I used Chaucer's passage on felony's "dark imagining" to observe that we define felony by the effects, motivations, and reactions that surround it, rather than by the act itself. But the passage also demonstrates the benefit of this arrangement: we are allowed to think we know what it means without ever being asked to say. It is:

> The pykepurs, and eek the pale Drede;
> The smylere with the knyf under the cloke;
> The shepne brennynge with the blake smoke;
> The tresoun of the mordrynge in the bedde;
> The open werre, with woundes al bibledde. (I.1995–2002)[22]

> The pick-pocket, and also the pale Dread;
> The smiler with the knife under the cloak;
> The sheepbarn burning with the black smoke;
> The treason of the murdering in the bed;
> The open war, with wounds all bled.

We know that felony is not built by concepts essential to the acts or perpetrators, and that it is by the historically and socially contingent choices of those who prosecute it. And yet this passage still seems coherent; as though felony can be both a smiler and black smoke, treason and open war. If we cannot quite trace its contours, we still leave the passage with the sense that we have grasped essential concepts, not historical contingencies. We assume that even if we did not recognize Felonye when we saw him, surely the law would. This assumption is what made the work of the people in this book possible, and it is what makes possible the modern prosecution of felony. It allows us to justify placing a wide and incoherent assemblage of crimes under felony's purview, and to punish them with a wide and incoherent assemblage of (permanent) consequences; don't worry, the law will know the difference.

When I began a version of this project years ago, I was interested in punishment, rather than investigation. I thought I might explore how medieval courts decided what punishment should follow what crime, and how this calculation was made. Should a punishment form an equivalence of harm? A deterrence? A satisfying retribution for the victim? Just like the questions that animate this book, it struck me that these were issues on which the law was unclear and for which literature provided the most guidance. The documents made this direction difficult, but I had a hard time giving it up. I realize now that my mind had

---

[22] Chaucer, "The Knight's Tale," in *The Riverside Chaucer*.

snagged on the standard statement of punishment's justification: that offenses should be punished. This is a live formulation in punishment theory today; Michael S. Moore (to name just one example) founds his comparison of different theories on the assumption that, "prima facie, all moral wrongs culpably done should be criminalized."[23]

While these statements aim to describe the reciprocity of action between crime and punishment, it is hard not to linger on their passivity ("should be punished"/"should be criminalized"). Once you do, you begin to notice that similar sentiments are almost always constructed in the same way. In a formal sense, a passive construction obscures the actor. In this case, the obscurity functions to make the actor seem larger than life, to give the impression that our system of punishment acts with such global and unified purpose that naming it would be unnecessary. But of course, the actual actors are discrete and identifiable, as we have seen throughout the examples in this book. It was not "the law" that punished the Northhamptonshire men of Chapter 3; their fine was the result of a specific, delicate compromise between Chief Justice Scrope on the one side and former mayor Simon Laushull on the other. Though so much has changed in the procedure itself, the actors today are not less identifiable. In the United States, the vast majority of criminal cases (felonies included) are decided by plea bargains, and these are each determined by the individual relationships and negotiations of local police, prosecutors, and judges.

Nothing could be more contingent. And yet when we talk about crime and punishment more broadly, we default to formulations in which there is no linguistic place for these actors, so that we can rid the law of any impression of contingency. Felony allows us to do this, despite its conceptual instability and lack of definition as a legal category. It allows us to assume—without requiring us to specifically describe—an archetype of crime and criminality that "should be punished," that conjures its own punishment against itself.[24] Berson has shown that prosecutors and defense attorneys rarely consider the collateral consequences of felony in the negotiation of plea deals, even though their effects can be the gravest on the convicted.[25] To consider these consequences would be to admit that, for us, felony is something more than "any crime punishable by more than a year in prison." We depend on Chaucer's

---

[23] Michael S. Moore, "A Tale of Two Theories," *Criminal Justice Ethics* 28, no. 1 (2009): p. 31.
[24] I am grateful here to Elizabeth Fowler's incisive question to me after I presented my fifth chapter: "You speak of 'the law' as a person. Is it a person?" This question allowed me to realize the centrality of felony to the fiction that the law operates independently and univocally.
[25] Berson, "Beyond the Sentence," p. 26.

"derke ymaginyng." The black smoke, the betrayed bed, and the cloak invoke our inchoate sense that felony exists and that it—by its very existence—calls up society's punishment. It allows us to conceive of the law in the passive voice; it is not people who punish crime, it is felony that brings the law down upon it. This is a fiction that would not survive any scrutiny, and so we leave it alone.

The fact that felony has retreated from nonlegal use has perhaps only made it easier to hide from ourselves what we believe it to mean, and to preserve a place in the law for our emotional reactions to what we perceive to be essential villainy. It is not through the Thief's punishment that we know that he is a felon. Instead, we know he is a felon because of Will's reaction, his disgust and horror that brings the Thief into view again and again, almost reflexively. Like Will, we deprive felons of a good life reflexively, habitually, with revulsion. It might be valuable to think about why we draw the boundaries of our society in this way, why we prefer not to look while we do it, and what a life worth living means in such a society.

Works Cited

Manuscripts

Kew, The National Archives
JUST 1/635 (Justices in Eyre, of Assize, of Oyer and Terminer, and of the Peace)
JUST 1/636
JUST 1/643
JUST 1/664
JUST 2/61 (Coroners' Rolls and Files, with Cognate Documents)
JUST 2/94
JUST 3/38 (Justices of Jail Delivery: Jail Delivery Rolls and Files)
JUST 3/48
KB 27/313 (Jail Delivery: King's Bench Plea Rolls)
KB 27/695

Edinburgh, National Library of Scotland
Adv. MS 19.2.1 (*The Pistil of Swete Susan*)

Lincoln, Lincoln Cathedral Library
MS 169

London, The British Library
MS Add. 10596 (*The Pistil of Swete Susan*)
MS Add. 22283 (Simeon Manuscript, *The Pistil of Swete Susan*)
MS Cotton Caligula A.ii (*The Pistil of Swete Susan*, missing first 104 lines)
MS Harley 2851 (Alan of Melsa, *Tractatus metricus de Susanna*)

London Metropolitan Archives
DL/C/B/043/MS09064 (commissary court act books)
COL/CS/01/002 (*Liber Horn*)

Oxford, The Bodleian Library
English Poet, a. 1 (Vernon Manuscript, *The Pistil of Swete Susan*)
Christ Church, MS 103 (*Placita corone*)
Exeter College, MS 115 (Year Books, 20 Henry 6)
Exeter College, MS 134 (*Placita corone*)
Tanner, MS. 13 (Year Books, 1 Edward 2–15 Edward 2)

Printed Primary and Reference Volumes

The Ancient Cornish Drama. Edited by Edwin Norris (Oxford: Oxford University Press, 1859).
The Anonimalle Chronicle, 1307 to 1334: from Brotherton Collection MS 29. Edited by Wendy Childs and John Taylor (Cambridge: Cambridge University Press, 2013).
An anonymous monk of Whitby. *The Earliest Life of Gregory the Great.* Edited and translated by Bertram Colgrave (Lawrence, KS: University of Kansas Press, 1968).
Thomas Aquinas. *The Sermon-Conferences of St. Thomas Aquinas on the Apostles' Creed*, Leonine Edition. Edited and translated by Nicholas Ayo (Notre Dame: University of Notre Dame Press, 1988).
Thomas Aquinas, *Summa Theologica*, 3 vols. Edited and translated by The Fathers of the Dominican Province (Cincinnati, OH: Benziger Bros., 1947).
John the Blind Audelay. *Poems and Carols (Oxford, Bodleian Library MS Douce 302).* Edited by Susanna Fein (Kalamazoo, MI: Medieval Institute Publications, 2009).
Augustine. *The Retractations.* In *The Fathers of the Church*, vol. 60, translated by Mary Inez Bogan (Washington, DC: Catholic University of America, 1968).
Augustine. *The Works of St. Augustine: Sermons.* Edited by John E. Rotelle and translated by Edmund Hill (New York: New City, 1995).
Barr, Helen, ed. *The Piers Plowman Tradition: A Critical Edition of Pierce the Ploughman's Crede, Richard the Redeless, Mum and the Sothsegger, and The Crowned King* (Letchworth: J.M. Dent and Sons, 1993).
Bentham, Jeremy. *The Rationale of Punishment* (London: Robert Heward, 1830).
Blackstone, William. *Commentaries on the Laws of England in Four Volumes* (Philadelphia: Lippincott Company, 1893).
Boethius. "De topicis differentiis libri quatuor." In *Patrilogia Latina*, vol. 64, edited by Jacques Paul Migne (Paris: Garnier, 1860), pp. 445–475.
Bonaventure. *St. Bonaventure's Commentary on the Gospel of Luke*, 8 vols. Edited and translated by Robert Karris (New York: Franciscan Institute Publications, 2004).
Bosworth, Joseph. *An Anglo-Saxon Dictionary* (Oxford: Oxford University Press, 1921).
Jean le Breton. *Summa de legibus Angliae que vocatur Bretone.* Edited by Francis Nichols (Oxford: Clarendon Press, 1865).
Robert of Brunne. *Robert of Brunne's "Handlyng Synne," A.D. 1303: With those Parts of the Anglo-French Treatise on which It Was Founded, William of Wadington's "Manuel des Pechiez,"* Edited by Frederick Furnivall. EETS, o.s. 119 (London: EETS, 1901).
Calendar of Patent Rolls, Preserved in the Public Record Office and Prepared under the Superintendence of the Deputy Keeper of the Records, 1216–1509, 55 vols. (London: HMSO, 1891–1916).
Cam, Helen M., ed. *Year Books of the Reign of Edward II*, vol. 26 (Part I): The Eyre of London (London: Bernard Quaritch, 1968).
Cameron, Christopher. "Saint Erkenwald" (MA thesis, Emporia University, 1993).
Geoffrey Chaucer. *The Riverside Chaucer.* Edited by Larry D. Benson (Boston: Houghton Mifflin, 1987).
Thomas Chaundler. *Liber Apologeticus de Omni Statu Humanae Naturae.* Edited and translated by D. Enright-Clark Shoukri (Oxford: MHRA Publications, 1974).
Childs, Wendy, and John Taylor, eds. *The Anonimalle Chronicle, 1307 to 1334: From Brotherton Collection MS 29* (Cambridge: Cambridge University Press, 2013).
Chobham, Thomas. *Summa Confessorum.* Edited by F. Broomfield (Paris: Louvain, 1968).

150 WORKS CITED

Davidson, Clifford, ed. *The York Corpus Christi Plays* (Kalamazoo, MI: Medieval Institute Publications, 2011).
de Lorris, Guillaume and Jean de Meun. *Roman de la Rose*, 3 vols., edited by Félix Lecoy (Paris: Champion, 1965).
de Walsingham, Thomas. *Historia Anglicana*, 2 vols., edited by Henry Thomas Riley (London: Longman et al., 1862–1864).
Dean, James M., ed. *Richard the Redeless and Mum and the Sothsegger* (Kalamazoo, MI: Medieval Institute Publications, 2000).
Doyle, A.I., ed. *The Vernon Manuscript: A Facsimile of Bodleian Library, Oxford, MS. Eng. Poet. a.1* (Cambridge: D. S. Brewer, 1987).
Elder, Carol. "Gaol Delivery in the Southwestern Counties, 1390–1416" (PhD diss., Carleton University, 2014).
Elder, Carol. "Gaol Delivery in the Southwestern Counties, 1416–1430" (MA thesis, Carleton University, 1983).
Fitzherbert, Anthony, ed. *La graunde abridgement* (London: John Rastell and Wynkyn de Worde, 1516).
John Fortescue. *De Laudibus Legum Angliae*. Edited and translated by Stanley Chrimes (Cambridge: Cambridge University Press, 2011).
Fowler, Herbert G., ed. *Calendar of the Roll of the Justices on Eyre, 1247* (Aspley Guise: Bedfordshire Historical Record Society, 1939).
Francis, W. Nelson, ed. *The Book of Vices and Virtues: A 14th-Century English Translation of the* Somme Le Roi *of Lorens d'Orléans* (London: EETS, 1942).
Furber, Elizabeth Chapin, ed. *Essex Sessions of the Peace, 1377–1379* (Colchester: Wiles & Sons Ltd for the Essex Archaeological Society, 1953).
Ginsberg, Warren, ed. *Wynnere and Wastour and The Parlement of Thre Ages*. (Kalamazoo, MI: Medieval Institute Publications, 1992).
Given-Wilson, Chris, P. Brand, A. Curry, et al., eds. *The Parliament Rolls of Medieval England*. (Leicester: Scholarly Editions, 2005). http://sd-editions.com/PROME/home.html.
John Gower. *The Complete Works of John Gower*, 4 vols. Edited by G.C. Macauley (Oxford: Clarendon Press, 1899–1902).
John Gower. *Confessio Amantis*, 3 vols. Edited by Andrew Galloway and Russell Peck (Kalamazoo, MI: Medieval Institute Publications, 2004).
Gregory. *Moralia in Iob*. Edited by M. Adriaen (Turnhout: Brepols, 1979).
Gross, Charles, ed. *Select Cases from the Coroners' Rolls, A.D. 1265–1413, With a Brief Account of the History of the Office of Coroner* (London: Bernard Quaritch, 1896).
Walter Guisborough. *The Chronicle of Walter of Guisborough*. Edited by H. Rothwell (London: Camden Society, 1957).
Hall, G.D.G., ed. and trans. *The Treatise on the Laws and Customs of the Realm of England Commonly Called Glanvill* (Oxford: Clarendon Press, 1994).
Hanawalt, Barbara A., ed. and trans. *Crime in East Anglia in the Fourteenth Century: Norfolk Gaol Delivery Rolls, 1307–1316* (Norwich: Norfolk Record Society, 1976).
Thomas Hoccleve. *The Regiment of Princes*. Edited by Charles Blyth (Kalamazoo, MI: Medieval Institute Publications, 1999).
Andrew Horne. *Mirror of Justices*. Edited by William Joseph Whittaker (London: Selden Society, 1895).
Horwood, Alfred John, ed. *Year Books of the Reign of King Edward the First* (London: Longmans, Greens, and Roberts, 1863).

Hunnisett, R.F., ed. and trans. *Bedfordshire Coroners' Rolls* (Streatley: Bedfordshire Historical Record Society, 1961).
Hunnisett, R.F., ed. *Sussex Coroners' Inquests* (Lewes: Sussex Record Society, 1985).
Johnstone, Hilda, and T.F. Tout, eds. *State Trials of the Reign of Edward the First, 1289–1293* (London: Royal Historical Society, 1906).
Kail, J., ed. *Twenty-Six Political and Other Poems*. EETS, o.s. 124 (London: EETS, 1904).
Kaye, Joel, ed. and trans. *Placita Corone or La Corone Pledee devant Justices* (London: Selden Society, 1966).
Kimball, Elisabeth G., ed. and trans. *A Cambridgeshire Gaol Delivery Roll, 1332–1334* (Cambridge: Cambridge Antiquarian Records Society, 1978).
Henry Knighton. *Knighton's Chronicle 1337–1396*. Edited and translated by G.H. Martin (Oxford: Oxford University Press, 1996).
Kölbing, E., ed. *The Romance of Sir Beues of Hamtoun* (London: N. Trübner, 1885).
William Langland. *Piers Plowman: A Parallel Text Edition of the A, B, C and Z versions*. Edited by A.V.C. Schmidt (Kalamazoo, MI: Medieval Institute Publications, 2008).
Laskaya, Anne and Eve Salisbury, eds. *The Middle English Breton Lays* (Kalamazoo, MI: Medieval Institute Publications, 1995).
Liebermann, F., ed. *Die Gesetze der Angelsachsen*, 4 vols. (Tübingen: Halle a.S. Max Niemeyer, 1898–1916).
Lindberg, Conrad, ed. *The Earlier Version of the Wycliffite Bible* (Stockholm: Almqvist and Wiksell, 1973).
Maitland, Frederic W., Leveson W. Vernon Harcourt, and William C. Boland, eds. *The Eyre of Kent of 6 and 7 Edward II (1313–1314)* (London: Selden Society, 1909).
Malcom, Andrew, and Ronald Waldron, eds. *The Poems of the Pearl Manuscript* (Liverpool: Liverpool University Press, 2008).
Mayhew, A.L. and W.W. Skeat. *A Concise Dictionary of Middle English from AD 1150 to 1580* (Oxford: Clarendon Press, 1888).
Maynard, John, ed. and trans. *Year Books, Liber Assissarum*, vol. 5 (London: G. Sawbridge, W. Rawlins, and S. Roycroft, 1678–80).
Meekings, C.A.F., ed. and trans. *Crown Pleas of the Wiltshire Eyre, 1249* (Devizes: Wiltshire Archaeological and Natural History Society, 1961).
Alan of Melsa. *Tractatus metricus de Susanna per fratrem Alanum monachum de Melsa de Beverlaco*. In J.H. Mozley, "Susannah and the Elders in Three Medieval Poems," *Studi Medievali* 3 (1930): pp. 27–52.
John Mirk. *Instructions for Parish Priests*. Edited by Edward Peacock. EETS, o.s. 31 (London: EETS, 1868).
Mills, David, ed. *The Chester Mystery Cycle* (East Lansing, MI: Colleagues Press, 1992).
Morris, Richard, ed. *Cursor Mundi (The Cursur O the World): A Northumbrian Poem of the XIVth Century in Four Versions*, 3 vols. (London: EETS by K. Paul, Trench, Trübner & Co., 1874–93).
Morris, Richard, and Pamela Gradon, eds. *Dan Michel's Ayenbite of Inwyt or Remorse of Conscience: Richard Morris's Transcription Now Newly Collated with the Unique Manuscript British Museum MS. Arundel 57*, 2 vols. (Oxford: EETS, 1965).
Mortier, Raoul, ed. *Les Textes de la Chanson de Roland* (Paris: La Geste Francor, 1940).
Mudie, James. *The Felonry of New South Wales: Being a Faithful Picture of the Real Romance of Life in Botany Bay* (London: Whaley and Co., 1837).
Nichols, Francis Morgan, ed. and trans. *Britton: The French Text Carefully Revised with an English Translation* (Washington: John Byrne & Co, 1901).
Norris, Edwin, ed. *The Ancient Cornish Drama* (Oxford: Oxford University Press, 1859).

Paris, Gaston, and Alphonse Bos, eds. *La Vie de saint Gilles, poème du XIIe siècle par Guillaume de Berneville* (Paris: SATF, 1881).
Peck, Russell, ed. *Heroic Women from the Old Testament in Middle English Verse* (Kalamazoo, MI: Medieval Institute Publications, 1991).
Peterson, Clifford, ed. *The Complete Works of the Pearl Poet*. Translated by Casey Finch (Berkeley: University of California Press, 1993).
Peterson, Clifford, ed. *Saint Erkenwald* (Philadelphia: University of Pennsylvania Press, 1977).
Pickering, Danby, ed. *The Statutes at Large, Anno duodecimo Georgii III. Regis. Being the Fifth Session of the Thirteenth Parliament of Great Britain* (Cambridge: John Archdeacon, Printer to the University, 1772).
Pike, Luke Owen, ed. *Year Books of the Reign of King Edward III: Years XIV and XV*, 14 vols. (London: Eyre and Spottiswoode, 1889).
Pugh, Ralph B., ed. and trans. *Wiltshire Gaol Delivery and Trailbaston Trials* (Devizes: Wiltshire Archaeological and Natural History Society, 1978).
Les Reports des Cases en ley que fuerunt argues en temps du roy Edward le Quart. Avec les notations de le tres reverend judges Brook & Fitz-Herbert. Et auter references n'unques devantiImprimee. Ovesque un table perfect des choses notables contenus en ycel (London: George Sawbridge, 1680).
Richardson, H.G., and G.O. Sayles, eds. *Fleta*, 4 vols (London: Seldon Society, 1955).
Rothwell, Henry, ed. *English Historical Documents*, vol. III (London: Eyre and Spottiswoode, 1975), 1189–1327.
John of Salisbury. *Metalogicon*. Edited by C.C.J. Webb (Oxford: Clarendon Press, 1929).
Seipp, David and Carol Lee, eds. *Medieval English Legal History: An Index and Paraphrase of Printed Year Book Reports, 1268–1535* (Boston, MA: Boston University School of Law, 2003).
Servius. *Servii grammatici qui feruntur in Vergilii carmina commentarii*, 3 vols. Edited by Georgius Thilo and Hermannus Hagen (Hildesheim: Georg Olms, 1961).
Sharpe, R.R., ed. *Calendar of the Letter Books of the City of London*, 11 vols. (London: John Edward Francis, 1899–1907).
Sharpe, Reginald, ed. *Calendar of Coroners Rolls of the City of London, 1300–1378* (Suffolk: Richard Clay and Sons, Ltd, 1913).
Sillem, Rosamond, ed. *Records of Some Sessions of the Peace in Lincolnshire, 1360–1375* (Hereford: Lincoln Record Society, 1936).
Skeat, William W., ed. *The Lay of Havelok the Dane* (London: EETS by N. Trübner, 1868).
Thomas Smith. *De republica anglorum*. Edited by L. Alston (Cambridge: Cambridge University Press, 1906).
The Statutes of the Realm, 11 vols. (London: HMSO, 1810–1828).
Stewart-Brown, R., ed. and trans. *Calendar of County Court, City Court and Eyre Rolls of Chester, 1259–1297* (Manchester: Chetham Society, 1925).
Stoljar, S.J. et al., eds. *Year Books of the Reign of Edward II*, vol. 27 (London: Selden Society, 1988).
Sugano, Douglas, ed. *The N-Town Plays* (Kalamazoo, MI: Medieval Institute Publications, 2007).
Sutherland, Donald, ed. *The Eyre of Northamptonshire 3–4 Edward III, A.D. 1329–1330*, vol. 1 (London: Selden Society, 1983).
Swanton, Michael, ed. *The Dream of the Rood* (Exeter: University of Exeter, 1987).
Trevisa, John. *Polychronicon*. Edited by Churchill Babington and Joseph Lumby (London: Longman et al., 1886).

Whitlock, Jill, ed. *The Seven Sages of Rome (Midland Version): Cambridge, University Library, MS Dd.I.17* (Oxford: Oxford University Press, 2005).
Whittaker, W.J., ed. *The Mirror of Justices* (Cambridge, MA: Selden Society by the Belknap Press of Harvard University Press, 1895).
Williams, C.H., ed. *Year Books of the Reign of Henry VI, 1422–1461* (London: Selden Society, 1895).
Wilson, Thomas. *Arte of Rhetorique*. Edited by G.H. Mair (Oxford: Clarendon Press, 1909).
Woodbine, George, ed. *Bracton on the Laws and Customs of England*, 4 vols., translated by Samuel Thorne (Cambridge: Belknap Press, 1968).
Year Books, Or Reports in the Following Reigns, with Notes to Brooke and Fitzherbert's Abridgments, 11 vols. (London: George Sawbridge, 1678, 1679–1680).

Secondary Sources

Allen, David. "The Dismas *Distinctio* and the Forms of Piers Plowman B.10–13." *Yearbook of Langland Studies* 3 (1989): pp. 31–48.
Allen, Elizabeth. "Episodes." In *Middle English (Oxford Twenty-First Century Approaches)*, edited by Paul Strohm (Oxford: Oxford University Press, 2007).
Altschul, Davis and Nadia, eds. *Medievalisms in the Postcolonial World: The Idea of "the Middle Ages" outside Europe* (Baltimore, MD: Johns Hopkins University Press, 2009).
Ashe, Laura. "1155 and the Beginnings of Fiction." *History Today* 65, no. 1 (2015): pp. 41–6.
Astell, Ann. *Political Allegory in Late Medieval England* (Ithaca, NY: Cornell University Press, 2002).
Baker, John. *The Common Law Tradition* (London: Hambledon Press, 2000).
Baker, John. *An Introduction to English Legal History*, 5th ed. (Oxford: Oxford University Press, 2019).
Barney, S.A. "The Ploughshare of the Tongue: The Progress of a Symbol from the Bible to *Piers Plowman*." *Medieval Studies* 35 (1973): pp. 261–293.
Barrington, Candace, and Emily Steiner, eds. *Cambridge Companion to Medieval English Law and Literature* (Cambridge: Cambridge University Press, 2019).
Barthes, Roland. *The Rustle of Language*. Translated by Richard Howard (Berkeley: University of California Press, 1986).
Bellamy, John G. *The Criminal Trial in Later Medieval England: Felony before the Courts from Edward I to the Sixteenth Century* (Toronto: University of Toronto Press, 1998).
Berson, Sarah. "Beyond the Sentence: Understanding Collateral Consequences." *National Institute of Justice Journal* 25 (2013): pp. 25–28.
Beven, Miranda, David Ormerod, and Samantha Magor. "*Time to Dispense with the Mute of Malice Procedure*." *Criminal Law Review* 10 (2020): pp. 912–930.
Binder, Guyora. "The Origins of American Felony Murder Rules." *Stanford Law Review* 57 (2004): pp. 59–208.
Black, Daisy. "Commanding Un-empty Space: Silence, Stillness and Scopic Authority in the York 'Christ before Herod'." In *Gender in Medieval Places, Space, and Thresholds*, edited by Victoria Blud, Diane Heath, and Einat Klafter (London: University of London Press: 2019): pp. 237–250.
Bloomfield, Morton W. *Essays and Explorations: Studies in Ideas, Language, and Literature* (Cambridge, MA: Harvard University Press, 1970).
Bolens, Guyllemette. "Narrative Use and the Practice of Fiction in *The Book of Sindibad* and *The Tale of Beryn*." *Poetics Today* 29, no. 2 (2008): pp. 309–351.

Bradbury, Nancy. "The Erosion of Oath-Based Relationships: A Cultural Context for 'Athelston'." *Medium Aevum* 73, no. 2 (2004): pp. 189–204.

Brand, Paul. "Dower Ex Assensu and Trial by Jury and Trial by Witnesses in the English Medieval Common Law." *Journal of Legal History* 42, no. 2 (2021): pp. 147–170.

Brand, Paul. "The Language of the English Legal Profession: The Emergence of a Distinctive Legal Lexicon in Insular French." In *The Anglo-Norman Language and its Contexts*, edited by Richard Ingham (York: York Medieval Press, 2010), pp. 94–101

Brand, Paul. *The Making of the Common Law* (New York, NY: Bloomsbury Academic, 1992).

Brazinski, Paul and Allegra Fryxell. "The Smell of Relics: Authenticating Saintly Bones and the Role of Scent in the Sensory Experience of Medieval Christian Veneration." *Papers from the Institute of Archaeology* 23, no. 1 (2013): pp. 1–15.

Brooks, Peter. "Law and Humanities: Two Attempts." *Boston University Law Review* 93 (2013): pp. 1437–1469.

Brooks, Peter and Paul Gewirtz, eds. *Law's Stories: Narrative and Rhetoric in the Law* (New Haven, CT: Yale University Press, 1996).

Burton, Alexander L., Velmer S. Burton, Jr., Francis T. Cullen, et al. "Beyond the New Jim Crow: Public Support for Removing and Regulating Collateral Consequences." *Federal Probation Journal* 84, no. 3 (2020): pp. 19–33.

Butler, Sara. *Forensic Medicine and Death Investigation in Medieval England* (Milton Park: Taylor & Francis, 2014).

Butler, Sara. *Pain, Penanace, and Protest*: Peine Forte et Dure *in Medieval England* (Cambridge: Cambridge University Press, 2022).

Camp, Cynthia Turner. "Spatial Memory, Historiographic Fantasy, and the Touch of the Past in *St. Erkenwald*." *New Literary History* 44, no. 3 (2013): pp. 471–491.

Cannon, Christopher. *The Grounds of English Literature* (Oxford: Oxford University Press, 2004).

Carruthers, Mary. *The Book of Memory: A Study of Memory in Medieval Culture* (Cambridge: Cambridge University Press, 2008).

Child, Claire K. and Stephanie A. Clark. "SNAP Judgments: Collateral Consequences of Felony Drug Convictions for Federal Food Assistance." *Berkeley Journal of Criminal Law* 26, no. 2 (2021): pp. 1–26.

Clanchy, Michael. "Law, Government, and Society in Medieval England: Review of *Crime and Public Order in England* in the Later Middle Ages by John Bellamy." *History* 59, no. 195 (1974): pp. 73–78.

Clopper, Lawrence. "Need Men and Women Labor? Langland's Wanderer and the Labor Ordinances." In *Chaucer's England: Literature in Historical Context*, edited by Barbara A. Hanawalt (Minneapolis: University of Minnesota Press, 1992), pp. 110–129.

Cockburn, J.S. and Thomas A Green, eds. *Twelve Good Men and True: The Criminal Trial Jury in England, 1200–1800* (Princeton: Princeton University Press, 2014).

Cohen, Jeffrey Jerome, ed. *The Postcolonial Middle Ages* (New York City, NY: St. Martin's Press, 2000).

Cole, Andrew. "Scribal Hermeneutics and the Genres of Social Organization in Piers Plowman." In *The Middle Ages at Work*, edited by Kellie Robertson and Michael Uebel (New York City, NY: Palgrave Macmillan, 2004): pp. 179–206.

Coleman, Janet. *English Literature in History, 1350–1400: Medieval Readers and Writers* (London: Hutchinson, 1981).

Copeland, Rita and Ineke Sluiter, eds. *Medieval Grammar and Rhetoric: Language Arts and Literary Theory, AD 300–1475* (Oxford: Oxford University Press, 2009).

Crassons, Kate. *Claims of Poverty: Literature, Culture, and Ideology in Late Medieval England* (Notre Dame: University of Notre Dame Press, 2010).
Craun, Edwin. *Ethics and Power in Medieval English Reformist Writing* (Cambridge: Cambridge University Press, 2010).
Crow, Martin M., and Clair C. Olson, eds. *Chaucer Life-Records, from Materials Compiled by John M. Manly and Edith Rickert, with the Assistance of Lilian J. Redstone and Others* (Oxford: Clarendon Press, 1966).
Dagenais, John and Margaret Greer. "Decolonizing the Middle Ages." *Journal of Medieval and Early Modern Studies* 30, no. 3 (2000): pp. 431–448.
David, Alfred. "The Man of Law vs. Chaucer: A Case in Poetics." *PMLA* 82, no. 2 (1967): pp. 217–225.
Davis, Kathleen. *Periodization and Sovereignty: How Ideas of Feudalism and Secularization Govern the Politics of Time* (Philadelphia, PA: University of Pennsylvania Press, 2008).
Davis, Robert Evan. "Medieval Law in The Tale of Beryn." *Classica and Mediaevalia* 36 (1985): pp. 261–74.
Dean, Trevor. *Crime in Medieval Europe, 1200–1500* (London: Routledge, 2014).
Devaux, Jean. "From the Court of Hainault to the Court of England: The Example of Jean Froissart." In *War, Government, and Power in Late Medieval France*, edited by Christopher Allmand (Liverpool: Liverpool University Press, 2000), pp. 1–20.
Demleitner, Nora V. "Preventing Internal Exile: The Need for Restrictions on Collateral Sentencing Consequences." *Stanford Law & Policy Review* 11 (1999): pp. 153–171.
Dinshaw, Carolyn. "The Law of Man and Its 'Abhomynacions.'" *Exemplaria* 1, no. 1 (1989): pp. 117–148.
Donahue, Charles Jr. "Proof by Witnesses in the Church Courts of Medieval England: An Imperfect Reception of the Learned Law." In *On the Laws and Customs of England: Essays in Honor of Samuel E. Thorne*, edited by Morris S. Arnold, Thomas A. Green, Sally Scully, et al. (Chapel Hill: North Carolina University Press, 1981), pp. 90–126.
Dunn, Caroline. *Stolen Women in Medieval England: Rape, Abduction, and Adultery, 1100–1500* (Cambridge: Cambridge University Press, 2013).
Dyer, Christopher. "*Piers Plowman* and Plowmen: A Historical Perspective." *Yearbook of Langland Studies* 8 (1994): pp. 155–176.
Erler, Mary C. *Women, Reading, and Piety in Late Medieval England* (Cambridge: Cambridge University Press, 2002).
Feld, Barry C. "The Youth Discount: Old Enough to Do the Crime, Too Young to Do the Time." *Ohio State Journal of Criminal Law* 11 (2013): pp. 107–148.
Fenster, Thelma and Daniel Lord Smail, eds. *Fama: The Politics of Talk and Reputation in Medieval Europe* (Ithaca, NY: Cornell University Press, 2018).
Fleischman, Suzanne. *Tense and Narrativity: From Medieval Performance to Modern Fiction* (Austin: University of Texas Press, 2010).
Fludernik, Monika. "Medieval Fictionality from a Narratological Perspective." *New Literary History* 51, no. 1 (2020): pp. 259–263.
Forrest, Ian. *Trustworthy Men: How Inequality and Faith Made the Medieval Church* (Princeton, NY: Princeton University Press, 2018).
Foucault, Michel. *Surveiller et punir: Naissance de la prison* (Paris: Gallimard, 1975).
Frank, Robert. Piers Plowman *and the Scheme of Salvation: An Interpretation of Dowel, Dobet, and Dobest* (New Haven, CT: Yale University Press, 1957).

Fryde, Natalie. "A Medieval Robber Baron: Sir John Molyns of Stoke Poges, Buckinghamshire." In *Medieval Legal Records, Edited in Memory of C.A.F. Meekings*, edited by R.F. Hunnisett and J.B. Post (London: Stationary Office, 1976), pp. 198–207.

Fuller, Lon. *Legal Fictions* (Palo Alto, CA: Stanford University Press, 1967).

Gabrovsky, Alexander. "The Good, the Bad, and the Penitent Thief: Langlandian Extremes, the Edge of Salvation, and the Problem of Trajan and Dismas in Piers Plowman." *Marginalia* 12 (2011), pp. 1–13.

Gallagher, Catherine. "The Rise of Fictionality." In *The Novel*, edited by Franco Moretti (Princeton: Princeton University Press, 2006), pp. 336–363.

Garay, K.E. "'No Peace Nor Love in England': An Examination of Crime and Punishment in the English Counties, 1388–1409" (PhD dissertation, University of Toronto, 1977).

Given-Wilson, Chris. "Service, Serfdom and English Labour Legislation, 1350–1500." In *Concepts and Patterns of Service in the Later Middle Ages*, edited by A. Curry and E. Matthew (Woodbridge: Boydell and Brewer, 2000), pp. 21–37.

Goodrich, Micah. "Lolling and the Suspension of Salvation in Piers Plowman." *Yearbook of Langland Studies* 33 (2019): pp. 13–42.

Gottschalk, Marie. *Caught: The Prison State and the Lockdown of American Politics* (Princeton, NJ: Princeton University Press, 2015).

Gradon, Pamela. "Trajanus Redivivus: Another Look at Trajan in Piers Plowman." In *Middle English Studies: Presented to Norman Davis in Honour of his Seventieth Birthday* (Oxford: University of Oxford Press, 1983), pp. 93–114.

Grady, Frank. *The Letter of the Law: Legal Practice and Literary Production in Medieval England* (Ithaca, NY: Cornell University Press, 2002).

Green, Richard Firth. *A Crisis of Truth: Literature and Law in Ricardian England* (Philadelphia: University of Pennsylvania Press, 1999).

Green, Thomas A. "The Jury and the English Law of Homicide, 1200–1600." *Michigan Law Review* 74 (1976): pp. 423–499.

Green, Thomas A. *Verdict According to Conscience: Perspectives on the English Criminal Trial Jury, 1200–1800* (Chicago: University of Chicago Press, 1985).

Hanawalt, Barbara. *Crime and Conflict in English Communities, 1300–1348* (Cambridge, MA: Harvard University Press, 1979).

Hanawalt, Barbara. *"Of Good and Ill Repute": Gender and Social Control in Medieval England* (Oxford: Oxford University Press, 1998)

Hanawalt, Barbara. "The Voices and Audiences of Social History Records." *Social Science History* 15, no. 2 (1991): pp. 159–175.

Hancock, Lauren N. "Another Collateral Consequence: Kicking the Victim When She's Down." *Washington and Lee Review* 77 (2020): pp. 1319–1374.

Hanna, Ralph III. *London Literature, 1300–1380* (Cambridge: Cambridge University Press, 2005).

Hanna, Ralph III. *Pursuing History: Middle English Manuscripts and their Texts* (Stanford, CA: Stanford University Press, 1996).

Hanna, Ralph III. "Robert the Ruyflare." In *Literature and Religion in the Later Middle Ages: Philological Studies in Honor of Siegfried Wenzel*, edited by Richard G. Newhauser and John A. Alford (Binghamton, NY: Center of Medieval and Early Renaissance Studies, 1995), pp. 81–96.

Harding, Alan. "The Origins of the Crime of Conspiracy." *Transactions of the Royal Historical Society* 33 (1983): pp. 89–108.

Harwood, Britton J. "The Plot of Piers Plowman and the Contradictions of Feudalism." In *Speaking Two Languages: Traditional Disciplines and Contemporary Theory in Medieval*

Studies, edited by Allen J. Frantzen (Albany: State University of New York Press, 1991), pp. 91–114.

Helmholz, R.H. "The Origins of the Privilege against Self-Incrimination: The Role of the European *Ius Commune*." *New York University Law Review* 65 (1990): pp. 962–990.

Holdsworth, William. *A History of English Law*, 7th edition, 17 vols., revised under the general editorship of A.L. Goodhart and H.G. Hanbury; with an introductory essay and additions by S. B. Chrimes (Mytholmroyd: Sweet & Maxwell Ltd., 1956–1966).

Hudson, John. *The Formation of English Common Law: Law and Society in England from King Alfred to Magna Carta* (Abingdon: Routledge Press, 2018).

Hunnisett, R.F. *The Medieval Coroner* (Cambridge: Cambridge University Press, 1961).

Hurnard, Naomi. *The King's Pardon for Homicide before 1307* (Oxford: Clarendon Press, 1969).

Hyams, Paul. *Rancour and Reconciliation in Medieval England* (Ithaca, NY: Cornell University Press, 2003).

Ingham, Patricia Clare, and Michelle R. Warren, eds. *Postcolonial Moves: Medieval through Modern* (New York, NY: Palgrave Macmillan, 2003).

Jahner, Jennifer. *Literature and Law in the Era of Magna Carta* (Oxford: Oxford University Press, 2019).

Jarvis, Paul and Michael Bisgrove. "The Use and Abuse of Conspiracy." *Criminal Law Review* 4 (2014): pp. 259–275.

Johnson, Eleanor. "English Law and the Man of Law's 'Prose' Tale." *Journal of English and Germanic Philology* 114, no. 4 (2015): pp. 504–525.

Johnson, Eleanor. "The Poetics of Waste." *PMLA* 127, no. 3 (2012): pp. 460–476.

Johnson, Eleanor. "Reddere and Refrain: A Meditation on Poetic Procedure in *Piers Plowman*." *Yearbook of Langland Studies* 30 (2016): pp. 3–27.

Johnson, Lynn Staley. "Chaucer's Tale of the Second Nun and the Strategies of Dissent." *Studies in Philology* 89, no. 4 (1992): pp. 314–333.

Jordan, William Chester. "A Fresh Look at Medieval Sanctuary." In *Law and the Illicit in Medieval Europe*, edited by E. Ann Matter, Joel Kaye, and Ruth Mazo Karras (Philadelphia: University of Pennsylvania Press, 2008), pp. 17–32.

Jusserand, J.J. *English Wayfaring Life in the Middle Ages*. Translated by Lucy Toulmin Smith (London: T. Fisher Unwin Ltd., 1889).

Justice, Steven. "Did the Middle Ages Believe in Their Miracles?" *Representations* 103, no. 1 (2008): pp. 1–29.

Justice, Steven. *Writing and Rebellion: England in 1381* (Berkeley: University of California Press, 1994).

Kamali, Elizabeth Papp. *Felony and the Guilty Mind in Medieval England* (Cambridge: Cambridge University Press, 2019).

Karnes, Michelle. *Imagination, Meditation, and Cognition in the Middle Ages* (Chicago: University of Chicago Press, 2017).

Karnes, Michelle. "The Possibilities of Medieval Fiction." *New Literary History* 51, no. 1 (2020): pp. 209–228.

Kelleher, Marie. "Later Medieval Law in Community Context." In *The Oxford Handbook of Women and Gender in Medieval Europe*, edited by Judith M. Bennett and Ruth Mazo Karras (Oxford: Oxford University Press, 2013), pp. 133–147.

Kelly, Douglas. "Fortune and Narrative Proliferation." *Speculum* 51, no. 1 (1976): pp. 6–22.

Kelly, H. Ansgar. "The Right to Remain Silent: Before and After Joan of Arc." *Speculum* 68, no. 4 (1993): pp. 992–1026.

Kerby-Fulton, Kathryn. *The Clerical Proletariat and the Resurgence of Medieval English Poetry* (Philadelphia: University of Pennsylvania Press, 2021).

Kesselring, K.J. "Felony Forfeiture in England, c.1170–1870." *Journal of Legal History* 30, no. 3 (2009): pp. 201–226.

Klerman, Daniel. "Was the Jury Ever Self-Informing?" *Southern California Law Review* 77 (2003): pp. 123–149.

Knapp, Ethan. *The Bureaucratic Muse: Thomas Hoccleve and the Literature of Late Medieval England* (University Park, PA.: Pennsylvania State University Press, 2001).

Kunkel, Nico. "Misogyny, Wisdom, and Legal Practice: On Narrative Flexibility across Different Versions of the Seven Sages of Rome." *Narrative Culture* 7, no. 2 (2020): pp. 181–197.

Lacey, Nicola. *In Search of Criminal Responsibility: Ideas, Interests, and Institutions* (Oxford: Oxford University Press, 2016).

Lacey, Nicola. "Psychologizing Jekyll, Demonising Hyde: The Strange Case of Criminal Responsibility." *Criminal Law and Philosophy* 4, no. 2 (2010): pp. 109–133.

Lake, Peter, and Michael Questier. *The Trials of Margaret Clitherow: Persecution, Martyrdom and the Politics of Sanctity in Elizabethan England* (New York, NY: Bloomsbury Publishing, 2011).

Langbein, John. *Torture and the Law of Proof: Europe and England in the Ancien Régime* (Chicago, IL: University of Chicago Press, 2012).

Levin, Benjamin. "Mens rea Reform and its Discontents." *Journal of Criminal Law and Criminology* 109, no. 3 (2019): pp. 491–558.

Lipton, Emma. *Cultures of Witnessing: Law and the York Plays* (Philadelphia: University of Pennsylvania Press, 2022).

Loar, Carol. "Medical Knowledge and the Early Modern English Coroner's Inquest." *Social History of Medicine* 23, no. 3 (2010): pp. 475–491.

Love, Margaret Colgate. "Deconstructing the New Infamy." *Criminal Justice* 16 (2001): pp. 30–62.

Lundt, Bea. "'Sieben weise Meister gegen eine Frau'. Ein populäres Volksbuch aus frauen- und geschlechtergeschichtlicher Perspektive." In *Begehren und Entbehren, Bochumer Beiträge zur Geschlechterforschung*, edited by G. Klein and A. Treibel (Pfaffenweiler: Centaurus, 1993), pp. 185–206.

Maddock, McCarley. "Done the Time, Still Being Punished for the Crime: The Irrationality of Collateral Consequences in Occupational Licensing and Fourteenth Amendment Challenges." *Duke Journal of Constitutional Law and Public Policy Sidebar* 18 (2022–2023): pp. 21–46.

Mann, Jill. *Feminizing Chaucer* (Woodbridge: Boydell and Brewer, 2002).

Masschaele, James. *Jury, State, and Society in Medieval England* (London: Palgrave Macmillan, 2008).

Matthews, Paul. "Involuntary Manslaughter: A View from the Coroner's Court." *Journal of Criminal Law* 60, no. 2 (1996): pp. 189–200.

McIntosh, Marjorie Keniston. "Finding Language for Misconduct: Jurors in Fifteenth-Century Local Courts." In *Bodies and Disciplines: Intersections of Literature and History in Fifteenth-Century England*, edited by Barbara Hanawalt and David Wallace (Minneapolis: University of Minnesota Press, 1996), pp. 87–122.

McKenzie, Andrea. "'This Death Some Strong and Stout Hearted Man Doth Choose': The Practice of Peine Forte et Dure in Seventeenth- and Eighteenth-Century England." *Law and History Review* 23, no. 2 (2005): pp. 279–313.

McLane, Bernard W. "Juror Attitudes toward Local Disorders: The Evidence of the 1328 Trailbaston Proceedings." In *Twelve Good Men*, edited by J.S. Cockburn and Thomas A. Green (Princeton, NJ: Princeton University Press, 1988), pp. 56–67.

McSheffrey, Shannon. "Jurors, Respectable Masculinity, and Christian Morality: A Comment on Marjorie McIntosh's *Controlling Misbehavior*." *Journal of British Studies* 37, no. 3 (1998): pp. 269–78.

Mellinkoff, David. *The Language of the Law* (Boston, MA: Resource Publications, 1963).

Middleton, Anne. "Acts of Vagrancy: The C Version Autobiography and the Statute of 1388." In *Written Work: Langland, Labor, and Authorship*, edited by Steven Justice and Kathryn Kerby-Fulton (Philadelphia: University of Pennsylvania Press, 1997), pp. 208–317.

Middleton, Anne. "Chaucer's 'New Men' and the Good of Literature in the *Canterbury Tales*." In *Literature and Society, English Institute Essays*, edited by Edward Said (Baltimore: Johns Hopkins University Press, 1978), pp. 15–56.

Middleton, Anne. "Narration and the Invention of Experience: Episodic Form in *Piers Plowman*." In *The Wisdom of Poetry: Essays in Early English Literature in Honor of Morton Bloomfield*, edited by Larry D. Benson and Siegfried Wenzel (Kalamazoo, MI: Medieval Institute Publications, 1982), pp. 91–122.

Milsom, S.F.C. *Historical Foundations of the Common Law* (London: Butterworths, 1969).

Moore, Michael S. "A Tale of Two Theories." *Criminal Justice Ethics* 28, no. 1 (2009): pp. 27–48.

Mulholland, Maureen. "Trials in Manorial Courts in Late Medieval England." In *Judicial Tribunals in England and Europe: The Trial in History*, vol. 1, edited by Maureen Mulholland and Brian Pullan (Manchester: Manchester University Press, 2003), pp. 81–101.

Musson, Anthony. *Medieval Law in Context: The Growth of Legal Consciousness from Magna Carta to the Peasant's Revolt* (Manchester: Manchester University Press, 2001).

Musson, Anthony. "Turning King's Evidence: The Prosecution of Crime in Late Medieval England." *Oxford Journal of Legal Studies* 19, no. 3 (1999): pp. 467–470.

Neville, C.J. "Common Knowledge of the Common Law in Later Medieval England." *Canadian Journal of History* 29, no. 3 (1994): pp. 461–478.

Nissé, Ruth. "'A Coroun Ful Riche': The Rule of History in *St. Erkenwald*." *English Literary History* 65, no. 2 (1998): pp. 277–295.

O'Connell, Brendan. "Struglyng Wel and Myghtily: Resisting Rape in the Man of Law's Tale." *Medium Aevum* 84, no. 1 (2015): pp. 16–39.

Olson, Greta. "Narration and Narrative in Legal Discourse." In *Handbook of Narratology*, vol. I, edited by in Peter Hühn et al., 2nd edition (Berlin: de Gruyter, 2014), pp. 371–383.

Orlemanski, Julie. "Who Has Fiction? Modernity, Fictionality, and the Middle Ages." *New Literary History* 50, no. 2 (2019): pp. 145–170.

Ormrod, W.M. "The Use of English: Language, Law, and Political Culture in Fourteenth-Century England." *Speculum* 78, no. 3 (2003): pp. 750–787.

Palmer, Robert. "Contexts of Marriage in Medieval England: Evidence from the King's Court circa 1300." *Speculum* 59, no. 1 (1984): pp. 42–67.

Phelan, Amy. "Trailbaston and Attempts to Control Violence in the Reign of Edward I." In *Violence in Medieval Society*, edited by Richard Kaeuper (Woodbridge: Boydell and Brewer, 2011), pp. 129–143.

Phillips, Susan. *Transforming Talk: The Problem with Gossip in Late Medieval England* (University Park: Pennsylvania State University Press, 2010).

Phipps, Teresa. *Medieval Women and Urban Justice: Commerce, Crime and Community in England, 1300–1500* (Manchester: Manchester University Press, 2020).

Pollack, Frederick and Frederic Maitland. *The History of English Law before the Time of Edward I*, 2 vols. (Cambridge: Cambridge University Press, 1895).
Post, J.B. "Crime in Later Medieval England: Some Historiographical Limitations," *Continuity and Change* 2, no. 2 (1987): pp. 211–224.
Post, J.B. "Jury Lists and Juries in the Late Fourteenth Century." In *Twelve Good Men*, edited by J.S. Cockburn and Thomas A. Green (Princeton, NJ: Princeton University Press, 1988), pp. 65–77.
Post, J.B. "Placita Corone." In *Legal Record and Historical Reality*, edited by Thomas G. Watkin (London: Hambledon Press, 1989), pp. 1–8.
Powell, Edward. "Jury Trial at Gaol Delivery in the Late Middle Ages: The Midland Circuit, 1400–1429." In *Twelve Good Men*, edited by J.S. Cockburn and Thomas A. Green (Princeton, NJ: Princeton University Press, 1988), pp. 78–116.
Pugh, R.B. "The Duration of Criminal Trials in Medieval England." In *Law, Litigants and the Legal Profession*, edited by E. W. Ives and A. H. Manchester (London: Royal Historical Society, 1983), pp. 104–115.
Rabin, Andrew and Anya Adair, eds. *Law, Literature, and Social Regulation in Early Medieval England* (Woodbridge: Boydell and Brewer, 2023).
Ristroph, Alice. "Farewell to the Felonry." *Harvard Civil Rights–Civil Liberties Law Review* 53 (2018): pp. 563–618.
Robertson, Kellie. "Branding and the Technologies of Labor Regulation." In *The Middle Ages at Work: Practicing Labor in Late Medieval England* (New York, NY: Palgrave Macmillan, 2004), pp. 133–155.
Robertson, Kellie. *The Laborer's Two Bodies: Literary and Legal Productions in Britain, 1350–1500* (Basingstoke: Palgrave Macmillan, 2005).
Robertson, Kellie and Michael Uebel, eds. *The Middle Ages at Work: Practicing Labor in Late Medieval England* (New York, NY: Palgrave Macmillan, 2004).
Rubin, Miri. *Charity and Community in Medieval Cambridge* (Cambridge: Cambridge University Press, 2002).
Sagui, Samantha. "The Hue and Cry in Medieval English Towns." *Historical Research* 87, no. 236 (2014): pp. 179–193.
Saunders, Corinne. "Medieval Law of Rape." *Kings College Law Journal* 11 (2000): pp. 19–48.
Saxonhouse, Elena. "Unequal Protection: Comparing Former Felons' Challenges to Disenfranchisement and Employment Discrimination." *Stanford Law Review* 56, no. 6 (2004): pp. 1597–1639.
Scase, Wendy. *Literature and Complaint in England, 1272–1553* (Oxford: Oxford University Press, 2007).
Scattergood, John. *The Lost Tradition: Essays in Middle English Alliterative Poetry* (Dublin: Four Courts Press, 2000).
Schlanger, Margo. "*Plata v. Brown* and Realignment: Jails, Prisons, Courts, and Politics." *Harvard Civil Rights–Civil Liberties Law Review* 48 (2013): pp. 165–215.
Schmitz-Esser, Romedio. *Der Leichnam im Mittelalter: Einbalsamierung, Verbrennung und die kulturelle Konstruktion des toten Korpers* (Berlin: Jan Thorbecke Verlag Gmbh & Co., 2014).
Schustereder, Stefan. "Coming to Terms with a Pagan Past: The Story of *St. Erkenwald*." *Studia Anglica Posnaniensia* 48, no. 2 (2013): pp. 71–92.
Schuurman, Anne. "Materials of Wonder: Miraculous Objects and Poetic Form in *Saint Erkenwald*." *Studies in the Age of Chaucer* 39 (2017): pp. 275–296.

Schwyzer, Phillip. "Exhumation and Ethnic Conflict: From *St. Erkenwald* to Spenser in Ireland." *Representations* 95 (2006): pp. 1–26.
Shapiro, Barbara. "Beyond Reasonable Doubt Doctrine: 'Moral Comfort' or Standard of Proof?" *Law and Humanities* 2, no. 2 (2008): pp. 149–173.
Shapiro, Barbara. *Beyond Reasonable Doubt and Probable Cause: Historical Perspectives on the Anglo-American Law of Evidence* (Berkeley, CA: University of California Press, 1991).
Shapiro, Barbara. *A Culture of Fact: England, 1550–1720* (Ithaca, NY: Cornell University Press, 2000).
Shoemaker, Karl. "Criminal Procedure in Medieval European Law: A Comparison between English and Roman-Canonical Developments after the IV Lateran Council." *Zeitschrift der Savigny-Stiftung für Rechtsgeschichte, kanonistische Abteilung* 85, no. 1 (1999): pp. 174–202.
Shoemaker, Karl. *Sanctuary and Crime in the Middle Ages, 400–1500* (New York City, NY: Fordham University Press, 2011).
Shoemaker, Karl. "Wrong: Toward a Cultural History of a Medieval Legal Concept." In *A Cultural History of Law in the Middle Ages*, edited by Laurent Mayali and Emanuele Conte (New York City, NY: Bloomsbury Press, 2018), pp. 113–124.
Sibilla, Nick. "Barred from Working: A Nationwide Study of Occupational Licensing Barriers for Ex-Offenders." Institute for Justice, 2020. https://ij.org/report/barred-from-working/.
Sisk, Jennifer L. "The Uneasy Orthodoxy of *St. Erkenwald*." *English Literary History* 74 (2007): pp. 89–115.
Skow-Obenaus, Katya. "The Whole is the Sum of its Parts: Misogyny as a Unifying Factor in *Die Sieben weisen Meister*." *Fifteenth-Century Studies* 26 (2001): pp. 169–182.
Smith, Carrie. "Medieval Coroners' Rolls: Legal Fiction or Historical Fact." In *Courts, Counties, and the Capital in the Later Middle Ages*, edited by Diana E.S. Dunn (London: St. Martin's Press, 1996), pp. 93–116.
Smith, D. Vance. "Crypt and Decryption: *Erkenwald* Terminable and Interminable." *New Medieval Literatures* 5 (2002): pp. 59–85.
Snyman, C.R. "The History and Rationale of Criminal Conspiracy." *The Comparative and International Law Journal of Southern Africa* 17, no. 1 (1984): pp. 65–77.
Spearing, A.C. "What Is a Narrator?: Narrator Theory and Medieval Narratives." *Digital Philology* 4 (2015): pp. 59–105.
Spiegel, Gabrielle M. "Forging the Past: The Language of Historical Truth in the Middle Ages." *History Teacher* 17, no. 2 (1984): pp. 267–288.
Staley, Lynn. "Susanna and English Communities." *Traditio* 62 (2007): pp. 25–58.
Stamato, Lydia. "Presentment of Englishry at the Eyre of Kent, 1313" (Honors Thesis, Syracuse University, 2007).
Steiner, Emily. *Documentary Culture and the Making of English Literature* (Cambridge: Cambridge University Press, 2003).
Steiner, Emily, and Candace Barrington. "Introduction." In *The Letter of the Law: Legal Practice and Literary Production in Medieval England*, edited by Emily Steiner and Candace Barrington (Ithaca, NY: Cornell University Press, 2002), pp. 1–11.
Stern, Simon. "Narrative in the Legal Text: Judicial Opinions and Their Narratives." In *Narrative and Metaphor in the Law*, edited by Michael Hanne and Robert Weisberg (Cambridge: Cambridge University Press, 2018), pp. 121–139.
Stevens, Martin, ed. *Four Middle English Mystery Cycles: Textual, Contextual, and Critical Interpretations* (Princeton, NJ: Princeton University Press, 2014).

Stones, E.L.G. "The Folvilles of Ashby-Folville, Leicestershire, and Their Associates in Crime, 1326–1347." *Transactions of the Royal Historical Society* 7 (1957): pp. 117–136.

Strohm, Paul. "Some Generic Distinctions in the Canterbury Tales." *Modern Philology* 68 (1971): pp. 321–328.

Summerson, H.R.T. "The Structure of Law Enforcement in Thirteenth Century England." *American Journal of Legal History* 23, no. 4 (1979): pp. 313–327.

Sunderland, Luke. *Rebel Barons: Resisting Royal Power in Medieval Culture* (Oxford: Oxford University Press, 2017).

Sutherland, Donald. "Review: *Placita Corone, or La Corone Pledee devant Justices* by J.M. Kaye." *Speculum* 43, no.1 (1968): pp. 167–170.

Symes, Carol. "When We Talk about Modernity." *American Historical Review* 116, no. 3 (2011): pp. 715–726.

Taylor, Jamie. *Fictions of Witnessing: Witnessing, Literature, and Community in the Late Middle Ages* (Columbus, OH: Ohio State University Press, 2019).

Thayer, James B. *A Preliminary Treatise on Evidence at the Common Law* (Boston: Little, Brown, and Co., 1898).

Toureille, Valérie. *Vol et brigandage de Môyen Age* (Paris: Presses Universitaires de France, 2006).

Uggen, Christopher and Robert Stewart. "Piling On: Collateral Consequences and Community Supervision." *Minnesota Law Review* 99 (2014): pp. 1871–1910.

van Dijk, Conrad. *John Gower and the Limits of the Law* (Suffolk: Boydell and Brewer, 2013).

Vitz, Evelyn Birge. *Medieval Narrative and Modern Narratology: Subjects and Objects of Desire* (New York: New York University Press, 1989).

Warren, Edward H. "Serjeants-at-Law: The Order of the Coif." *Virginia Law Review* 28, no. 7 (1942): pp. 911–950.

Whitman, James. *The Origins of Reasonable Doubt: Theological Roots of the Criminal Trial* (New Haven, CT: Yale University Press, 2008).

Wigmore, John H. *A Treatise on the Anglo-American System of Evidence*, 10 vols. (Boston: Little, Brown, and Co., 1940).

Willard, James F. and William Alfred Morris. *The English Government at Work: 1327–1336* (Cambridge, MA: Medieval Academy of America, 1940).

Yeager, Stephen. *From Lawmen to Plowmen: Anglo-Saxon Legal Tradition and the School of Langland* (Toronto: University of Toronto Press, 2014).

Yorke, Barbara. *Kings and Kingdoms of Early Anglo-Saxon England* (Oxford: Taylor & Francis, 2002).

Zumthor, Paul. *Toward a Medieval Poetic*. Translated by Philip Bennett (Minneapolis: University of Minnesota Press, 1992).

Index

For the benefit of digital users, indexed terms that span two pages (e.g., 52–53) may, on occasion, appear on only one of those pages.

'n.' after a paragraph number indicates the footnote number.

A

accusation, 96
    Chaucer's "Man of Law's Tale": knight's false accusation, 66–67
    sheriff's tourns, 10, 14–15
accused
    confession, 119
    fleeing, 9–10, 14–15, 115
    as pleader, 10–11, 53, 69, 72
    reputation and judgement, 37, 49, 104–105
    see also consent; offender; *peine forte et dure*; standing mute; suspect
acquittal, 96
    coroner's inquest and, 28
    jury trial and, 25–26 n.6, 139
    Langland's Good Thief in *Piers Plowman*, 19, 96–97, 111–112
    in robbery cases, 99, 99–100 n.13, 100–101, 103, 111–113, 115
acts of Parliament, 3, 19–20, 98
adultery, 18–19, 75–76, 90, 90 n.42
Albertus Magnus, 115–116
Allen, David, 97–98, 106
Allen, Elizabeth, 60
Aquinas, Thomas, 38–39, 99–100, 105–106 n.25
Aristotle, 59
arson, 3–5, 8–9
Ashe, Laura, 59–60 n.38
assize, 8–9, 12, 113–114 n.41
Audelay, John, 133
Augustine, 84–85, 106

B

Baker, John, 14, 53 n.8
Barr, Helen, 133

Barthes, Roland, 56–57
Bellamy, John, 8–10 n.27, 19 n.46, 54, 71, 99 n.9, 112–113
Bentham, Jeremy, 1
Berson, Sarah, 146–147
betrayal, felony as, 4–5, 8–9, 141–142
Beves of Hamtoun, 4, 60
Black, Daisy, 126
Blackstone, William, 1 n.1, 121
body (dead body)
    coroner's inquest: examination of the body, 29, 31, 35
    first finders: duties towards the body, 9, 33–34
    punishments for people who fail to preserve the body, 41
    St. Erkenwald: judge's dead body, 16–17, 27–28, 33–34, 38, 46
Boethius, 38–39
Bohun, Joan, 87
Bonaventure, 105–106 n.15
Book of Vices and Virtues, The, 85–86, 129–130
Bracton (*De legibus et consuetudinibus Angliae*)
    on evidence, 42–43 n.35, 66
    on false witnessing, 85–86, 92
    on indictment by way of rumor, 37–38
    on rape, 55 n.17
    on robbery, 71–72
Bradbury, Nancy, 82
Brand, Paul, 76 n.3, 121
Braybrooke, Gerard, 80–81
Britton (*Summa de legibus Anglie que vocatur Bretone*), 4–5, 41
    on delay of justice, 44–45 n.38
    on *peine forte et dure*, 124
    on robbery, 99–100 n.13

164 INDEX

Brooks, Peter, 61
Butler, Sara, 13, 25–26
  on consent principle, 137
  on coroner's inquest, 27–29
  on evidentiary standards, 25–26 n.5, 42–43
  on *peine forte et dure*, 6–7, 121, 128, 137

C
Cannon, Christopher, 59
canon law/court system
  oathworthy witness and, 75 n.1, 82
  witness/witnessing, 76–77
capital punishment, 1, 8–9
  hanging, 11, 71, 135–136, 142–143
  robbery, 71–72, 99–100, 117, 142–143
  see also punishment
Chaucer, Geoffrey: *Canterbury Tales*, 60
  "Canon's Yeoman's Tale, The", 77
  "General Prologue", 44–45
  "Knight's Tale, The", 1–2, 4–5, 145–147
  "Manciple's Tale, The", 129–130
  "Parson's Tale, The", 77, 85–86, 141–142
  robbery, 102–103, 113–114
  "Wife of Bath's Tale, The", 86–87
  see also Chaucer, Geoffrey: "Man of Law's Tale"
Chaucer, Geoffrey: "Man of Law's Tale", 18, 68–69, 72, 120–121
  Custance, 52–53, 65–67
  Custance, rape attack and homicide conviction, 67–68
  factual and narrative satisfaction, 68
  idleness, 45–46
  knight's false accusation, 66–67
  Man of Law as pleader, 61, 65–68
  self-defense argument, 67–68
Chaundler, Thomas: *Liber Apologeticus de Omni Statu Humanae Naturae*, 129–130
Chobham, Thomas de, 70
Christ's silence (Mystery Plays), 20, 122, 125, 139
  one's power over one's speech, 125, 129–131
  peine forte et dure, 126 n.25, 127–128
  see also standing mute
Cicero, 58–59
Cole, Andrew, 111
Commissions of Trailbaston, 83

common law (medieval English)
  common law court, 85, 90
  felony, 1–3
  felony procedure records and, 96, 105
  witness/witnessing, 76–77
community (local)
  community members as jury, 89
  felony procedure and, 2–3, 6, 9–11, 138
  law enforcement and, 32
  local community/royal power struggle, 5–6, 36–37, 79–80, 83, 94–95
  St. Erkenwald: community's investigation, 16–17, 24, 27, 32, 48
  self-investigation, 48
  witnessing, role in creating and sustaining medieval communities, 75
confession, 119
  Placita Corone: Hugh de M's case, 70–72
  religious confession, 70–72
  torture and, 119
consent (to jury trial), 20, 123
  as coercive/non-voluntary, 125, 136
  as essential to English law, 137
  need of, 120–121, 123–124, 137–138
  peine forte et dure and, 120–121, 137
  "put himself upon the country", 123, 128–129, 137
  standing mute and, 120–121, 123–124, 137
  see also peine forte et dure; standing mute
conspiracy as crime, 83 n.23, 90–91, 113–114, 128–129
conviction, 1
  conviction rates, 96, 140–141
  coroner's inquest and, 28
  fama and, 88–89, 113
  language of afforcement and conviction rates, 88, 113
  quality of "feloniousness" as bar for conviction, 141–142
  robbery: low conviction rates, 19 n.46, 96 n.2, 98–99
  see also punishment
conviction: collateral consequences, 1, 142–143, 145–147
  critique of, 141, 143
  denial of social services, 1 n.3, 143
  disenfranchisement, 1 n.3, 140–141, 143
  divorce, 1 n.3, 143

legal underclass, 143
professional consequences, 1 n.3, 143
property forfeiture, 124
termination of parental rights, 1 n.3, 140–141
coroner
  crown's coroner, 8–9
  medical knowledge, 41
  as "tax gatherer", 5–6
coroner's inquest (enrollments, records, rolls), 2–5, 9–10, 13, 27, 81–82
  dialogue format, 29–30
  evidence/material evidence, 31–32
  examination of the body, 29, 31, 35, 41–42
  as felony procedure record, 11
  inquest on Alice's death, 30–31, 35–36, 41–42, 48
  inquest on Robert Curteys' death, 28–29, 31–32, 35–36, 41–42, 88
  JUST 2 series, National Archives, 12
  language, 13
  limitations of, 30
  local jury and, 12, 24, 27–32, 35–36, 41–42
  narrative, 28–29
  preservation of, 105
  purposes, 28, 30
  St. Erkenwald, 16–17, 24, 27, 48
  St. Erkenwald: bishop Erkenwald as coroner, 24, 27, 38–42, 44, 46
  time between the discovery of a body and the coroner's arrival, 27–28, 33, 44
  trial jury and, 29–30
  verification and corroboration practice, 31–32
  white bags, 11
  witness credibility, 30–32
corruption
  local big men, 81
  oathworthy witness and system's vulnerability to corruption, 18–19, 75–76, 93
  "Outlaw of Trailbaston, The", 5–6
  power structures and, 78
  testimonial system, economic/social power and corruption, 75
  see also power
court

church court, 90, 125, 136–137
common law court, 85, 90
English language in the courtroom, 14
eyre court, 79–80
itinerant court, 12
laxity of, 6
overzealousness of, 6
oyer and terminer tribunal, 12
royal court, 5–6, 83, 86–87
crown
  crown's coroner, 8–9
  crown's justice, 8–9
  felony, royal purview over, 2–3, 8–9
  local community/royal power struggle, 5–6, 36–37, 79–80, 83, 94–95
  pleas of the crown, 53
  royal court, 5–6, 83, 86–87

D
Davis, Robert, 11
De Dorley, John, 126
delay
  complaints of, 44–45
  delay in narrative, 45
  as endemic feature of medieval trial, 44–45
  idleness and waste: spiritual implications, 45–46
  justice delay as akin to denial of justice, 44–45
  Middle English Breton Lays, The: "Sir Orfeo", 45
  Poems of the Pearl Manuscript, The: Gawain's delay, 45
  St. Erkenwald, 27, 43
De Lorris, Guillaume: *Roman de la Rose*, 99–100
De Meun, Jean: *Roman de la Rose*, 99–100
Dinshaw, Carolyn, 65
Doyle, A.I., 87
Dream of the Rood, 132
Dunn, Caroline, 90

E
Edward I (King of England), 99–100
Edward III (King of England), 101
Eland, Sir Hugh, 102–103, 114–115
Elder, Carol, 88
embalming, 41

evidence, 5
  Bracton on, 42–43 n.35, 66
  collection of, 2–3
  concept of, 2–4
  evidentiary standards, 17, 20–21, 25–26 n.5, 42–43
  indictment and evidence-weighing, 10
  jury and, 37
  laws of evidence, 75–77
  material evidence, 17, 27, 31–32, 38, 40–43
  reputation vs evidence, 42–43, 49, 76–78
  self-interpreting evidence, 41–42
  St. Erkenwald: evidence procedure, 17, 24–26, 37
  see also felony procedure
eyre, 2–3
  1339-40 Northamptonshire Eyre, 11
  eyre court, 79–80
  eyre records, 12, 81–82 n.16
  felony prosecution and, 8–9, 12

F
false appeal, 103–104
false witnessing, 75–76
  Bracton on, 85–86, 92
  penitential literature on, 85
  Susannah and the Elders, 18–19, 75–78, 85
  see also oathworthy witness; testimony; witness/witnessing
fama (common opinion/reputation), 75–76 n.3, 76–77
  conviction and, 88–89, 113
  Pistil of Swete Susan, The, 78, 87–91, 93
  robber's *fama*, 104–105, 117
  see also reputation
felony: definition, 1 n.1, 8–9, 138, 140
  as betrayal, 4–5, 8–9, 141–142
  "bōtlēas" crimes, 8–9
  Britton, 4–5
  built collaboratively, 4
  conceptual dynamic, 140
  conceptual history of felony, 141–142, 144
  as crime rather than feudal offense, 4–5
  cultural concepts, 2–3, 122, 138
  "dark imagining", 1–3, 5, 145–147

  defined by effects, motivations, and reactions surrounding it, 1–2, 145
  defined by its practice, 2–4, 122, 140–141, 145
  defined by its punishment, 2, 140–141, 146–147
  duplicity, 4
  felony procedure and, 2–4, 138, 140, 145
  grave, violent offenses, 6
  lack of definition as conceptual strength, 144–147
  legal concepts, 2–3
  medieval flawed definition as preserved in modern times, 140–141, 143–147
  quality of "feloniousness", 141–142
  quality of a person/villainy, 1–2, 4, 142–144, 147
  resilience as category, 140–141, 144, 146–147
  United States, 2, 140–141
felony procedure, 3, 10, 119
  definition of felony and, 2–4, 138, 140, 145
  determining guilt, 2–3, 138
  as intellectual project, 5
  law and literature, 7–8, 17
  local community/townspeople and, 2–3, 6, 9–11, 138
  as matter of the public, not lawyers, 9–10
  medieval poets and, 3–4
  in modern times, 145
  Mystery Plays and English procedure, 125–126, 130
  sources examined and, 3–4
  stages of, 20
  torture, 120–121
  see also evidence; indictment; investigation; pleading; proof; standing mute; testimony; trial; witness/witnessing
felony procedure records, 12, 16, 19–21, 96
  common law and, 96, 105
  documentary technology, 11, 96
  eyre records, 12, 81–82 n.16
  gaol delivery records, 12, 20–21, 96
  language of, 13, 16
  organization and preservation, 11
  plea rolls, 12
  purposes, 28

Year Books, 12–13, 54
  see also coroner's inquest; robbery records
first finders, 9, 28, 35–36
  duties of, 9, 33–34, 86–87
  as primary investigators, 35–36
Fitzherbert, Anthony, 113
Fleishmann, Suzanne, 47
Fleta, 99–100 n.13
Fludernik, Monica, 58
Folville brothers, 80–81 n.15, 82
Forrest, Ian, 7–8, 72–73 n.71, 75, 82–84
Fortescue, Sir John, 14
Foucault, Michel, 120–121
Fuller, Lon, 73

G
Gabrovsky, Alexander, 97–98
Gallagher, Catherine, 57–58
gaol delivery, 12, 44–45, 108–109
Garay, Kathleen, 19 n.46, 96 n.2
Gascoigne, William (Chief Justice), 100–101, 104, 131
gender issues, 89–90
  see also women
Glanvill
  on oathworthy witness, 76
  on rape, 55 n.17, 87
  on robbery, 3, 99
gossip, 24, 35, 75 n.1, 77, 114, 139
  false talk, 18, 77
Gottschalk, Marie, 144
Gower, John, 111–112
Gower, John: *Confessio Amantis*, 52–53, 60, 73
  Cataline's trial, 52–53, 64
  Cillenus, 64–66
  ideal pleader, 18, 63–65
  plain style of pleading, 64, 69–70
  pleader as tale-teller, 64–65
  "Tale of Constance", 65–68
Gradon, Pamela, 97–98
Grady, Frank, 134
Gregory the Great, 105–106, 131
Green, Richard Firth, 5–6 n.16, 25–26 nn.6–7, 37, 54, 71
Green, Thomas A., 99–100, 103 n.21, 119

guilt
  as a binary/as spectrum, 5
  determining guilt, 2–3, 138
  putting the question to God, 123–124

H
Hanawalt, Barbara, 50 n.2, 55 n.17, 89–90
Handlyng Synne, 4
Hanna, Ralph, 59, 97–98
Harding, Alan, 83 n.24
hearsay, 18, 42–43, 75–77, 85–86
Helmholz, R.H., 127
Hobart (Chief Justice), 141–142
Hoccleve, Thomas, 87
  Regement of Princes, 131–132
Holdsworth, William, 121
Hudson, John, 99 n.9
hue and cry, 9, 20–21, 32, 35–36
  St. Erkenwald, 24, 33–34
Hurnard, Naomi, 39
Hyams, Paul, 119

I
imprisonment, 9–11, 104
  felony as defined by its punishment, 2, 140–141, 146–147
  as punishment for felony, 1–2, 141
  see also punishment
indictment, 3–5, 10
  Bracton (indictment by way of rumor), 37–38
  local community/townspeople and, 10
  for robbery, 99, 112–113
  voices heard in different forms of, 80 n.11
  see also felony procedure
investigation, 20–21
  first finders as primary investigators, 35–36
  investigation practices, daily life, and literature, 26
  St. Erkenwald: community's investigation, 16–17, 24, 27, 32, 48
  St. Erkenwald as death investigation, 16–17, 23–27, 32
  St. Erkenwald as ideal investigation, 24–27, 41–42, 48
  see also felony procedure

J

Jerome, 84–85
Johnson, Eleanor, 45–46 n.46, 66, 96–97
Judas, 4, 142–143
judgment, 20
    reputation and, 37, 49, 104–105
    St. Erkenwald: 47–48
    see also felony procedure; jury trial; trial
judicial comment, 4–5, 98–99
    on robbery, 19–20, 98–101
    "self-defense" argument, 29–30 n.15
judicial treatises, 3–5, 18
jurisdiction (criminal)
    local community/royal power struggle about, 5–6, 36–37
    as overlapping and complex, 12
jury, 5
    community members as jury, 89
    coroner's inquest and local jury, 12, 24, 27–32, 35–36, 41–42
    evidence and, 37
    good faith engagement, 5
    integrity and rigor, 5
    mens rea, sense of, 6–7, 141–142
    modern juror, 5, 48–49
    "moral comfort" vs "factual proof", 25–26 n.6
    need for the accused's consent to jury trial, 123–124
    own definitions/theories of crimes, 103, 103 n.21
    robbery and jury nullification, 99–100, 103–104
    self-dealing and mixed motives, 5
    "self-informing" nature of, 25–26
    trial by ordeal and, 119 n.1
    as witness, 25–26, 25–26 n.5
    see also oathworthy witness
jury trial, 20, 28, 37, 119 n.1, 123
    acquittal, 25–26 n.6, 139
    coroner's inquest and trial jury, 29–30
    trustworthy men and, 119
    see also consent; trial
justice (officer)
    crown's justice, 8–9
    delay of justice and, 44–45
    need for the accused's consent to jury trial, 123–124

Placita Corone: justice's unjust role in pleading, 68–73
pleading, justice's role in, 53
standing mute and, 124–125, 135–139
unjust conduct of, 71
Justice, Steven, 5–6 n.16

K

Kamali, Elizabeth, 6–7, 71–72, 99–100 n.9, 141–142
Karnes, Michelle, 59–60, 111
Kaye, Joel, 53–54 n.9, 54 n.12, 71
Kelly, H. Ansgar, 127
Kesselring, K.J., 121 n.10
Klerman, Daniel, 25–26
Kunkel, Nico, 61–62
Kyroun, John, 113–114

L

Lacey, Nicola, 48–49
Langbein, John, 121 n.10
Langland, William: Good Thief in *Piers Plowman*, 105
    cross-referencing, 98–99, 106–107, 109
    Good Thief as felon, 96–98, 108–109, 117, 147
    Good Thief as legal record, 106–107
    Good Thief's acquittal, 19, 96–97, 111–112
    Imaginatif, 105–106, 109–111, 114–116, 144
    legal failure: robber's salvation, 97–98
    poem's repetitions, 19–20, 96–97, 105–107, 115–118
    punishment, 105–106, 109–111, 114–118, 144, 147
    Repentence, 107, 116–117
    Roberd the Robbere, 97–98, 105–111, 116–117
    scholarship on, 97–98
    unresolved robber, 117–118
    Will, 19, 106, 109–111, 116, 144, 147
    see also robbers; robbery
Langland, William: *Piers Plowman*, 80–81, 83, 86–87
Piers Plowman tradition, 20, 131, 134
language, 8, 14
    1362 Statute of Pleading, 14–15
    Anglo-Norman, 8, 13–16, 50–51

English, 8, 14
felony procedure records, 13, 16
French, 14
language of afforcement, 88, 112–113
Latin, 8, 13–16, 50–51, 77, 84
pleading, 14
St. Erkenwald: language issue, 17, 36
testimony, 15
vernacular, 13–16, 87
Lateran Council IV (1215), 15, 38–39, 119
Laushull, Simon of, 81–82, 94, 146
law and literature, 3, 6–8, 75, 77
conceptual history of felony, 141–142
felony procedure, law and literature in the making of, 7–8, 17
narrative theories and law, 50–51
Placita Corone, 73–74
robbery, 98–99
St. Erkenwald, 24–27
Lay of Havelok the Dane, The, 142–143
legal history, 6–8, 16, 25–26, 78, 119, 121
Anglo-American law, 76–77, 119, 121
Legenda aurea, 60
Lipton, Emma, 6–7, 75, 119, 126
Lisle, Thomas de, 80–82
Loar, Carol, 32

M
Magna Carta, 3
Maitland, Frederic, 2, 50–51, 120 n.5
Mann, Jill, 67
Marie de France: *Lanval*, 86–87
Masschaele, James, 121 n.10, 123–124, 137
medieval literary theory, 57–58
fabula, argumentum, historia, 58–59
medieval narrative theory, 7–8, 18, 51–53
Melsa, Alan of, 77 n.7
mens rea, 6–7, 141–142, 141–142 n.11
methodology, 5–8, 20–21
language, 8, 14
legal and literary sources, 12, 16
limitations of the project, 20–21
Michel, Dan: *Ayenbite of Inwit*, 85, 102
Middle English Breton Lays, The: "Sir Orfeo", 45
Middleton, Anne, 65, 106–107
Milsom, S.F.C., 2–3, 37
Mirk, John, 39, 70
Mirror of Justices, The, 41, 99–100

modern times
felony: medieval flawed definition as preserved in modern times, 140–141, 143–147
felony case, 48–49
felony conviction, 1
felony procedure, 145
juror, 5, 48–49
narrative theory, 51–52
pleading, 146
trial, 48–49
United States, 2, 140–141, 146
Molyns, Sir John, 80–82, 102–103
Moore, Michael S., 145–146
Mudie, James, 142–143
Mulholland, Maureen, 103
Mum and the Sothsegger (Silence and the Truth-Sayer), 131
Mum as personification of silence, 20, 132–135
Mum/Silence as the villain, 20, 131–134
narrator's silence, 135
obligation to speak out, 131–135, 137–138
Piers Plowman tradition, 20, 131, 134
political literature and, 20, 132–133
silence, disruptive power of, 20, 122, 131, 135, 139
silence as aggressive, 134–135, 137–138
silence and anti-social recalcitrance, 20, 131, 133–134, 137–138
silence as opacity and provocation, 135–136
see also standing mute
murder, 3, 8–9, 143
Musson, Anthony, 49, 113–114
Mystery Plays, 15, 20, 125–126, 139
Christ's silence, 20, 122, 125, 139
English procedure and, 126, 130
Herod, 126 n.25, 127–129
N-Town plays, 126 n.25
Ordinalia, 127–128, 130
Pilate, 125–129
political critique of felony procedure, 125
trials of Christ, 15, 125–126
tyrants, 126
York Mystery Plays, 20, 75 n.1, 126–129
see also Christ's silence

N

narrative
  audience expectations and, 51–52
  believable lies, 68
  Chaucer's "Man of Law": factual and narrative satisfaction, 68
  coroner's inquest, 28–29
  delay in, 45
  episodic, discontinuous, and repetitive medieval narratives, 51–52, 60
  love for good stories and truth/justice, 5, 61, 68–69, 73–74
  medieval literary theory, 57–59
  medieval narrative theory, 7–8, 18, 51–53
  medieval reader and story/truth relationship, 52–53, 57
  modern narrative theory, 51–52
  narrative expectations and investigative process, 47
  narrative theories and law, 50–51
  pleading and audience expectations, 18, 52
  pleading and narrative in medieval criminal procedure, 17–18, 50–51
  pleading and narrative satisfaction, 51–53, 56–57, 73–74
  present tense's markedness and, 47
  prose as designation of truth, 66, 66 n.53
  St. Erkenwald, 38, 40, 44, 46–47, 75
  Seven Sages of Rome: narrative satisfaction, 61–63
  see also Placita Corone
Neville, C.J., 108–109
Nissé, Ruth, 23–24
Northampton case, 18–19, 78–79, 146
  assault case, 78–79, 93–94
  case records, 81–84, 94–95
  fine as punishment, 79, 83–84, 93–94, 146
  lies, 93–94
  offenders as local big men, 79–82
  Pateshull, Walter (coroner), 79–80, 93–94
  power structures and corruption, 78
  presentment, 79–80, 83–84, 94–95
  proof procedure and local power structures, 94
  Scrope (Chief Justice), 11, 79–80, 83–84, 93–95, 146
  testimonial system, critique of, 18–19, 79–80, 83–84, 94–95
  victim, 79–80
  see also oathworthy witness

O

oath, 13, 82
oathworthy witness, 9–10, 18–19
  canon court system and, 75 n.1, 82
  "common knowledge" and, 76–77, 112–113
  creation of reputation in the law by, 74
  cross-jurisdictional power of, 18, 74, 75 n.1, 75–76, 91
  Glanvill on, 76
  oath (Gratian's *Decretum*), 82
  social power of, 18, 82
  system's vulnerability to corruption, 18–19, 75–76, 93
  trustworthy status, 82–84
  viri fidedigni (trustworthy men), 7–8, 75 n.1, 82–84, 119
  see also false witnessing; Northampton case; *Pistil of Swete Susan, The*; witness/witnessing
O'Connell, Brendan, 67
offender
  escaping punishment by way of their power, 6
  local big men as, 79–82
  see also accused; suspect
One Thousand and One Nights, 63
Orlemanski, Julie, 58–59
Ormrod, W.M., 14
"Outlaw of Trailbaston, The", 5–6 n.15, 6
oyer and terminer commission, 12

P

pardon, 11
  Cecily's standing mute and pardon, 125, 130–131
  coroner's inquest and, 28–30
Peasant Rebellion (1381), 5–6
Peck, Russell, 86–87, 91–92
peine forte et dure
  Britton on, 124
  Butler, Sara on, 6–7, 121, 128, 137

Cecily's case, 123–124, 138–139
Christ's silence (Mystery Plays), 126
  n.25, 127–128
Clitherow, Margaret, 128–129
consent and, 120–121, 137
end of, 136–137
justifications for, 121 n.10, 137
methods of torture, 120–121, 123–124
robbers' case, 131
standing mute, 10–11, 20
as torture designed to coerce
  compliance, 20, 120–121, 124,
  136–137
see also standing mute
penitential literature, 4, 6–7, 15, 45–46
  on false witnessing, 85
  penitential manuals, 38–39
  on robbery, 102–103
  Susannah and the Elders story, 18–19,
  75–77
Phelan, Amy, 83 n.22
Phillips, Susan, 129–130
Pistil of Swete Susan, The, 18–19, 84
  biblical story/poem comparison, 78, 84,
  86–93
  Elders as corrupt oathworthy witnesses,
  78, 84, 87–92, 94
  fama/common opinion, 78, 87–91, 93
  as legal critique, 18–19, 78, 84, 91–94
  manuscripts, 86–87
  popularity of, 86
  proof procedure, shortcomings of, 78, 94
  sources for, 77 n.7, 86, 93
  Susanna as model of female witness, 78
  Susannah's spotless reputation as legal
  truth, 78, 84, 87–88
  testimonial system, critique of, 78,
  83–84, 89–90, 92–94
  see also oathworthy witness; Susannah
  and the Elders
Placita Corone, 17–18, 37, 73–74
  Alice and Adam: plea regarding rape,
  55–57, 61
  as criminal pleading manual, 17, 51,
  53–54, 57
  explanatory matter, 54–55
  Hugh de M: plea regarding
  horse-thievery, 68–73
  justice's unjust role in pleading, 68–73

law and literature, 73–74
legal fiction, 73
as literary training of the medieval
  pleader, 51
manuscripts, 17, 53–54 n.9, 54–55, 69
  n.60, 74
narrative construction, 51–53
narrative expectations of the courtroom,
  17, 51
negative perception of, 54–55
Nicholas: plea regarding cattle-stealing,
  72–73
pleading and narrative satisfaction,
  51–53, 56–57, 73–74
popularity of, 17, 53–55
prioritizing good stories over procedural
  accuracy, 52–55
procedural inconsistencies and mistakes,
  17, 51, 53–54
prologue, 54–55, 74
Thomas's plea, 72
see also pleading
pleader
accused as, 10–11, 53, 69, 72
Chaucer's Man of Law as pleader, 61,
  65–68
duty of, 63
Gower's *Confessio Amantis*: ideal
  pleader, 18, 63–65
literary pleaders, 18, 65, 68–69
professional pleader (*narrator*), 10–11,
  50–51, 53, 61, 63
as tale-teller, 64–65
pleading, 20, 50–51
1362 Statute of Pleading, 14–15
audience expectations and, 18, 52
finding truth in medieval literary pleas,
  61
justice's role in, 53
language of, 14
narrative satisfaction and, 51–53, 56–57,
  73–74
plain style of, 64, 69–70
plea and narrative in medieval criminal
  procedure, 17–18, 50–51
plea rolls, 12
pleas of the crown, 53
revised plea, 50–51, 53
successful plea, 52, 55, 63–64

pleading (*Continued*)
  US plea bargains, 146
  see also felony procedure; *Placita Corone*; pleader
Poems of the Pearl Manuscript, The:
  Gawain's delay, 45
poets (medieval), 3–4, 7–8
Pollack, Frederick, 120 n.5
Post, J.B., 30, 53–54, 55 n.17
Powell, Edward, 113
power
  abuse of, 78
  local abuse of power, 79–81, 83–84
  local big men, 79–84
  local community/royal power struggle, 5–6, 36–37, 79–80, 83, 94–95
  oathworthy witness, 18, 74, 75 n.1, 75–76, 91
  offenders escaping punishment by way of their power, 6
  power structures and corruption, 78
  proof procedure and local power structures, 94
  robbery and abuse of the powerful, 19–20, 102–103, 114–115
  testimonial system, economic/social power and corruption, 75
presentment, 83
  Northampton case, 79–80, 83–84, 94–95
  procedure description, 80 n.12
proof, 2–3
  Pistil of Swete Susan, The: critique of proof procedure, 78, 94
  proof procedure and local power structures, 94
  robbery and proof procedure, 105, 117
  St. Erkenwald: proof procedure, 17, 25–26, 42–43, 49
  see also felony procedure
punishment, 143, 145–147
  crime/punishment reciprocity, 145–147
  felony as defined by its punishment, 2, 140–141, 146–147
  fine, 79, 83–84, 93–94, 99–100, 146
  Langland's Good Thief (*Piers Plowman*), 105–106, 109–111, 114–118, 144, 147
  loss of goods and property, 1, 8–9
  see also capital punishment; conviction; imprisonment; robbery, punishment for

R
rape
  Bracton on, 55 n.17
  Chaucer's "Man of Law": rape attack and homicide conviction, 67–68
  definition of, 55 n.17
  as felony, 8–9
  Glanvill on, 55 n.17, 87
  Placita Corone: plea regarding rape, 55–57, 61
  Seven Sages of Rome: plea regarding rape, 61–62
  Statute of Westminster on, 55 n.17
reputation
  accused: reputation and judgement, 37, 49, 104–105
  factors affecting reputation, 89–90
  reputation vs evidence, 42–43, 49, 76–78
  as source of truth, 42–43
  woman's reputation as fragile, 89–90
  see also fama
Richard II (King of England), 23–24
Ristroph, Alice, 1 n.1, 140–141
robbers, 101–102, 111–113
  as approvers, 113–114
  biblical Good Thief, 105–106
  fama of robber, 104–105, 117
  Richard Taylor's case, 103–104, 108–109, 111, 115
  robber barons, 102–103, 114
  unresolved robber, 111
  William le Just de Clyda's case, 104–105, 112–113, 115, 117
  see also Langland, William: Good Thief in *Piers Plowman*
robbery
  abuse of the powerful and, 19–20, 102–103, 114–115
  acquittal, 99, 99–100 n.13, 100–101, 103, 111–113, 115
  acts of Parliament on, 19–20, 98
  Bracton on, 71–72
  Britton on, 99–100 n.13
  burglary, 99–100 n.9, n.13

definition of, 19–20, 99–101, 104, 111–112
distinction between serious and lesser theft, 99–100, 142–143
as felony, 8–9
first-time offenses, 71–72
Fleta, 99–100 n.13
Glanvill on, 3, 99
indictments, 99, 112–113
judicial comment on, 19–20, 98–101
jury nullification, 99–100, 103–104
larceny, 99–100, 99–100 n.9
law and literature, 98–99
low conviction rates, 19 n.46, 96 n.2, 98–99
malice of, 101–102, 111–113, 131
motives for, 100–101
penitential literature, 102–103
Placita Corone: Hugh's plea, 68–73
Placita Corone: Nicholas: plea, 72–73
poverty as driver of, 71–72, 99–100, 99–100 n.13
proof procedure, 105, 117
theories of robbery crime, 99
theories of robbery crime, contradictions, 99–101, 104–105, 111, 114–115
as trespass, 99–100
vagrancy and, 101, 105, 111–112
violence, 99–101
see also Langland, William: Good Thief in *Piers Plowman*
robbery, punishment for, 19, 111–112
capital punishment, 71–72, 99–100, 117, 142–143
fine, 99–100
mutilation, 99–100
pillory, 99–100
robbery records, 19–20, 98–99, 101, 103, 105, 112–114
memory and preservation of, 115–116
recordkeeping that keeps a thief "evermore in danger", 112–115, 117

S
St. Eorcenwald, 24–25, 24–25 n.3
St. Erkenwald, 16–17, 23, 32
community's inadequacy for investigation, 36–37

community's investigation ("crowdsourced" investigation), 16–17, 24, 27, 32, 48
coroner's inquest, 16–17, 24, 27, 48
as death investigation, 16–17, 23–27, 32
delays, 27, 43
emphasis on procedure, 38, 42–44
England's non-Christian past and Christianization, 23–24, 39–40
Englishness, 23–25, 49
Erkenwald, bishop of London, 16–17, 23, 24–25 n.3
Erkenwald as confessor, 38–40
Erkenwald as coroner, 24, 27, 38–42, 44, 46
evidence procedure, 17, 24–26, 37
historicist reading of, 16–17, 23–25
hue and cry, 24, 33–34
as ideal investigation, 24–27, 41–42, 48
judge's baptism, 16–17, 23, 43–44, 46–47
judge's dead body, 16–17, 27–28, 33–34, 38, 46
judge's dead body decay and salvation of soul, 23, 47–48
judge's reanimation, 16–17, 23, 38–42
judgment, 47–48
language issue, 17, 36
law and literature, 24–27
material evidence, 27, 38, 40–43
mayor, 33–34
miraculous investigative procedure, 17, 24
narrative, 38, 40, 44, 46–47, 75
"now", 46–47
proof procedure, 17, 25–26, 42–43, 49
scholarship on, 16–17, 23–24
time between the discovery of the body and Erkenwald's arrival, 27–28, 33
witness/witnessing, 26
Saunders, Corinne, 55 n.17
Scase, Wendy, 5–6 n.15, 80 n.11
scene of the crime: first finders' duty to protect the scene, 9, 33
Schmitz-Esser, Romedio, 41
Scrope (Chief Justice), 11, 79–80, 83–84, 93–95, 146
self-defense argument, 25–26 n.6, 29–30, 81–82, 135–136, 138–139
Chaucer's "Man of Law Tale", 67–68

sermons, 2–3, 15, 60, 138
Servius, 58–59
Seven Sages of Rome, 18, 52–53, 68
   Empress, 61–63, 73
   love for good stories and truth, 61
   narrative satisfaction, 61–63
   plea regarding rape, 61–62
Shapiro, Barbara, 25–26, 42–43
Shareshull, William (Chief Justice), 100–101
sheriff's tourns, 10, 14–15, 89
Shoemaker, Karl, 89, 119
silence, *see* standing mute
Smail, Daniel Lord, 88
Song of Roland, 142–143
"Song on the Venality of Judges, The", 5–6, 5–6 n.15
Spearing, A.C., 58
Staley, Lynn, 77 n.7, 78
standing mute, 20–21, 121–123, 136–139
   1772 Criminal Law Act, 136–137
   Cecily's case, 123–125, 128–131, 137–139
   Cecily's pardon, 125, 130–131
   Christina's case, 128, 136
   Christlikeness of those standing mute, 127–128, 130–131
   Christ's silence (Mystery Plays), 20, 122, 125, 139
   consent to jury trial, 120–121, 123–124, 137
   disruptive power of silence, 20, 122, 125, 127, 131, 135, 137–139
   Isabel of Bury's case, 135–139
   justice (officer) and, 124–125, 135–139
   loose talk, 129–130
   "nihil dicit"/"rien dit", 121–122
   peine forte et dure, 10–11, 20
   self-incrimination, 127
   silence as choice, 130–131
   silence as failure to appear (church courts), 125, 136–137
   silence in literary sources: dramatic staging and allegorical personification, 122
   silence as plea of guilty (civil and trespass law), 125, 136–137
   silence as protest, 125, 128–129
   silence as speaking that did not fit the plea/consent pattern, 135–136
   women, 124, 128
   see also consent; *Mum and the Sothseggerz*; *peine forte et dure*
Steiner, Emily, 96
Stevens, Martin, 126
Strohm, Paul, 58–59
Susannah and the Elders (biblical story), 18–19, 75–76, 84
   adultery, 18–19, 75–76, 90
   Augustine on, 84–85
   Chaucer's "The Parson's Tale", 77
   Daniel, 18–19, 75–76, 84–86, 92–93
   false witnessing, 18–19, 75–78, 85
   Jerome on, 84–85
   lust and lying, 92
   penitential literature and, 18–19, 75–77
   traditional interpretation: triumph of procedure over aberrations of bad actors, 84–86
   Vulgate, 84, 86–88, 90–91, 93
   witness procedure and, 77
   Wycliffite Bible, 84–87, 90
   see also Pistil of Swete Susan, The
suspect, 9–10
   abjuration, 10, 14–15
   claiming sanctuary in a church, 9–10, 128–129
   see also accused; offender
Sutherland, Donald, 53–54 n.9, 54 n.14, 81–82 n.16

T

Taylor, Jamie, 6–7, 78, 87, 90
testimony
   common knowledge/consensus and, 76–78
   common opinion/*fama* and, 75–76 n.3, 76–78, 87–91, 93
   English language and testimony in religious matters, 15
   Northampton case: testimonial system critique, 18–19, 79–80, 83–84, 94–95
   oral testimony, 25–26
   Pistil of Swete Susan, The: testimonial system critique, 78, 83–84, 89–90, 92–94
   supremacy over all forms of evidence, 75

testimonial system critique, 75–77, 83, 85
trusted testimony, 3–4
see also false witnessing; felony procedure; hearsay; oathworthy witness; witness/witnessing
torture
   confession and, 119
   distaste for, 120
   felony procedure and, 120–121
   hypocrisy around, 121
   judicial torture, 120, 121 n.10
   see also peine forte et dure
Toureille, Valérie, 99–100 n.9
treason, 8–9, 138–139, 141–142
Tresilian (Chief Justice), 113
Trevet, Nicholas: "Tale of Constance", 65–66, 68
trial, 8–9
   beginning of, 10–11
   brevity of, 11, 48–49
   crown's justice and, 8–9
   delay as endemic feature of medieval trial, 44–45
   modern trial, 48–49
   priests, involvement in, 119
   stages of the felony trial, 20
   trial by battle, 20, 123
   trial by ordeal, 20, 119 n.1, 123
   trial scenes in medieval English literature, 11
   verdict, 11
   witness/witnessing, 11
   see also felony procedure; jury trial
trustworthy men, *see* oathworthy witness

V
victim (local), 6
   of local abuse of power, 79–81

W
Whitman, James, 25–26 n.6, 123–124
Wilson, Thomas, 45
witness/witnessing, 20
   canon law on, 76–77
   common law on, 76–77
   jury as, 25–26
   reliability of, 76–77
   role of witnessing in creating and sustaining medieval communities, 75
   St. Erkenwald, 26
   witnessing, concept of, 2–3
   witness procedure, 77
   see also false witnessing; felony procedure; first finders; oathworthy witness; testimony
women
   misogyny, 92–93
   standing mute, 124, 128
   Susanna as model of female witness, 78
   women's reputation as fragile, 89–90
Wynnere and Wastoure, 45–46 n.46

Y
Yeager, Stephen, 134
Year Books, 12–13, 54
   Vulgate edition, 12–13